# RICHARD GREENHAM

## PORTRAIT OF AN ELIZABETHAN PASTOR

# RICHARD GREENHAM

## PORTRAIT OF AN ELIZABETHAN PASTOR

John H. Primus

Mercer University Press
Macon, Georgia
1998

ISBN 0-86554-578-2
MUP / H432


© 1998 John H. Primus
All rights reserved
Mercer University Press
6316 Peake Road
Macon, Georgia 31210-3960


The paper used in this publication meets the minimum requirements of
American National Standard for Permanence of Paper for Printed Library
Materials ANSI Z39.48–1984.


*Library of Congress Cataloging-in-Publication Data*


Primus, John H.
Richard Greenham: portrait of an Elizabethan pastor / John H. Primus.
p. cm.
Includes bibliographical references and index.
ISBN 0-86554-578-2 (alk. paper)
1. Greenham, Richard. 2. Church of England—Clergy—Biography.
3. Puritans—England—Biography. 4. Anglican Communion—England—
Clergy—Biography. I. Title.
BX5199.G725P75 1998
283'.092—dc21
[B] 98-5027
CIP

# TABLE of CONTENTS

TO JUNE

# ACKNOWLEDGMENTS

My wife June, to whom this book is dedicated, is gifted with an exceptionally good memory coupled with an unusual measure of curiosity about the past. She is a historian by instinct. Consequently, she has not only been my constant companion throughout my professional life and the person chiefly responsible for providing the context of love and moral support in which I do my work; she has also maintained a special interest in this Richard Greenham project.

June spent three sabbatical leaves with me in Cambridge, England, where most of the research and writing for this book were done. On all three occasions her positive attitude and spirit of adventure contributed immensely to making them such memorable and pleasurable experiences. She never wearied of the countless times we took the short drive from Cambridge to Dry Drayton, where Greenham spent the bulk of his ministry four centuries ago. There in the little parish church of St. Peter and St. Paul we attempted to absorb the spirit of Greenham by historical osmosis. One spring afternoon, June spent some five hours on her knees in that chilly old church–not praying, but rubbing the memorial brass of Thomas Hutton and his family, a brass still to be found under the carpet in the aisle near the chancel. That brass rubbing and–thanks to the generosity of our friends, David and Laurie Vander Ark–a lovely picture of the church now adorn our living room thousands of miles from Dry Drayton as constant reminders of the place where a puritan ministry was born.

When we reminisce about our sabbaticals, a number of special friends and experiences come immediately to mind. We occasionally attended worship services in Dry Drayton and we remember with gratitude the warmth and hospitality of the current parishioners there, especially Rosemary and David Gardiner. Twice they invited me to give the homily, and I am grateful for those opportunities to hold forth in the very place where Richard Greenham preached some six thousand sermons. Others in Cambridge who were especially kind, thoughtful, and hospitable to us were Susan and John Wilson, Rosamond and John Long, Leslie and Graham Maile, and Jill and Tony Barker. They contributed significantly to our sabbatical tranquility.

For providing the sabbatical leaves I thank the administration and board of trustees of Calvin College. The Calvin Alumni Association made several travel grants available, and I am grateful for the fine support and encouragement they give to faculty scholarship. Others in the Calvin community who deserve special mention are my colleague, Ken

Pomykala, who cheerfully(?) took over as chairperson of the religion and theology department during my most recent sabbatical, and the entire department for their helpful responses to portions of the work presented in seminars. Above all, I am grateful to our secretary, Esther Vander Tuig, who, with some summer-time assistance from Donna Quist, spent innumerable hours getting the manuscript ready for the publisher.

There are a number of institutions and people in England whom I wish to acknowledge and thank. In London, the staffs of the Guildhall Library, the Manuscripts Room in the British Library, the Greater London Record Office and History Library, and the St. Bartholemew's Hospital Archives, all provided help in locating documents pertaining to Greenham's closing years. In Cambridge, the librarians at Caius and Pembroke Colleges, and the staffs of the Cambridgeshire Record Office and Cambridge University Library–especially in the Manuscripts and Rare Book Rooms–consistently provided friendly and efficient service. I thank also the administration and staff of Westminister Theological College for providing me with an academic home while in Cambridge.

Of the many others who contributed in some way to this work, three should be acknowledged by name. I am deeply appreciative of the contacts I had with the premier historian of Elizabethan Puritanism, Patrick Collinson, and I thank him for his hospitality, insights, and advice. I also thank Kenneth Parker, whose English puritan interests coalesce uncannily with my own, and who graciously provided me with his transcript of Greenham's tabletalk. And it was a distinct pleasure to work with Marc Jolley of Mercer University Press, who was exceptionally congenial and helpful in bringing this work to publication.

Finally, I gratefully acknowledge posthumously the one person without whom this book most certainly could not have been written: Richard Greenham, 1540-1594. I know by experience that this remarkable man is still capable of making an impact four hundred years after his death. But, modest and pious as he was, Greenham would not want me to end on that note. He would insist that we give God the glory and thank Him for His love and faithfulness to all generations.

John H. Primus
Grand Rapids, Michigan

# ABBREVIATIONS

| | |
|---|---|
| APC | Acts of the Privy Council |
| BL | British Library |
| CRO | Cambridgeshire Record Office |
| DNB | Dictionary of National Biography |
| EDR | Ely Diocesan Records |
| GLMS | Guildhall Library Manuscripts |
| GLRO | Greater London Record Office |
| HTR | *Harvard Theological Review* |
| OED | Oxford English Dictionary |
| REM | Rylands English Manuscript |
| SBHA | St. Bartholomew's Hospital Archives |

# INTRODUCTION

In the twentieth century's explosion of books on sixteenth century English Puritanism, there are relatively few monographs that focus exclusively on a single, early puritan preacher. And yet if the universal lies embedded in the particular, such concentrated study of a proto-typical puritan seems warranted. Richard Greenham is an excellent candidate. He is on everyone's short list of the most important English puritan pioneers. Patrick Collinson, in his landmark work on Elizabethan Puritanism, calls him "the model puritan," and elsewhere refers to him as the "quintessentially puritanical Richard Greenham."[1] William Haller, in his earlier ground-breaking work, calls Greenham the "patriarch" of those puritans whom Richard Baxter dubbed, the "affectionate practical English writers."[2] M. M. Knappen observes that Greenham was one of the greatest pastoral ministers of the era,[3] and H. G. Owen, commenting on Greenham's move in 1592 from his parish in Dry Drayton to Christ Church in London, calls it an "ecclesiastical scoop" for the London church to have secured the services of "perhaps the leading Puritan preacher of the day."[4] Gordon Wakefield honors Greenham as one of those who began the Reformed study of pastoral theology in England, and places him in the company of the "Country Parson," George Herbert, alleging that Greenham's ministry in Dry Drayton "is as attractive as that of George Herbert later at Bremerton..."[5]

Given such positive press, it seems odd that no monograph on Greenham has yet been published. He gets a few paragraphs here and

---

[1] *The Elizabethan Puritan Movement* (Berkeley: University of California Press, 1967) 128; *The Religion of Protestants* (Oxford: Clarendon Press, 1982) 109.

[2] *The Rise of Puritanism* (New York: Columbia University Press, 1938) 26.

[3] Marshall M. Knappen, *Tudor Puritanism* (Chicago: University Press, 1939) 382-386.

[4] H. Gareth Owen, "Tradition and Reform: Ecclesiastical Controversy in an Elizabethan London Parish," *Guildhall Miscellany*, Vol. II, No. 2 (July, 1961) 69.

[5] *Puritan Devotion* (London: Epworth Press, 1957) 3.

there, sometimes a page or more, but heretofore, apart from one unpublished dissertation back in the 1920s,[6] there has been no attempt at what might be called a full treatment of his life and thought. Such is the aim of this work, written with the conviction that Greenham is a superb example of the "moderate" Puritanism of the Elizabethan era, that is, a Puritanism that was completely loyal to church and crown, that was at most selectively non-conformist, and that had no intention of separating from the Church of England. In the study of Greenham lies the opportunity to see Puritanism in its most positive and untarnished form, not as a quarrelsome, negative political force reacting against the English church and state.

The focus of this study is not political, but theological, for Richard Greenham was a parish pastor who, in his written works at least, seems almost oblivious to the ecclesiastical and civil skirmishes of his time. His writings infrequently refer to such battles, but are more simply and single-mindedly focussed on the personal struggles of individual believers and on building up godliness in the community of faith. He was a pastoral, rather than systematic, theologian. Among his treatises are many "grave counsels and divine directions for the attaining and retaining of faith and a good conscience."[7] Also included are practical directions for reading the Scriptures, treatises for "afflicted consciences," and even pre-marital counsel. There are homilies on hypocrisy, anger, humility, prayer and fasting, Christian warfare, and of course, on keeping the Sabbath. Clearly, practical theology was his forte; Greenham was first and foremost a puritan *pastor*, whose specialty was the care and cure of troubled consciences.

And yet, in his writings there is a discernible doctrinal theology as well. The godliness with which the puritans were so preoccupied is rooted, after all, in a certain view of God and a particular understanding of the Bible. Theology is intimately related to piety, at least it was for the puritans. Henry Holland, the editor of Greenham's works, states that Greenham wrote for two purposes: to "teach and informe the mind in sundry arguments...concerning truth and error," and "to edifie the heart and conscience, being well assured, that this

---

[6] Marshall M. Knappen, *Richard Greenham and the Practical Puritans under Elizabeth* (Ph.D diss., Cornell University, 1927).

[7] *Workes* (London, 1612) 51.

part hath most neede in most Christians of direction and consolation."[8] In Puritanism, theological concern and passion for piety constantly interact and feed upon each other. It is difficult to say which comes first; for Greenham they are correlative. On the one hand, his religious experience is the soil in which his theological formulations grow and thrive; on the other, his piety—the way of being religious—is grounded upon a certain view of God, humanity, and the universe. Although his own view of the importance of intellectual endeavor is somewhat ambiguous, he demonstrates considerable scholarly acumen. Samuel Clarke's contention that Greenham at Pembroke "followed his Studies so hard" that he became eminent for " his proficiency in learning,"[9] is reflected in his works.

Dewey Wallace appropriately calls for more careful study of Puritanism as a theological movement to balance the rapt attention already given it as an economic and socio-psychological phenomenon.[10] Perhaps that imbalance is due to a philosophy of history that has difficulty knowing what to do with matters of faith, but surely the faith of the puritans was also an historical reality and needs analysis. What ultimately constituted the driving force of Puritanism and accounted for the puritans' revolutionary energy was not their view of work, but their vision of God; not their economics, but their theology. In the words of A. G. Dickens, Puritanism was an "obstinately religious phenomenon," deeply resistant to all later attempts to secularize it.[11] This is clearly reflected in Richard Greenham. The power source at the center of his thought and life was his faith in God. Consequently, there is something profoundly theological in his writings. This is an important dimension to consider, for behind the puritan effort to bring the Church of England to further reform lay a clear vision of what the Christian faith is, or ought to be; that is, a theological vision. In these early years of Puritanism, this vision was not particularly well defined, but was fluid

---

[8] *Workes*, "The Preface to the Reader."

[9] *The Lives of Thirty-two English Divines* (London, 1677) 12.

[10] *Puritans and Predestination* (Chapel Hill: University of North Carolina Press, 1982) vii.

[11] *The English Reformation* (London: B. T. Batsford LTD, 1964) 319. Cf. Patrick Collinson, *English Puritanism* (London: The Historical Association, 1983) 5.

and dynamic. Richard Greenham illustrates this as well, for his theology is not entirely predictable and sometimes provokes questions about its inner consistency. Some of these problems will be considered later in this book.

This introduction would not be complete without the inevitable discussion of the terms "puritan" and "puritanism." Professor Collinson's wry comment that a "secondary academic industry has arisen, devoted to the search for an acceptable definition,"[12] suggests both the profound difficulty and the mysterious appeal of the defining enterprise. Some day, no doubt, an entire dissertation will be devoted to the history of efforts to define Puritanism. One hesitates to get caught up in this maelstrom of the "definition problem," but a few observations seem nonetheless appropriate.

First, Peter Lake's comment about defining Puritanism, early in his book on "moderate" Puritanism, is eminently sensible. It also conveniently obviates the need to say much more. He argues that to define Puritanism "at the outset of an inquiry which is, in a sense, an extended exercise in definition would perhaps be inappropriate." To do so is "to indulge in a circular process whereby the results of the entire enterprise would be determined by its initial terms of reference." Such solecism, he suggests, has bedeviled the entire history of the study of Puritanism and should be put to a halt. Lake advocates a more "nominalist" or inductive approach, i.e., understanding or defining Puritanism in terms of the puritans, not vice-versa.[13] This approach is particularly applicable to this study of Richard Greenham. No one challenges the contention that Greenham embodied that common core of beliefs and values that have come to be named "puritan." What precisely that means, however, should be allowed to develop as the study unfolds. In other words, the concept of Puritanism as a more or less coherent entity will presumably gather meaning in the process of the study of such individuals as Richard Greenham. Consistent with this approach, some conclusions about Greenham's Puritanism will appear near the end of the book in chapter eight.

---

[12] Collinson, *English Puritanism*, 6.
[13] *Moderate Puritanism and the Elizabethan Church* (Cambridge: University Press, 1982) 11.

Second, Nicholas Tyacke has argued compellingly that it is virtually impossible to make sharp theological distinctions between Puritanism and Anglicanism during the years covering Greenham's career, roughly the last half of the sixteenth century.[14] Indeed, as a coherent entity, Anglicanism did not emerge until the Laudian years of the following century as a "defensive response to the puritan challenge."[15] And yet, there were divergent points of view already in the sixteenth century Church of England that need to be described. While it is true that the ostensible, visible disputes in Greenham's day involved seemingly non-theological issues such as vestments and church government, the differing views on these matters did have theological implications.[16] The non-puritan ones also need a label, and "anglican" (with a lower case "a") seems as good as any. So, the sin of anachronism notwithstanding, the terms "puritan" and "anglican" will both be used in this study as labels for the emerging theological differences in early English protestantism—differences in temperature Collinson calls them—with the understanding that the terms are not mutually exclusive.

Both words are problematic when applied to specific persons or parties, for there are larger areas of agreement than of disagreement among most of the disputants in the sixteenth century English church, but generalizations are inevitable, and the labels are generalizations that must be taken for what they are: artificial constructs applied to a reality too messy to be forced into neat compartments. Categories are necessary, but no individual will conform completely to the one in which he is placed. Richard Greenham, for example, will be called a puritan, but by some definitions of "anglican," he is that as well. The terms will be used in full recognition of their deficiencies, to describe subtle differences in

[14] "Puritanism, Arminianism and Counter-Revolution" in Conrad Russell, ed., *The Origins of the English Civil War* (London: Macmillan, 1973) 121. Cf., Nicholas Tyacke, *Anti-Calvinists: The Rise of English Arminianism* (Oxford: Clarendon Press, 1987) 7,8. See also the debate between Tyacke and Peter White, "Debate: The Rise of Arminianism Reconsidered," *Past and Present*, 115 (May 1987) 201-229.

[15] Dewey Wallace, *Puritans and Predestination*, 71.

[16] J.S. Coolidge, among others, has analyzed various theological nuances that surfaced early in the English Reformation. *The Pauline Renaissance in England* (Oxford: Clarendon Press, 1970). Cf. Ronald J. Vander Molen, "Anglican Against Puritan: ideological origins during the Marian exile," *Church History*, xlii (1973) 45-57, and J.F.H. New, *Anglican and Puritan; the Basis of their opposition, 1558-1640* (London: Adam and Charles Black, 1964).

attitude vis á vis the need for additional reform, and for differences in religious fervor when it came to matters of godliness, holiness, and purity.

Finally, the term "moderate puritanism," commonly used in the trade over the past twenty years or so to describe the peace-loving, conformist puritans, is meaningful, but only when it is clearly understood that the adjective "moderate" has *political* reference. Puritanism was, at its core, radically spiritual. To speak of "moderate puritanism," therefore, is arguably oxymoronic. If it was moderate in the temperature of its spiritual dynamic, it was not Puritanism. Perhaps the term "cooperative Puritanism" is preferable. This label leaves intact the strong puritan zeal for godliness, and at the same time unambiguously suggests a puritanism that was not separatist, non-conformist, or in any way disrespectful or disobedient to lawful, established authority of either church or state. It was, on the contrary, fully cooperative, promoting peace, harmony, and unity both in the ecclesiastical and political realms.

This study is based primarily on Richard Greenham's *Workes,* published posthumously through the prodigious editing efforts of Henry Holland, a clerical colleague and Cambridgeshire neighbor of Greenham. With the help of a number of "godly and learned friends," Holland painstakingly collected spiritual treatises and wise sayings of Greenham, some of which "were taken from his mouth when he preached, the rest written...with his owne hand, but no part revised or corrected by himselfe with intent and purpose to be published."[17] It was Holland who compared the collected copies, and then revised, corrected, organized, and reorganized the wide variety of materials, lovingly nursing them through three editions, and nearly ready to go to press with the fourth at the time of his death in 1604. Holland's wife finished the fourth edition, published in 1605, and dedicated it to King James I, the recent successor of Queen Elizabeth. A fifth and final edition, virtually identical to the fourth, appeared in 1612. Unless indicated otherwise, all references in this study will be to the fifth edition.

In "The Preface to the Reader," repeated in all the editions, Henry Holland's love and respect for Greenham knows no bounds. He feels

[17] *The Workes of M. Richard Greenham,* (third edition, 1601) 254.

himself unworthy to write about "this reverend mans life" and of his work in the Church. Simply to have known him was the rarest of privileges, "for that the most rare graces of Gods spirit did shine in him...." Greenham was an ecclesiastical titan, who used his extraordinary gifts to make enormous contributions to God's church and kingdom. "He was the special instrument and hand of God to bring many, both godly and learned, to the holy service of Christ," Holland declares. Greenham, in Holland's judgment, had a rare capacity for dealing with "afflictions of the mind," which are "very great and dangerous." Holland believes that Greenham "could have given best rules for this unknowne facultie," for he restored many from unspeakable torments, and terrors of minde." Holland quotes Greenham himself as having expressed special interest in such pastoral psychology. In fact, "many godly learned friends" had urged him to take up this study, train others in it, and "leave unto posteritie a commentarie of such particular maladies, as through Gods blessing hee hath cured, together with the meanes used to that end." Holland also praises Greenham for being a great leavening influence in a turbulent Church of England that seemed constantly threatened with dissension. He was very effective at restraining radicals "from schisme and error, striving alwaies to retaine such in obedience of lawes, and pretiouslie to esteeme and regard the peace of Church and people of God." To close the Preface, Holland extols Greenham's two-fold literary contribution:

> This good servant of Christ in all these workes, doth not onely teach and informe the mind in sundry arguments handled in this volume, concerning truth and error, that so in judgement wee might receive the one and reject the other: but most principally respecteth in the whole, to edifie the heart and conscience, being well assured, that this part hath most neede in most Christians of direction and consolation: and as we be in this part affected, so be we in substance and veritie before God. For this cause hee desireth and laboureth most in all these workes, to stirre up the heart, and to quicken the affections to embrace true godlines, that so being freed from sin by the blood of Christ, and made the servants

of God, we might have our fruit in holines, and in the end
eternall life.

Although God has "translated this Elias from us," it was Holland's
great hope that the legacy of Richard Greenham would live on
through these written works. This hope was realized, for the
posthumous publication history itself is testimony to Greenham's
continuing significance and influence. His *Workes* went through five
editions in a mere thirteen years, 1599-1612. A half century later they
were still popular. In 1673, Richard Baxter, in answer to the question,
"What Books Especially of Theologie should one choose, who for
want of money or time, can read but few?" responded with a list of
books and authors who should be included "in the Poorest or
Smallest Library that is tolerable." Under authors on the topic, "The
Practice of Piety," Greenham is high on the list.[18] His *Workes* were to
be found on the shelves of many a seventeenth century home, and
Baxter suggests that his writings were in the libraries of all the puritan
pastors.

The first edition appeared in 1599, five years after his death. It was
a small, quarto volume of 476 pages. The editions were gradually
expanded to become 875 folio pages in the fourth (1605) edition,
repeated in the fifth. Henry Holland was passionate for good order—
"methodical manner" he calls it—and so was constantly at work
reshuffling the contents. The fifth and final edition is divided into five
parts. The organizational principle is not readily apparent, but the
first part seems to be the result of Holland's attempt to bring the
brief, pithy, pedagogical material together in one unit. It is made up
largely of "grave counsels" and "divine aphorisms," and concludes
with Greenham's catechism, an exceptionally important document for
understanding his theological approach. The second part consists of
seventeen treatises of various lengths and of considerable variety in
content. Many of these deal with practical matters of spiritual life and
devotion: prayer, fasting, reading Scripture, etc. There are also two
treatises on comfort for afflicted consciences. Another of the more
significant documents in this section is on the "sending of the Holy
Ghost." The lengthiest one in the second part, however, is
Greenham's famous "Treatise of the Sabaoth," one of the earliest

---

[18] *A Christian Directory* (London, 1673) 921-2.

extensive treatments of the fourth commandment and the one that prompted and inspired the classic volumes on the Sabbath written by his step-son, Nicholas Bownd.

Part three is made up entirely of sermons—seventeen of them—which provide excellent insight into the nature and style of Greenham's preaching. They are thoroughly biblical, yet more topical than exegetical, focussing on a variety of practical issues. The sermons are typically devotional and somewhat introspective. Concluding this section are two sermons on the cross of Christ, both very positive and joyful in tone. Part four includes five "meditations" on various portions of Scripture. They are quite similar in style to the sermons, but typically much briefer in scope. These meditations include, however, the lengthiest treatise in the *Workes*, meditations on Psalm 119, more than 220 pages in all.

The fifth and last part might well be called the "commonplaces" of Richard Greenham. It contains a vast number of "godly instructions for the due examination and direction of all men, to the attayning and retayning of faith and good conscience." It is truly a handbook for the Christian life, with seventy-five items arranged in alphabetical order from "admonition" to "zeal." Having a problem with pride? Check it out in Greenham's manual, page 741. Want a biblical answer to your questions on "Physicke and Diet"? Turn to page 794.

These then are the published works of Richard Greenham, "a holy monument for posteritie," in the words of Henry Holland, who is still to be acknowledged with gratitude for his tireless efforts. For all his conscientious attempts to collect every last fragment of Greenham's written wisdom, however, he missed one item of immense significance: Rylands English Manuscript 524 located in the John Rylands Library in Manchester, England.[19] Patrick Collinson discovered this manuscript in 1954, when he was a young scholar embarking on what turned out to be a most illustrious career. The document is untitled and will be referred to in this book simply as "tabletalk." It appears to be the work of one of Greenham's students

---

[19] Kenneth L Parker has produced an unpublished transcription, dated 1989, under the title, *Rylands English Manuscript 524: Authur [sic] Hildersham's Commonplace Book of the Sayings of Richard Greenham 1581-1584.* He has kindly provided me with a copy which I have used after comparing it both with a microfilm copy of the original document and with my own transcription of it.

at the rectory, probably Arthur Hildersham,[20] written during the years 1581-1584, the first few years of Greenham's final decade in the Dry Drayton parish. It is essentially a compilation of the accumulated wisdom of Richard Greenham, gleaned from discussions around the dinner table, other informal conversation, and from Hildersham's observations of the master at work.

The document is an unedited, handwritten, rough, first draft, 135 folio pages in length, consisting of single paragraph items pertaining to Greenham, his ministry, and his insights into the Christian life. Its only organization is chronological; in terms of subject matter it is a totally random collection. There are 450 items in all, ranging in length from one or two lines to three pages. Most of these are short summaries of Greenham's views on a wide array of topics; for example, church sacraments and ceremonies, preaching, pastoral work, practical problems of faith, and the ongoing struggle with sin and evil. These normally begin with "he said" or "he observed" or "his judgement was."

About a hundred items are explicitly presented as Greenham's answers to questions put to him by parishioners and others who came to him for advice. These typically begin with the following or similar formula: "To one with an afflicted conscience, he said...." There are also a number of short morality stories, accounts of striking episodes that contain some lesson for life.[21] In addition, there are some sixty spiritual aphorisms attributed to Greenham, such as, "The promises of god must bee to our prayers as a double string to our bow";[22] "many are barren in grace beecaus they are barrain in prayer";[23] "wee cannot hartily bee greeved for that sin in others whereof wee have not made great conscience in ourselves."[24] Finally, there is a substantial number of Hildersham's own observations of Greenham—his personality, conduct, style of ministry, manner of dealing with people and issues—presented as sterling examples for others to follow. Much of the document reads like a "how to" manual on the Christian life with rules for behaviour, advice about interpersonal relationships, the

---

[20] On Hildersham, see DNB.
[21] See, for example, fols. 56v, 57v, 59r, 60r, 61r, and 64r&v. Most of these, as well as the aphorisms, appear in the last (1584) section of the table talk.
[22] Fol. 57r.
[23] Fol. 58v.
[24] Fol. 60v.

technique of self-examination, instructions for ministry, worship in private or in the church, and of course, the pathway to comfort for afflicted consciences. All in all, REM 524, along with the published *Workes,* are invaluable resources for understanding the pastoral work and the protestant thought of Richard Greenham.

The following chapters contain a description of Greenham's ministry and an analysis of his thought. Chapter one is a brief account of the decade he spent gaining a formal education at Pembroke College, Cambridge. Chapter two surveys his extremely difficult ministry in the small Cambridgeshire village of Dry Drayton. Chapter three takes a look at Greenham's attitude toward and involvement in the political controversies rampant in the young protestant Church of England in the latter half of the sixteenth century. Chapters four through seven contain an analysis of the focal points of Greenham's theology. Chapter eight delineates a number of conclusions, followed by a closing epilogue describing the final few years of his ministry in London until 1594, the year of the death of "this reverend man of God."

# 1

# THE CAMBRIDGE YEARS

## I

One spring day in 1559, young Richard Greenham stepped through the main gate of Pembroke Hall in Cambridge, and went looking for his room. He makes his very first appearance in the historical record as a sizar at Pembroke, where he enrolled on May 27, 1559.[1] Before that date we know nothing for sure about Greenham. Like ancient Melchizedek of biblical lore, he is without father or mother or genealogy.[2] Even his birthyear is a matter of guesswork. *The Dictionary of National Biography* gives it as 1535 (with a question mark), but that is almost certainly too early, for in his tabletalk Greenham himself is quoted as saying that he was "a child in Q Maries daies."[3] Mary reigned from 1553-58, so it is unlikely that Greenham was born before the early 1540s. This would also bring him closer to the normal age of matriculation at Cambridge and Oxford in the sixteenth century—14-16. That he was a sizar suggests that his family was not well-to-do and that he worked for his room and board, possibly by doing chores for the master or fellows of the college.

Whence he came to Cambridge is even more of a mystery. Marshall Knappen says he hailed from Lancashire, but leaves the statement undocumented.[4] Another possibility is that his surname

---

[1] Charles H. and Thompson Cooper, *Athenae Cantabrigienses* (Cambridge: Deighton, Bell, and Co. and Macmillan and Co., 1861) II, 103, 143, 356, 546.

[2] Hebrews 7:3.

[3] REM 524, 16v.

[4] Marshall M. Knappen, *Tudor Puritanism* (Chicago: University of Chicago Press, 1939) 382.

was derived from the English hamlet where the family once resided. Currently there are two villages called Greenham in England, one in Berkshire, the other in Somerset. Perhaps Richard came from Greenham, but the records in neither of the villages yield positive evidence. Thomas Fuller, always quick to seize a rhetorical opportunity, uses the mystery surrounding Greenham's early life to good advantage.

> It may be said of some persons in reference to their history, that they were born men, namely, such of whose birth, and youth, we finde no particular account. Greenham is one of these, for, for want of better intelligence we finde him full grown at the first, when...he was admitted into Pembroke Hall in Cambridge.[5]

From 1559-1570, Cambridge was Greenham's home. Sixteenth century Cambridge was far different from the busy, crowded city it is today.[6] With its sixteen colleges in 1559, it was a university town, but with a decidedly rural atmosphere. The pollution problems in Greenham's day were not the result of exhaust emission from thousands of automobiles. Sanitary regulations of 1575 indicate the presence of livestock—pigs, cows, and geese—in the streets and alleys, and even in the colleges themselves, with the resultant dirt and smell. There were dunghills in Cambridge, as well as unclean slaughter-houses, and every summer saw a recurrence of the plague, interrupting the educational enterprise. Some things, however, never change. Foreign visitors (e.g., Erasmas and Bucer) complained bitterly about the climate. And just like today, there was great natural and cultural beauty in and around Cambridge: rolling fields, trees, and gardens, the striking architecture of the colleges, the courtyards, and the visually overwhelming King's College Chapel, then, as now, the chief landmark of the town. Religiously, the Cambridge of the mid-sixteenth century has been called the "Wittenburg" of England, in recognition of its important role in the genesis of the English

---

[5] *The Church History of Britain* (London: William Tegg, 1868) III, 146.

[6] Harry C. Porter gives a brief, physical description of sixteenth century Cambridge in *Reformation and Reaction in Cambridge* (Cambridge: University Press, 1958) 18-19.

Reformation.[7] Earlier in the century, an important visiting scholar at Queen's College, by the name of Desiderius Erasmus had opened up the Scriptures for serious study in Cambridge. By the 1520s, a reform movement was underway, led especially by Thomas Bilney, Hugh Latimer, and Robert Barnes.[8] This trio constituted the core of the early Cambridge reformers and of the famous White Horse Inn group where the ideas of Luther were discussed. Other important Cambridge religious leaders in the 1520s were Miles Coverdale, William Tyndale, John Frith, John Rogers, Richard Taverner, Matthew Parker, and Thomas Cranmer. They put the Bible first, and relegated the medieval philosophers to the background. The royal injunctions of 1535, shaped by Henry VIII's problems with the pope, stipulated that the traditional lectures in canon law were to be replaced with teaching "according to the true sense" of Scripture, and students were encouraged to read the Bible privately. Melanchthon's *Loci* became prescribed reading in that same year. Cambridge was on its way to becoming "the creative theological centre and the most important seminary of the Elizabethan Church."[9]

The reform movement continued apace in the 1540s, especially under the more openly protestant regime of young King Edward VI. Late in the decade, Martin Bucer, the Strasbourg reformer who significantly influenced John Calvin's thought, was appointed at Cambridge. His arrival in 1549 "set the seal upon the success of the Cambridge reformers,"[10] even though his tenure was brief. Bucer died in 1551, and his remains became a symbol of the religious vacillation that followed: buried with honor in Great St. Mary's; disinterred in 1557 by Mary and burned on Market Hill; restored to honor in 1560 under Elizabeth not long after Greenham arrived in Cambridge. Young Greenham most likely attended that ceremony.

Upon Edward's death in 1553, Mary, the devout Roman Catholic daughter of Henry VIII and Catherine of Aragon, came to the throne, determined to stamp out Protestantism from the realm. Although she attempted to strip Cambridge of protestant leadership as well as of

---

[7] James B. Mullinger, *A History of the University of Cambridge* (London: Longmans, Green, and Co., 1888) 79ff., 113. See also Mullinger's "Preface."
[8] St. Edward's Church, in the heart of the city center, contains a tablet dedicated to the memory of these three.
[9] Patrick McGrath, *Papists and Puritans Under Elizabeth I* (London: Blandford Press, 1967) 34.
[10] Porter, *Reformation and Reaction*, 51.

protestant worship, it was during her reign that "the English Reformation came of age" through the dual impact of the protestant martyrs and protestant exiles.[11] Many of the martyrs and at least one fifth of the exiles were from Cambridge. When Elizabeth came to the throne in 1558, the Reformation, which had continued as an underground movement, resurfaced and became permanently established in the Church of England.

Greenham matriculated at Pembroke Hall in 1559, graduated B.A. in 1563-64, commenced M.A. in 1567, and was elected a fellow at about that time.[12] This "model puritan" was schooled and shaped for the ministry during the early Elizabethan years, in part before the label "puritan" had even been coined, so he must be interpreted and understood in a religious context formed by Edward and Mary as well as Elizabeth. He was reading theology at Pembroke when memories of popery were fresh and when, in Cambridge especially, a strong protestant consensus had developed against Marian Catholicism. In 1559, earnest protestant reformers in England were filled with mixed emotions. They were mourning the death of the martyrs who were victims of the Marian persecutions, and rejoicing in the accession of the new protestant queen, Elizabeth. Mary died in November of 1558, just six months before Greenham arrived in Cambridge. The fires she had lit at Smithfield in London, where many of England's leading protestants perished in the flames, had barely been extinguished. The last martyrs were burned on November 11, six days before Mary died, prompting this entry in the register recording the final executions: "Six days after these were burned to death, God sent us our Elizabeth."[13]

During the early years of the new regime, hopes and expectations ran high among England's protestants. Although the nature and depth of Greenham's religious convictions at this time are unknown, he probably shared these hopes, and at Pembroke Hall, when he and his friends took their tea breaks and discussed national and ecclesiastical politics, their conversations must have turned quickly to such matters as the Elizabethan settlement, the new Prayer Book, and Parliament's treatment of the church. 1559 was a landmark year in

---

[11] Ibid., 74.
[12] *Grace Book Delta*, ed. Jon Venn (Cambridge: University Press, 1910) 171, 173, 203.
[13] Elizabeth Jenkins, *Elizabeth the Great* (London: Panther Books, 1958) 64.

which power swiftly shifted to the protestants. The new, protestant queen was officially crowned on Sunday, January 15, just four months before Greenham matriculated at Pembroke Hall. She immediately appointed protestant sympathizer William Cecil as Chancellor of Cambridge University, and later in the year, Matthew Parker of Cambridge and Landbeach as Archbishop of the Church of England.[14] An Act of Uniformity was adopted as part of the Elizabethan settlement, enforcing protestant worship in churches throughout the land. The new Book of Common Prayer was used for the first time on May 14, just two weeks before Greenham's arrival in Cambridge. Soon after, the Geneva Bible arrived in England with the returning exiles. When Greenham began his theological training, such privileges as reading the Scriptures in the vernacular were still relatively new and exciting experiences, and devout protestants were keenly aware that these privileges had been restored at a very high price: the lives of the protestant martyrs.

In Cambridge, where several of those martyrs had been resident members of the university and leaders in the colleges, awareness of the devastation wrought by Mary, and anticipation of new opportunities represented by Elizabeth must have been keen indeed. There is no better expression of protestant hopes and expectations to be found than in the prefatory letter printed in the Geneva Bible. It was written by English exiles and addressed to Queen Elizabeth. The homiletical opportunity of comparing their return from exile with that of the ancient Israelites was not lost on these devout churchmen. God has appointed the new queen to be "our Zerubbabel," they declared, with admirable gender blindness. She will lead in the rebuilding of the temple in England, and will "plante and maynteyne" God's Word in the land, for it is her task to feed the Church of England "both in body and soule." There is no better way to fight the papists and to build the church than through the holy scripture, which is a "fyre and hammer to breake the stonie heartes of them that resist Gods mercies offred by the preaching of the same." The two fundamental requirements for the reestablishment of the protestant temple are aptly stated: "First that we have a lyvely and stedfast faith

---

[14] Parker resisted this appointment but the Queen prevailed. She was returning a favor. Parker had been her mother's chaplain, and he had promised Ann Boleyn before her death that he would look after Elizabeth.

in Christ Jesus," who "is the only meanes and assurance of our
salvation," and second, "that our faith bring forthe good fruites, so
that our godly conversation may serve us as a witnes to confirme our
election and to be an example to all others...." For training to be a
co-worker in the temple's reconstruction, Richard Greenham entered
Pembroke Hall.

## II

Pembroke Hall was the fifth of the Cambridge colleges, founded in
1347 by the Countess of Pembroke.[15] It boasted the first college
chapel in Cambridge, erected in 1357. Judging from the illustrious
list of fellows and masters of Pembroke Hall, it appears that this
college played an important role in the English reformation.[16] It had
been the academic home of such notables as John Rogers, Nicholas
Ridley, and John Bradford—all outstanding protestant leaders who
were martyred in 1555. Before he was executed at Smithfield, Ridley
delivered a brief farewell to his *alma mater,* in which he reflects on
Pembroke's established reputation for protestant, Christian learning.

> Farewell, Pembroke Hall, of late mine own college, my cure
> and my charge! What case thou art in now, God knoweth, I
> know not well. Thou wast ever named sithens [since] I knew
> thee (which is now a thirty years ago,) to be studious, well
> learned, and a great setter forth of Christ's gospel and of
> God's true word: so I found thee, and, blessed be God! so I
> left thee indeed....[17]

Fittingly for the "Pauline renaissance" in England, Ridley
memorized all of St. Paul's letters while at Pembroke, and prayed that
"this zeal and love toward that part of God's word, which is a key and
true commentary to all the holy Scriptures, may ever abide in that

---

[15] Robert Hawes and Robert Yoder report that the Countess "in one day, (that
is) the day of her marriage, was a maid, a wife, and a widow, her husband being that
day slain in a tilt, or tournament," *The History of Framlingham* (Woodbridge,
1798) 208. This work includes lists of "Masters and Fellows of Pembroke Hall" in
Chs. 9 and 10. Greenham is mentioned on p. 232.
[16] Cf., "The Glory of Pembroke Hall," Ch. 2 in Patrick Collinson, *Archbishop
Grindall* (London: Jonathan Cape, 1979) 35-46.
[17] *Works* (Parker Society, 1841) 406.

college so long as the world shall endure."[18]

John Bradford, who was appointed Fellow of Pembroke Hall in 1550, was also martyred at Smithfield in 1555. It was Bradford who uttered the famous line to a fellow victim as the flames licked up around them, "Be of good comfort brother: for we shall have a merry supper with the Lord this night."[19] Bradford had been a friend of Hugh Latimer, a tutor of John Whitgift (later Master of Pembroke Hall, and still later, Archbishop), and a close friend and disciple of Martin Bucer. He was a prominent leader at Cambridge, and his heroic martyrdom guaranteed that his memory would linger on at Pembroke Hall during Greenham's years there. Greenham's writings, in fact, show much affinity to those of Bradford. Their approaches to such topics as law and gospel, repentance, faith, providence, election, meditation, and prayer are strikingly similar. They share the same devotional spirit, and the same emphasis on the good life leading from faith.[20]

Bucer's presence at nearby Corpus Christi College from 1549-51 was certainly important for the shaping of protestant thought at Pembroke Hall. Patrick Collinson, who believes that "it was in England that the echo of Bucer's voice resounded longest," speculates that Bucer spent long hours conferring with his friends at Pembroke, just across the street from Corpus.[21] Ridley, Bradford, Sampson, and Grindall were all friends and disciples of Bucer. Bradford, appointed fellow at Pembroke Hall in 1549, referred fondly to Bucer as, "My father in the Lord," sat with him day and night during his last illness, and in his farewell to Cambridge left this admonition: "Remember the readings and preachings of Gods true prophet and true preacher, Martin Bucer."[22] Bucer's legacy to generations of English puritans in the following century is suggested by August Lang, when he calls the Strasbourger, "the pietist among the Reformers."[23]

---

[18] Ibid., 407.
[19] John Foxe, *The Book of Martyrs* (London, 1732) 291.
[20] See Carl R. Trueman, *Luther's Legacy* (Oxford: Clarendon Press, 1994) esp. 243-88.
[21] *Godly People: Essays on English Protestantism and Puritanism* (London: The Hambledon Press, 1983) 25, 31.
[22] *The Writings of John Bradford* (Parker Society, 1848) I, 31, 355, 445; II, 352-4. Cf., Collinson, ibid.
[23] *Der Evangelienkommentar Martin Butzers* (Leipzig: Dieterich'sche Verlags-Buchhandlung, 1900) 14.

Thomas Sampson, one of the earliest "non-conformists," was also a Pembroke man in the 1540s. He refused vestments at his ordination in 1549, and was an exile on the continent during part of Mary's reign. In 1564, he was cited for nonconformity along with Laurence Humphrey. Pembroke Hall was by no means a nursery for reactionaries, however. It was broadly evangelical, moderate, mainstream, and centrist in the Church of England's political spectrum, a position that would be modelled by Greenham. No less than three Masters of Pembroke Hall went on to become archbishops under Elizabeth: Edmund Grindal, John Whitgift, and Matthew Hutton.[24] Pembroke also produced Lancelot Andrewes, who "was well acquainted with Mr. Greenham,"[25] became a Master of the college, and, in the following century, a prominent bishop in the Church of England.

Regarding Greenham's formal studies at Cambridge, for his B.A. he would have studied the seven liberal arts contained in the basic Trivium of Grammar, Logic, and Rhetoric; followed by the Quadrivium made up of Music, Arithmetic, Geometry, and Astronomy. He became fluent in Latin and Greek, and his works reveal acquaintance with classical philosophy. For his M.A. the curriculum would have included Logic and Metaphysics, besides Theology, but the teaching was handled on an *ad hoc* basis in the individual colleges and was largely dependent upon the wishes and whims of the current Master. Matthew Hutton was Master of Pembroke during Greenham's middle years there, 1562-67. Hutton was a sound scholar, who was appointed Professor of Divinity in 1562, and was entrusted to lead the theological disputation before Queen Elizabeth on the occasion of her visit to Cambridge in 1564. Greenham may have learned about moderation from Hutton—in the vestments controversy he was one of the Cambridge leaders who recommended compromise.[26]

The theological curriculum at Cambridge also included serious, academic study of the Bible. Samuel Clarke reports that Thomas

---

[24] Hutton became Archbishop of York; Whitgift succeeded Grindal as Archbishop of Canterbury.

[25] Thomas Fuller, *The Church History of Britain*, III, 146. Fuller adds, "if Greenham gained any learning by Andrews, Andrews lost no religion by Greenham." According to Fuller, Andrews may have been one of those friends who helped Henry Holland compile Greenham's *Workes*.

[26] Ibid., 43.

Wilson, early in the following century, "had read the whole Bible, with the Annotations of Junius and Tremelius three times over," before he finished his B.A.[27] One of Greenham's contemporaries at Cambridge, Laurence Chaderton, drew up an "Order to be used for the trayning upp and exercising of Students in Divinitye,"[28] with a heavy emphasis on biblical exegesis and proclamation. The order included "mutual conference," in which the whole Bible was examined, interpreted and discussed over a two year period. Students were required to "diligentlye searche out by them selves the trewe sense and meaning of the text appointed...." Knowledge of Hebrew and Greek, the arts of Rhetoric and Logic, internal comparison of Scripture with Scripture, study of learned commentators, and familiarity with Greek and Roman History, were also required. In the mutual conferences, two students were assigned to deliver the meaning of the text; the others listened, evaluated, and responded. Chaderton's order also required "disputation," by which, over the course of two years, all controversial points "betweene us and the Papists and other hereticks" were to be examined and discussed. Greenham learned these lessons well. Nothing is more evident from his *Workes* than his thorough grounding in the Scriptures.

The daily routine and the spartan conditions of a Cambridge college in the mid-sixteenth century is described in a sermon by Thomas Lever, who, after lamenting the "secular" state of the university, conceded there were still "a small number of poore godly dylygent students" in the colleges who were serious, God-fearing, and well disciplined.

> There be dyvers ther whych ryse dayly betwixte foure and fyve of the clocke in the mornynge, and from fyve untyll syxe of the clocke, use common prayer wyth an exhortacion of gods worde in a commune chappell, and from sixe unto ten of the clocke use ever eyther pryvate study or commune lectures. At ten of the clocke they go to dynner, whereas they be contente wyth a penye pyece of byefe amongest, iiii. havying a fewe porage made of the brothe of the same byefe, wyth salte and

---

[27] *The Lives of Sundry Eminent Persons* (London, 1683) 19.
[28] Albert Peel, ed., *The Seconde Parte of a Register*, 2 vols. (Cambridge: University Press, 1915) I, 133-4.

otemell, and nothynge els. After thys slender dinner they be
either teachynge or learnynge untyll v. of the clocke in the
evenyng, when as they have a supper not much better then
theyr dyner. Immedyatelye after the whyche, they go eyther to
reasonyng in problemes or unto some other studye, untyll it
be nyne or tenne of the clocke, and there beying wythout fyre
are fayne to walk or runne up and downe halfe an houre, to
gette a heate on their feete whan they go to bed.[29]

Lever was Master of St. John's when he preached this sermon, but
routines in the various colleges tended to be similar, and his
description is worded in such a way as to suggest life at the university
in general. Greenham no doubt followed a similar schedule and
experienced the same austere conditions.

By the time of Greenham's matriculation, Pembroke Hall had
developed a solid academic reputation. Gabriel Harvey wanted to
keep it that way. Harvey became a fellow at Pembroke in 1570,
shortly before Greenham left his teaching position there. Reflecting
on his illustrious predecessors at Pembroke Hall, Harvey urged that
Greek lectures be instituted, so that we may "in time grow to that
ripenes of learning, wisdom and eloquens whitch thos our
predecessors grew unto, that at length it mai pass for a gud
consequent he is a Pembrook Hal man, ergo a good schollar."[30]

It is virtually impossible to know for sure what Greenham read
while at Pembroke in the 1560s, but Matthew Wren and Elisabeth
Leedham-Green provide some clues. Wren in 1617 compiled an
important manuscript history of the Pembroke library which includes
a catalogue of holdings.[31] From this can be gained a fairly clear
picture of the library's contents in the 1560s. Works of Aristotle,
Seneca, Josephus, and Plutarch are mentioned, along with a number

---

[29] *Sermons*, ed. by Edward Arber (London, 1870) 121-2. This description of
student life at Cambridge is from a sermon preached at Paul's Cross on 14
December 1550.

[30] Quoted in Aubrey Attwater, *Pembroke College Cambridge: A Short History*
(Cambridge: Pembroke College, 1973) 47. Harvey became a life-long friend of the
poet, Edmund Spenser, who enrolled at Pembroke Hall in 1569. Greenham may
have been Spenser's tutor, and Marshall M. Knappen speculates that Greenham was
the source of some of Spenser's ideas, *Richard Greenham and the Practical
Puritans under Elizabeth*, 87ff.

[31] *Memoriae, Veritati, Virtuti, Sacram LAVRUM Pembrochianam*, 1617,
located in the Pembroke library.

of church fathers, Irenaeus, Chrysostom, Jerome, Tertullian, Ambrose, and Lactantius. Josephus, Eusebius, and the Venerable Bede are among the historians, and Augustine is included along with later authors from the medieval period—Aquinas, Albertus Magnus, and Erasmus. Writings of the reformers do not appear in the earliest lists, but are included later in benefactors' bequests. In the 1560s, Calvin's *Institutes*, Bullinger's *Decades*, Musculus's *Commonplaces*, and Melanchthon's *Loci*, were standard fare for Cambridge students of theology. Judging from the Cambridge private library inventories compiled by Leedham-Green, the works of Aristotle, Cicero, Augustine, Aquinas, Erasmus, Melanchthon, Bullinger, Calvin, and Musculus were especially popular in Cambridge.[32] Most of these authors are mentioned, however briefly, in the text of Greenham's *Workes*. He also makes explicit reference to Plato, Hymineus, Philetus, Athanasius, Hilary, Luther, Bucer, Martyr, Beza, and Tremelius. But Greenham lived before footnotes, and at a time when rules regarding attribution, quotation, and plagiarism were almost non-existent.

The influence of his peers, who were also studying at the university in the 1560s, was probably as important as his formal training for the shaping of Greenham's theology. He had many colleagues with the same ministerial aspirations. John Whitgift claimed that from the beginning of Elizabeth's reign until 1573—just a fifteen year span—"the number of known preachers, which this university hath bred...are at least 450." In 1573 alone, according to Whitgift, there were 102 aspiring preachers at Cambridge.[33] Patrick Collinson has gathered a "rough-and-ready list" of 228 Cambridge students and fellows, who showed some evidence of puritan convictions between the years 1565 and 1575.[34] Among the leading lights were Laurence Chaderton, Edward Dering, John More, and Walter Travers at Christ's College; John Knewstub and William Fulke (later Master of Pembroke) at St. John's; and Thomas Cartwright and Edmund Chapman at Trinity. Cambridge was rapidly developing into the intellectual center of Puritanism precisely during Greenham's most formative years at the university. The list of influential

---

[32] *Books in Cambridge Inventories*, 2 vols. (Cambridge: University Press, 1986).
[33] *Works* (Parker Society, 1851-1853) I, 313.
[34] *The Elizabethan Puritan Movement*, 127.

acquaintances could be expanded considerably when taking into account the fact that Greenham actually spent far more than a decade in the environs of Cambridge. He did not leave the area until 1591, and throughout his long tenure in Dry Drayton, he maintained regular contact with old friends and acquaintances at the university. He also formed new, important friendships, such as the one with William Perkins, English Puritanism's first systematic theologian, who became a dominant figure at Cambridge in the 1580s.

It is impossible to overestimate the significance of Cambridge in the shaping and early development of Greenham's protestant convictions. He himself gives testimony to the importance of the university for the building of God's temple in England in the following soliloquy, which was undoubtedly inspired by his own experience.

> Universities are the eyes of the Common-wealth, and a mote in the eyes is a great trouble. Briefly, Universities be the Lebanon of the Lorde, from whence timber must be fetched to build the Temple. They be the Conduits, to derive water into the whole land. They be the Rocks or Bayes, where Salt is prepared to season. They be the polished Saphires to garnish the house of the Lord.[35]

And yet, for Greenham, the university was but a place of preparation for ministry. If the puritan vision for full reformation was to become a reality, it had to be carried out to the people of the land. So in the fall of 1570, Richard Greenham left the relative security of the academic womb to engage in the harsh realities of ministry in an English country parish.

---

[35] *Workes*, 734.

# 2

# MINISTRY IN DRY DRAYTON

## I

In the autumn of 1570, Richard Greenham left Pembroke Hall to take up the challenge of ministry in an English protestant parish. He did not have far to travel. Five miles northwest of Cambridge, just a mile off the Huntingdon Road, lies the little village of Dry Drayton. Today, the A 14 to Huntingdon is multi-laned and heavily trafficked, but within moments of taking the left turn on to the narrow road that snakes across the fields to the village, there is stillness and peace. Pulling up on the side street in front of the Church of St. Peter and St. Paul is like entering a time warp. It is the only pre-sixteenth century building left in the village, and it was here that Greenham was instituted as rector on November 27, 1570,[1] a clerical post he would hold for the next twenty-one years.

The name of the village is unusual, and the cynic may wonder why any place in England should have "dry" in its name, but with respect to Dry Drayton, there is a rational explanation. It lies in the Cambridgeshire uplands and was probably described as "dry" in contrast to Fen Drayton, another village not far off in the much wetter fenlands. The name "Drayton" suggests "town by the hill," and Dry Drayton is precisely that, with houses nestled against and built upon a sizeable ridge along the north side of town. Greenham must often have watched the dray horses pull ("draeg" in old English) heavy loads of hay and grain up that hill. Hence the name Drayton (draeg-town).[2] Picturesque farmlands surround the village to this day, a rural setting reflected in Greenham's writings where agricultural

---

[1] EDR, G/1/8, fol. 160.
[2] Percy H. Reaney, *The Place-Names of Cambridgeshire and the Isle of Ely* (Cambridge: Cambridge University Press, 1943) 152.

metaphors for the Christian life are common.

Dry Drayton was probably founded in the twelfth century by the abbots of Crowland Abbey who held the parish lands until the dissolution of the monasteries under Henry VIII in 1539.[3] The layout of the village is somewhat atypical, for it reflects a more rational and deliberate plan than is true of most English villages. In addition to the usual High Street, there are a few streets and lanes that run in almost parallel lines.[4] Along these streets lived Greenham's parishioners, most of them in very modest dwellings. Just to the east of the church, however, stood a large manor house originally built by the Crowland abbots and later expanded to become the mansion of the Duke of Bedford. Demolished in 1817, it was recently the site of an archeological excavation.

Parts of the parish church of St. Peter and St. Paul date to the thirteenth century although it has been restored and revamped several times since then.[5] The original building was made of fieldstone and clunch covered by a slate roof. The chancel was reconstructed and the tower restored in the nineteenth century. The font is thirteenth century, but the pulpit is a nineteenth century replacement of the old wooden original from which Greenham preached some six thousand sermons. The seating capacity of the building today is approximately 125 and was likely less than that in the sixteenth century.[6]

According to the most recent census figures, the population of Dry Drayton in 1991 was 563. In Greenham's day, it was a little less than half that size. According to the Bishop's Return of 1563, the parish was then made up of thirty-one households with an estimated population of 255.[7] There is evidence of considerable growth during

---

[3] Frances M. Page, *The Estates of Crowland Abbey* (Cambridge: Cambridge University Press, 1934) 155.

[4] I am indebted to Mr. Christopher Taylor of the Royal Commission on Historical Monuments for this observation and other suggestions concerning Dry Drayton.

[5] For a nineteenth century description of the church (and of Dry Drayton flora and fauna) see Francis A. Walker, *A History of the Parish of Dry Drayton* (London: T.P. Newman, 1876).

[6] This assumes the church had been "impewed" by Greenham's time; there is no definite evidence either way.

[7] William M. Palmer and Herbert W. Saunders, eds., *Documents Relating to Cambridgeshire Villages*, VI, (December, 1926) 102. A survey of 1603 suggests that the average size of all English parishes was 243 communicants, cf., Christopher Haigh, *Reformation and Resistance in Tudor Lancashire* (Cambridge: Cambridge University Press, 1975) 231.

Greenham's tenure. According to the parish register, in the two decades of the 1570s and 80s, baptisms outnumbered burials 203 to 64, about a three to one ratio.[8] Although data from parish registers must be handled cautiously, the growth suggested is consistent with that to be found in other Cambridgeshire villages and even throughout the nation during that period.[9] Since the population increase in Dry Drayton took place without corresponding growth in the material resources of the 2400 acre parish, the people had significant economic as well as spiritual needs. Greenham responded to both in creative ways and with exemplary compassion.

He first lived alone in the rectory, arriving there as a young bachelor about thirty years of age. But, like Luther, a Katherine entered his life. Nothing is known of their courtship, but in August of 1573 Greenham married Katherine Bownd, widow of Dr. Robert Bownd, personal physician to the Duke of Norfolk.[10] She had four children by her first marriage: Nicholas (who later gained fame through his treatises on the Sabbath) Alexander, Richard, and Ann. Ann became the bride of John "Decalogue" Dod in 1585— sabbatarians abounded in Greenham's extended family. His marriage to Katherine produced no additional offspring, but, as Henry Holland observed, "God gave him (to recompence his want of naturall children) many sons and daughters begotten by the Gospell...."[11]

## II

When Greenham took up his work in Dry Drayton, only eleven years had passed since the coronation of Elizabeth and the adoption of the Act of Uniformity governing the religious life and thought of the Church of England. The church was again officially protestant but this did not translate automatically into genuine reform. Parish pastors with a passion for completing the reformation faced a

---

[8] CRO, P/58/I/I
[9] Cf., Margaret Spufford, *Contrasting Communities* (Cambridge: Cambridge University Press, 1979) 228; David Underdown, *Revel, Riot, and Rebellion* (Oxford: Clarendon Press, 1985) 18ff.; and William G. Hoskins, "The Rebuilding of Rural England 1570-1640," *Past and Present*, 4 (1953) 459.
[10] William P. W. Phillimore and Evelyn Young, eds., *Cambridgeshire Parish Registers—Marriage*, Vol. III (London: Phillimore and Co., 1909) 70; *Dry Drayton Parish Register*, CRO, P/58/I/I.
[11] "Epistle Dedicatorie," *The Works of...Richard Greenham* (1599 edition.)

daunting challenge, for at the grass roots there was little evidence of enthusiasm for reform.[12] Greenham's parish was composed largely of subsistence level tenant farmers and poor labourers along with a few yeomen and a few small trades people for whom the ecclesiastical twists and turns of the previous generation must have seemed utterly baffling. Some of the most significant and genuine movements toward reform in all England were taking place in Cambridge, only five miles away, but culturally and intellectually—and perhaps religiously—Dry Drayton and Cambridge were light years apart.

Liturgically, the churches had been brought into conformity to protestant standards by the settlement of 1559, but in theology, doctrinal instruction, and formation of distinctive protestant piety, there was still a long and rugged road to travel. The best evidence suggests very little interest in theological differences between Rome and the reformers. Doctrines like justification by grace through faith alone and the priesthood of all believers probably meant very little to the roughhewn labourers of Dry Drayton and it must have been a herculean task simply to generate interest in the finer theological differences between Rome and the reformers. Lawrence Stone may have overstated the case when he called the Elizabethan period the "age of greatest religious indifference before the twentieth century,"[13] but it is nonetheless certain that zealous reformers like Richard Greenham had their work cut out for them.

His two immediate predecessors in Dry Drayton,[14] who served there after the Elizabethan settlement of 1559, undoubtedly used the new Church of England liturgy, but Greenham was the first to attempt the formation of a fully protestant, evangelical parish based upon the comprehensive teachings of the Reformation. Medieval Catholicism was a religion of ritual and ceremony, and, on the popular level at least, one that put more emphasis on proper

---

[12] Eamon Duffy, *The Stripping of the Altars* (New Haven and London: Yale University Press, 1992) 573. On the progress of reform at the grassroots level, see Keith Wrightson, *English Society* (London: Hutchinson, 1982) 200ff.; Keith Thomas, *Religion and the Decline of Magic* (London: Weidenfeld and Nicholson, 1971) Chs. 3-6; and Margaret Spufford, *Contrasting Communities*, Ch. 10.

[13] *English Historical Review*, Vol. LXXVII, (April, 1962) 328.

[14] John Clever (1541-1567) and William Fayrelough (1567-1570) cf., Walker, *A History of the Parish of Dry Drayton*, 7-8. Fayrelough's tenure was cut short by his involvement in an adulterous affair, EDR, D/2/8, fols. 9v, 11,20,27. Cf., Spufford, *Contrasting Communities*, 327.

observance than it did on correct belief. Protestantism, on the other hand, diminished the importance of ceremonial ritual and emphasized text and doctrine more than sign.[15] It was a religion of the word rather than of rites. Protestant convictions had verbal content, which had to be learned and internalized by all believers. In England, therefore, as on the continent, there was from the beginning of the Reformation a powerful emphasis on catechizing, indicating the large intellectual dimension of this religious revolution.[16] Furthermore, the Christian life, in the Protestant view, involved much more than collective ritual observances. Good works had to be performed personally and individually, in daily adherence and conformity to the will of God expressed in the Scriptures.

The task facing parish pastors like Richard Greenham, therefore, was overwhelming. It was the task of overcoming the natural religious inertia of the masses, leading people to reject a system of religious practices that had been ingrained in them through centuries of tradition, and replacing that system with a word-centered faith that had to be proclaimed to people who were for the most part unlettered and even illiterate. As Keith Thomas has observed, it was not simply a matter of replacing a religious system that had become meaningless with one that was obviously more meaningful. Even when religious ritual becomes utterly a matter of form, it is not necessarily meaningless to those who engage in it. It still may provide a method of survival in a world fraught with insecurity and anxiety. In sixteenth century England, people were exceedingly liable to pain, sickness, and premature death; many had to cope with a precarious food supply; they lived in conditions of poor hygiene and sanitation that brought death-dealing plagues; and their lives and goods were constantly threatened by consuming fire. One of the ways they had learned to cope was the way of religious ceremony and ritual. Holy water, candles, relics, visits to shrines, prayers to saints, the sign of the cross, and use of the sacrament—these were sources of comfort and protection for many who felt they were living in a hostile environment.[17]

What Reformed Protestant pastors like Greenham faced, therefore,

---

[15] Duffy, *The Stripping of the Altars*, 532.
[16] See below, 93-94.
[17] See Thomas, *Religion and the Decline of Magic*, Ch. 1.

was a twofold problem: the persistence of Roman Catholic rituals and devotions in an officially non-Roman Catholic nation; and a religious vacuum of ignorance and indifference on the part of those who had left Catholicism but were only nominally protestant. Throughout England, according to one estimate, not more than one person in forty was a "true gospeller" in the early 1570s.[18] Thomas Cartwright, in a 2500 word prayer of uninterrupted confession written in 1580, declared that there were "heaps" of people in the land who had turned away from Roman Catholicism but "stil abide in an utter ignorance of the truth" and are "as raw in the knowledge of the true service of [God], as they were expert before, in the service of the Devill."[19] According to a document dated 1584, three fourths of England's protestants "were wedded to their old superstitions still," an observation based not on a scientific sampling, but nonetheless reflecting both puritan impatience and the natural religious inertia of the people.[20] Dry Drayton lay within the diocese of Ely, whose visitation articles and injunctions of this period give evidence of the lingering practices of venerating images and relics and visiting Catholic shrines.[21] There is no reason to believe Greenham's parish was unlike other English villages, where, if his contemporaries are to be believed, the parishioners seemed virtually impervious to the gospel.

Josias Nichols complained about his parish of four hundred communicants in Eastwell, Kent, that he "skarse found tenne in a hundred, to have anie knowledge" about such basics as the person and office of Christ, how sin entered the world, what is the punishment for sin, "what becomes of our bodies being rotten in the graves," and whether it is possible for people to "winne heaven" by their good works.[22] Arthur Dent, a preacher in South Shoebury in Essex, complained that many of his parishioners "despise the word of God," regard sermons merely as "good tales," and are "utterly voyd of

---

[18] Patrick Collinson, *English Puritanism* (London: The Historical Association, 1983) 19.
[19] Albert Peel and Leland Carlson, *Cartwrightiana* (London: Allen and Unwin, 1951) 144.
[20] Albert Peel, ed., *The Seconde Parte of a Register* (Cambridge: Cambridge University Press, 1915) i. 254.
[21] Walter H. Frere, ed., *Visitation Articles and Injunctions* (London: Longman, Green and Co., 1910) II, 6, 28, 115, 116.
[22] *The Plea of the Innocent* (n.p., 1602) 219.

all true knowledge of God, and of his word."²³ He implies that secularism is the greatest problem, for when his parishioners "minde, dreame, and dote on nothing else day and night, but this world, lands, and leases, grounds and livings, kine and sheepe, and how to waxe rich,"²⁴ they are likely to ignore Scripture and despise sermons. The only religious exercises they are willing to engage in are the occasional recital of the Lord's Prayer, the ten commandments, and the creed, "without all this running to sermons, and pratling of the scriptures."²⁵ In Dent's grim assessment the nation was rife with people who have no true fear of God, seldom hear the word preached, are content with ignorant ministers, have no family exercises, do not observe the Sabbath, curse and swear oaths, and are better described as gamesters, rioters, drinkers, alehouse haunters, and whore hunters, than as Christians.²⁶

Greenham's stepson, Nicholas Bownd, in 1585 became rector of Norton, a small Suffolk village about thirty miles east of Dry Drayton. Under the inspiration of his stepfather, Bownd wrote the definitive treatises on Sabbatarianism. In one of those volumes, Bownd laments "how few of the common sort can read, or have Bibles, or doe use them at home." He grumbles about the people's ignorance of the most common biblical stories, and claims they are more knowledgeable in the stories of Robin Hood.²⁷ Bownd's complaints are reminiscent of John Jewel's famous comment earlier in the reformation: "Many are so ignorant, they know not what the scriptures are, they know not that there are any scriptures."²⁸

George Gifford paints one of the most graphic and detailed portraits of a sixteenth century rural congregation in his classic treatise on country divinity.²⁹ It is precisely what Greenham must have encountered in Dry Drayton. Gifford first identifies the underlying problem as he sees it: "there is a flood of ignorance and

²³ *The Plaine Mans Path-way to Heaven* (London: 1601) 20.
²⁴ Ibid., 21.
²⁵ Ibid., 27.
²⁶ Ibid., 274-5.
²⁷ *Sabbathum Veteris* (London, 1606,) 338-9.
²⁸ *Works* (Cambridge: Parker Society, 1845-50) II, 1014.
²⁹ *A Briefe discourse of certaine points of the religion, which is among the common sort of Christians, which may be termed the Countrey Divinitie* (London, 1612). Cf., Dewey D. Wallace, "George Gifford, Puritan Propaganda and Popular Religion in Elizabethan England," *The Sixteenth Century Journal*, IX, 1, (1978) 27-49.

darknesse, overflowing the most part of the land," for the people have had "Poperie taken from them" with nothing to replace it. This has resulted in widespread religious indifference.[30] Popular country religion, in Gifford's view, is blindly tradition-bound, stresses works more than faith and knowledge, is ignorant of the Scriptures, and is generally suspicious of knowledgeable "Scripture men."[31] Gifford's country divine believes he can keep some of God's commandments perfectly, and yet despises puritans for their moral hypocrisy.[32] Those who stress preaching are suspect for they are too "hot and severe," and tend to meddle with abstruse doctrines such as election and reprobation which only confuse people and make matters worse.[33] Gifford lashes out at the typical pseudo-religious parishioner who can sit at cards all night, but "if the Preacher do passe his houre but a little, your buttockes begin for to ake, and you wish in your heart that the pulpet would fall."[34] Country divinity is shot through with pelagianism, emphasizing doing more than believing, and hoping that God "will not forget the good deedes which I have done."[35] The archetypal rural believer is ignorant, "crammed as full of Popish drosse as you can hold," and absolutely without knowledge of the true God.[36]

Gifford's analysis highlights particularly the sharp difference between medieval and reformation religion on the issue of knowledge. True repentance, said Gifford, involves right understanding, for repentance is "a returning home unto God from all evill vices and corrupt desires" and to be renewed in repentance "cannot be but where a man is renued in knowledge, for that is one part of the image which must be restored in us."[37] In sum, Gifford's country divine was suspicious of learning, leaned on tradition, despised preaching, de-emphasized knowledge of the word of God, was self-reliant, and had an inadequate grasp of sin, repentance, and faith. He had built up an impenetrable wall of indifference that made it exceedingly difficult for the godly, zealous, puritan pastors to succeed in bringing about their

---

[30] *Countrey Divinitie*, A3r.
[31] Ibid., 15.
[32] Ibid., 25.
[33] Ibid., 43-4.
[34] Ibid., 46.
[35] Ibid., 56.
[36] Ibid., 69.
[37] Ibid., 203-4.

primary objective: increased knowledge and understanding of the Scriptures.

One of the more significant problems encountered by Greenham and others is suggested by Arthur Dent when he points to the gap between preachers and parishioners. In his church the people believed that the scriptures are not really for "plain folke, they are too high for us,...they belong to Preachers and Ministers."[38] Perhaps the preachers were as guilty as the parishioners in perpetuating that problem, but it is nonetheless true that there were vast differences in educational levels in the sixteenth century creating a cultural and intellectual chasm exceedingly difficult to bridge. Imagine Richard Greenham in 1570—fresh out of university where he had been steeped for a decade in rhetoric, logic, classical thought, languages, biblical studies, and theology; where he had associated with like-minded colleagues and engaged in learned disputations—now suddenly translated into another universe, an alien from the outer space of Cambridge University thrust into the earthy realities of Dry Drayton, where male illiteracy was at least seventy percent and female illiteracy virtually one hundred percent.[39] Even the Dry Drayton churchwardens, during all of Greenham's years there, signed the parish registers with a mark. How could his unlettered parishioners be expected to become instantly interested in hearing learned sermons and in sorting out the theological intracacies of justification, sanctification, predestination, and the nature of Christ's presence in the Eucharist?

Although the Book of Common Prayer had been introduced well before Greenham arrived, there were still liturgical problems to be addressed. Sixteenth century worship services in the village churches were little short of chaotic. Ecclesiastical court presentments of that era indicate that rude and unruly behavior of congregants was not uncommon. Members jostled for pews, nudged their neighbors, spat on the floor, knitted, made coarse remarks, told jokes, fell asleep, and even fired guns.[40] In his treatises on the Sabbath, Nicholas Bownd makes reference to various sorts of disorder he encountered in his Suffolk church. People apparently drifted in and out of church during the service, for he explicitly insists that congregants must come on

---

[38] *The Plaine Mans Pathway,* 29.
[39] David Underdown, *Revel, Riot, and Rebellion,* 1; Keith Wrightson, *English Society,* 190, 220.
[40] Keith Thomas, *Religion and the Decline of Magic,* 161.

time and stay until the end. "Some tarrie at home a great part of the service and others departe away before the blessing and the sacrament." He urges his worshippers to "bee present at the whole action." He admonishes hunters for coming to worship with their falcons on their wrists, and requests that dogs be left outside during the service so that the sermon not be interrupted by their barking.[41]
Bishop Cox's 1571 injunctions to the parishes of Ely include a mandate to the churchwardens to check on church attendance and to present the names of those who sit in ale houses during the time of common prayer, or who otherwise absent themselves whether "negligently or willfully," or "come very late to the church upon the Sundays and Holy Days, and especially on the Sundays." He also mandates the wardens "to present and certify the names of such of your parishioners as walk, talk, or otherwise unreverently behave themselves in the church...."[42]

Complaints about church attendance are common in puritan literature. William Warde, for example, laments that "sometimes not halfe of the people in a parish [are] present at holy services upon the Sabbath day, so hard a thing it is to drawe them to the meanes of their salvation." The attitude toward church going is "cold and carelesse," he says, for "some lie in their beds, some about their ordinarie businesses, others follow vanities, whooring, & drunkennesse...."[43] Attending church followed class lines, with poorest attendance by the poorest classes.[44] The size of the church buildings did not encourage maximum attendance, especially considering the population expansion in the second half of the sixteenth century. In the Dry Drayton church, for example, it would have been impossible to accomodate the entire parish.

Greenham himself does not specifically refer to problems he may have encountered in church attendance and behavior in worship, but he does speak occasionally in more general terms of "prophaning the holy exercises," shortcomings in the practices of prayer and hearing the word, superstitious use of the sacraments, and negligence of the

---

[41] *The Doctrine of the Sabbath* (London, 1595) 132.
[42] Walter H. Frere, ed., *Visitation Articles and Injunctions* (London: Longmans, Green and Co., 1910) II, 299, 302.
[43] *Gods Arrowes* (London, 1607) fol., 23v.
[44] David Underdown, *Revel, Riot, and Rebellion*, 30-1

Sabbath.[45]

Perhaps his parishioners were not always faithful, but in their defense it must be said that although Greenham established a reputation as a competent preacher, his somewhat erudite sermons must have been difficult for the uneducated to comprehend.

## III

Greenham's tabletalk is an excellent resource for a deeper and more detailed understanding of his Dry Drayton ministry.[46] It provides helpful information regarding the attitudes and concerns of his parishioners, as well as Greenham's pastoral response to them.

A random list of topics included in the tabletalk gives some indication of the range of questions raised by sixteenth century believers in the newly formed protestant Church of England: how heresies like the Family of Love arise; whether Protestants may secure medical help from "popish" physicians; how better to remember sermons; whether ungodly places may be frequented by Christians simply to keep their sense of disgust fresh; how to hear the Word with profit; what to do about troubles in daily work; how to deal with conscience attacks from sin; how to admonish sinners; what to do with the problem of unbelief and persistent doubts about God's love and promises; whether usury is permissible and how money should be used ("give even more, the tenth to the pore"); the efficacy of sacraments administered by heretical or incompetent ministers; whether unjust ordinances should be disobeyed; vestments, the sign of the cross and other ceremonies in church; demon possession; the want of "affection" in one's faith; consciences afflicted by thoughts of a secret sin; where to bury the dead; how to deal with fear; comfort for one whose son had drowned; avoiding worldly thoughts; dietary and medical advice; how to make plasters for physical ailments; the sin against the Holy Spirit; whether the Apocrypha is canonical; how to deal with affliction and cope with death; the reality of angels, fairies, and evil spirits; the authenticity of visions; provision for the poor; the dangers of prosperity; questions about marriage and family; and proper administration of the sacraments.

---

[45] "A third portion...of grave counsels," *Workes,* 54.
[46] See introductory chapter, 9ff..

This list indicates that the issues addressed to and by Greenham were primarily practical questions of a religious or spiritual nature, although, as indicated, there are also occasional references to ailments, diet, and "physick." Questions and answers concerning Christian doctrine are almost non-existent in the tabletalk; and, even more striking, given the years during which Hildersham compiled the document, is the total absence of any reference to disputes over church government. The tabletalk is an account of the daily work of a rural pastor who was not particularly interested in ecclesiastical politics. His attention was focused single-mindedly on his parish and its needs.

In addition to the material regarding Greenham's views on a wide variety of practical problems, the tabletalk contains Hildersham's hagiographic commentary on Greenham himself—his personality, conduct, style of ministry, manner of dealing with people—all presented as sterling examples for others to follow. The portrait of Richard Greenham that emerges is one of monumental wisdom, stability, compassion, and composure. More specifically, it is the picture of an utterly dedicated, hard-working, self-disciplined, parish pastor who loved to *preach* but who found even greater satisfaction in *dealing with afflicted consciences.*[47] These were the two main dimensions of his ministry in Dry Drayton.

## IV

According to Samuel Clarke, Greenham was short in stature, but long on energy, a virtual incarnation of the puritan work ethic. He preached twice on Sunday, with young people's catechism prior to the evening service. In addition, he preached four times during the week in the early morning, at daybreak, "so soon as he could well see," before the farmers took to the fields. His punishing preaching schedule of six sermons a week required diligent study, so he arose every day, winter and summer, at four in the morning.[48]

Greenham's reflections on preaching appear frequently in the tabletalk. It obviously consumed much of his time and attention. He

---

[47] Fol. 61r.
[48] Samuel Clarke, *The Lives of Thirty-Two English Divines* (London, 1677) 12. The following pages will focus on Greenham's *practice* of preaching. For his *theory* of preaching, see below, 131 ff.

describes preaching as "the painfullest thing,"[49] and confesses to
doing it with "sharp and trembling fears" which he sought to
overcome by prayer and by "speaking boldly the word of the
lord...."[50] Especially on Sabbath mornings, he would engage in fervent
prayer accompanied by such sighing and groaning that his wife
thought him to be ill.[51] He displayed such "great zeal and fervency of
speaking" in the pulpit that he was advised to calm down.[52] Samuel
Clarke reinforces this image of the high-energy preacher, stating that
Greenham "was so earnest, and took such extraordinary pains in his
preaching, that his shirt would usually be as wet with sweating, as if it
had been drenched in water...."[53] Greenham complained that many
preachers are too "cold" and their teaching "glassy, bright, and
brickle."[54] Yet he personally could profit even from an incompetent
preacher, for his message would cause Greenham to meditate on the
"truth whereof the speaker failed...."[55] The gift of eloquence in
preaching is helpful when "joyned with the power of the word," but
too often it is merely a "carnal" manifestation of human skill.[56]

Although Greenham gained a reputation as a premier preacher,
and in spite of his express desire for more "salty" preaching,[57] his
published sermons seem wordy, repetitive, and dull.[58] They are
generally topical rather than expository, ostensibly based on one brief
text, and well-sprinkled with biblical references. Many of the
seventeen sermons that have been preserved deal with very practical
aspects of Christian life, for example, "murmuring," zeal, humility,
swearing, the importance of a good reputation, and of keeping good
company. Others are somewhat more doctrinal in character, treating
such issues as the meaning of repentance, the quenching of the Spirit,
and the effects of the Cross of Christ. Four of the sermons are based
on passages from Proverbs; others on verses in Genesis, Exodus,
Psalms, Matthew, Acts, the Epistles, and Revelation. They are well

---

[49] Fol. 37v.
[50] Fol. 43v.
[51] Fol. 40v.
[52] Fol. 5v.
[53] *Thirty-Two English Divines* , 12.
[54] Fol. 39r.
[55] Fol. 6r.
[56] Fols. 38r,v.
[57] "Of the Ministerie," ibid., 747.
[58] They constitute the third part of his *Workes*, 241-379.

organized and clearly outlined, often with an introduction summarizing the thrust of the message. Individual sentences, however, are long and labored—very difficult to deliver orally in a clear and interesting way. To spark interest, he occasionally uses illustrations and similes drawn from rural life, but his sermons are largely made up of lengthy, unbroken, didactic passages of dense prose that must have proved formidable for the unlettered parishioners of Dry Drayton. The seventeen published sermons average about eight large folio pages in length. The mean time for oral delivery is about one hour.

Greenham was well aware of the wide range of preaching ability within the English church and longed for more and better preaching throughout the land. Still, he charitably defends even the preacher with "great wants," arguing that his hearers may be prompted "to meditate inwardly of that truth, whereof the Preacher failed."[59] Indeed, Greenham places as much responsibility upon the hearers as on the preachers. He complains of negative attitudes and despairs of rampant fickleness with the church.

> Some will say, if doctrine be too much used, we cannot understand, he is too profound: some, if perswasion be urged, we can learne little, he is alwaies about one matter: some, when one is vehement, say, he is an Heremite too precise for us to follow, he had neede of a new world: some if the Preacher be comfortable, thinke, he is a clawbacke[60] and seeketh for living: some say, if they hear one for the peace of the Church tolerating some ceremonies, that he is a time-server and man-pleaser: if they heare one zealous and unwilling to give any little credit to superstitions, then they say, he is factious: if he be young and vehement, then they say, he will grow wiser and colder in time: if he be old and still faithfull, then he wants wisedome and is but a doting foole.[61]

Greenham, however, finds benefits in such variety of preaching.

---

[59] "The first portion of grave Counsels," ibid., 26.
[60] Old English meaning "flatterer."
[61] "A third portion...of an hundred grave counsels," Workes, 59.

... if doctrine be used, we learne; if perswasion, we are moved;
if threatnings, we are humbled; if promises, we are comforted;
if lenitie, we thinke God calleth us in mercie; if severitie, God
calleth us out of securitie, and so we profit by all in
something, though by some in more things and oftner.[62]

Regarding preaching method, "His manner was first to intreat
generally, and more breefly of a text to his people as it were, to
unbowel it before ther faces, and then with deeper meditation, and
larger amplification to discours of it...."[63] The law/gospel doctrine
was the principal analytical tool Greenham used to measure and
divide the content of his preaching. Both law and gospel must be
proclaimed, for the threatenings of the law drive sinners to Christ,
while the sweet sound of the gospel assures them of the love and
mercy of God. The tabletalk contains a few hints indicating that he
used the whip more than the honey. He confessed to some concern
about not emphasizing the gospel sufficiently, but then dismissed
such thoughts by attributing them to "sathan." People need to hear
the law when they are feeling "secure," he observes, apparently
convinced that security was a greater spiritual threat than insecurity.
This is followed by an interesting comment that suggests a very
moderate rather than hyper-Calvinist doctrine of salvation: "by the
law I drive men out of themselves and send them to christ if they wil,
but if they refuse they go worthily to hel." In a sobering assessment of
the preacher's pivotal role, the tabletalk scribe adds, "to whom hee
could not bee the messenger of salvation for ther unbeleef, unto them
hee was an instrument of condemnation prepared for them."[64]

Preaching that was so important in the plan of salvation required
meticulous preparation, not only on the part of the preacher, but also
the hearers. Greenham frequently voiced doubts about the latter.[65]
He complained that his parishioners would receive the Word with
apparent reverence in the public service, but in private call his
preaching into question.[66] In the face of criticism and resistance,
however, "hee would not as many do use once any bitter words, but

---

[62] Ibid.
[63] REM 524, fol. 33r.
[64] Fols. 7v, 8r.
[65] Fol. 9v.
[66] Fol. 4r.

with love and levity sought to reform his adversary...." He believed such love was sadly "wanting in many ministers," a lack that contributed to dissension in the churches.[67] He practiced what he preached in terms of his personal, daily, spiritual exercises, praying twice a day with his family, and, after his sermons, calling his servants together to quiz them about what they had heard, and what they remembered.

# V

Despite all his emphasis on preaching, Greenham believed it was an even greater thing for "a Pastor to deal wisely and comfortably with an afflicted conscience...."[68] This was his specialty and the tabletalk provides evidence of his consummate pastoral and psychological skills. Greenham established a farflung reputation for these skills, and was sought out by many, rich and poor alike, who were suffering acutely from "spiritual Afflictions and Temptations," so empathizing with them "as if he had been afflicted with them."[69] Henry Holland was convinced of the need for the development of these skills into a sixteenth century science of pastoral psychology, and believed that if "the Lord had not so soone translated him to rest," Greenham would have undertaken the task. According to Holland, the matter was on Greenham's long-range academic agenda, for "many godly learned friends" had urged him to engage in a scientific study of cases of conscience, so that he might "traine up some younger men to this end, and communicate his experience" to them, and "leave unto posteritie a commentarie of such particular maladies, as through Gods blessing hee hath cured, together with the meanes used to that end." Holland quotes Greenham as expressing the desire to develop a "method and Art" of treating afflicted consciences.

> ...because precepts are wanting, rules of direction in such cases (by a through [sic] searching,  with  a  diligent  and continuall observation and conference with others learned

---

[67] Fols. 34v, 35r.
[68] Fol. 61r.
[69] Samuel Clarke, *Thirty-two Divines*, 13, 14.

and experienced) might in this age, or in the age following, be brought to some forme of method and Art, whereby the knowledge and experience of these things might be made common to many, not onely to the fruitfull curing, but also the healthfull preventing of manifold mischiefes.[70]

It is evident from the tabletalk that Greenham devoted more than ordinary reflection to counselling techniques. His insights into the human condition and the psychology of sin are sometimes stunning in their perceptiveness. Hildersham observes that Greenham had such "great sight of inward corruptions, and in laying out the vainnes of mens secret consciences," that others wondered if he had special powers bestowed by "Spirits and magical arts."[71] This extraordinary ability came in part from deep introspection. He "watched so narrowly over his own hart, that making an anatomy of it, hee could unrip the secret courses of sin in others."[72] He recommended, especially to those who declaimed against other sinners, to apply their "speaches" to themselves and to consider their own condition.[73] In the same vein, since children often inherit the sins of their fathers, he advised parents, when correcting their children, to "first consider, if it were not a syn which they gave them as it were, which now they are about to correct." Such an approach results in more effective discipline, for parents then carry it out humbly, with prayer, and "in love of ther own conversion" and self-correction.[74]

Greenham, three centuries before Freud, was intrigued by dreams and ventured an explanation of their significance. Many dreams that come from "natural causes" quickly fade away and are forgotten, "but if our dreams dwel longer upon us and leav some greater impression in us, they may bee thought either to proceed from god or from the devil." Spiritual profit may be gained from dreams. An "evil dream" for example, may indicate "an evil hart either in some sin already committed, or in some sin which may bee committed." Through dreams God may be correcting some unknown sin of the past, or

---

[70] Greenham's *Workes*, "The Preface to the Reader."
[71] Fols. 23r,v.
[72] Ibid.
[73] Fol. 52r
[74] Fol. 20r.

revealing some sin to come.[75] So do not quickly "condemn a dream, nor yet too superstititiously...thinck of a dream," but "make some godly use and instruction of it." If the dream is of some terrible evil, "avoid al the occasions of that evil" and engage in fervent prayer. Greenham recommends a balanced approach to dreams and their interpretation.

> If wee give too great credit to dreams they are dangerous to weaken faith. The best is neither to bee too remis nor too wyse in them. It is good to observ them, but not too much to perswade ourselves of any great things if they bee good, neither too much to fear them if they bee evil, and yet not to cast of the use which may bee made of them, seing the lord by leaving such long impressions in us doth as it were cal upon the consciences of men to profit by them.[76]

Greenham's style, when dealing with sinners, was honest confrontation tempered by gentleness, for his aim was to win the sinner back to the fold. When he felt compelled to pronounce God's judgment, he did so with a compassionate heart and a prayer that the judgment might be averted.[77] His boldness in confronting sinners was tinged with a measure of self-doubt. He frequently examined his own heart and motives.[78] Greenham distinguished between the general course of the Christian life and the occasional falling into sin. It is the "pollicy of sathan" to get his victims to focus on the "little offenses." Sorrow for sin should be proportionate to the sin: "greater in greater sins, les in lesser sins." There is an obvious difference, says Greenham, between a generally healthy person who experiences occasional "fits of sicknes," and a generally sick person who has "fits of health." The same difference pertains to the Christian life. Occasionally the godly, whose "general cours is to please god," have "a violent fit of syn." This is far less serious than those whose entire lives are characterized by sin and who have only occasional "fits" of godliness.[79]

---

[75] Fol. 62v.
[76] Fol. 63r.
[77] Fol. 4r.
[78] Fol. 4v.
[79] Fols. 24r,v.

## VI

Greenham also engaged in a teaching ministry in Dry Drayton. This cannot be completely separated from his preaching, for through his sermons he was constantly teaching his people throughout the week. But Clarke mentions explicitly that each Sunday, before the evening sermon, it was his custom "to Catechize the young people of the Parish." He instructed the youth on Thursday also, the day on which he normally omitted the early morning sermon. For teaching purposes he wrote a catechism, as was typical of Elizabethan pastors.[80] The tabletalk mentions children rarely, however, except in several excerpts on baptism. In one brief, cryptic paragraph Hildersham suggests that Greenham was willing to teach young children whom some regarded as deprived because of neglectful parents and poor education, for he had faith in the promises of God, and was confident that "evil natures cannot hinder gods purpose in calling if the means with his mercy and blessing bee purely and painfully used."[81] Since children are baptized in the name of the Trinity, they should be instructed about "things concerning the father the son and the holy ghost, that so they might bee trayned up in religion, according to that same order, which the lord Jesus himself both taught and practized."[82] In another reference to children, it is mentioned that Greenham believed in postponing instructions in the meaning and significance of their baptism until they are able to comprehend.

There was another important teaching ministry in which Greenham was engaged: the "seminary" in his rectory. It was common for puritan clergy in the Elizabethan church to assist in the training of divinity students.[83] With Cambridge so near by, and given Greenham's exceptional abilities, it is not surprising that students sought him out and came to reside in Dry Drayton for a time of internship. Greenham himself regarded it as a "happy nourcery" for the church, and expressed the hope that "every grounded pastor"

---

[80] "Of Catechizing and Instruction of Youth," *Workes*, 662-6. For an analysis of his catechism, see below 93ff.

[81] REM 524, fol. 17r.

[82] Ibid., fol. 47r.

[83] Patrick Collinson alludes to a "formal resolution" of puritan clergy that every minister entertain a student of divinity to train for ministry, *The Religion of Protestants* (Oxford: Clarendon Press, 1982) 118-19.

would engage in this effort and at the same time gain an assistant minister for help in the parish. Apparently he took them on one at a time, and at the completion of their training would recommend them to the church at large. He would then "draw some other out of the university, to bee framed in like manner fit for the work of the lord."[84] Greenham drew upon eminent biblical examples for support of this tutorial arrangement, for this, he said, is the way "Josua ministred to Moses, Elisha to Elijah, Samuel to Heli, Gehesi to Elisha, Baruck to Jeremiah, the disciples to christ, and Timothy to Paul...." So, he said, "every godly learned minister should trayn up some yong schollar to commend him the better, and to enable him the more to the church."[85]

Several of these students went on to make their mark on the church. The "pathologically prickly" Robert Brown was one, who later, certainly to Greenham's dismay, became leader of the radical separatist movement that bore his name.[86] Another was Henry "Silvertongued" Smith, who later gained the reputation of being one of the greatest preachers in England.[87] Marsden calls him the "Chrysostom of England," and, even more effusively, "the most eloquent preacher in Europe."[88] And still another was Arthur Hildersham, himself, the scribe of Greenham's tabletalk.

The historical record includes nothing about the formal dimension of these internships. Perhaps, by their very nature, the training was informal, consisting of hands-on, practical experience in ministry. The tabletalk implies that it was largely instruction by observation and example, for the manuscript focusses precisely on Greenham's pastoral example and practical wisdom about parish ministry. Hildersham indicates that much was learned from dinner-time

---

[84] REM 524, fol. 57v.
[85] Ibid., fol. 58r.
[86] Cf., Harry Porter, *Reformation and Reaction*, 216. John Marsden said that Brown was "chiefly remarkable for carrying through life the heat and rashness of untamed childhood," *The History of the Early Puritans* (London: Hamilton, Adams, & Co., 1850) 141. See also Ephraim Pagitt, *Heresiography or, A description of the Hereticks and Sectaries of these latter times* (London: 1645) 49; and Robert Browne, *A True and Short Declaration* (1583) in Albert Peel and Leland Carlson, eds., *The Writings of Robert Harrison and Robert Browne* (London: Allen and Unwin, 1953) 398.
[87] R. B. Jenkins, *Henry Smith: England's Silver-Tongued Preacher* (Macon: Mercer University Press, 1988).
[88] *The History of the Early Puritans*, 178. Cf., 238. Smith, upon Greenham's recommendation, became lecturer at St. Clement Danes in London.

conversations.

Occasional references to tabletalk protocol appear, giving some insight into Greenham's personality and style. He regarded it as "unchristian courtesy" when others simply waited for him to talk, for, he said, all christians are equally "annointed with the same spirit." So he encouraged others to speak, but asked them to do so "reverently" and without "passing the bounds of ther knowledge." If nothing else, they should ask questions. If they could find nothing at all to say, then "they should complain of ther dul minds" and from their dullness "rayse quicknes and life of speach again."[89] Sometimes at the table he would admonish others for certain sins, but in such a way as "to reform rather than rebuke." Putting it another way, his concern was to "rebuke the sin as zealous of gods glory, and yet correct thoffender as pitying his brother...."[90] His advice to others too, was to use "gentle and courteous speaches before vehement and sharp speaches and threatnings."[91] Such was his own example. He did not exhibit a contentious or controversial spirit at the table, but calmly reasoned with others without drawing undue attention to himself.[92] In conversation he tended to avert his eyes. Hildersham notes that Greenham did not usually "look any much in the face," and therefore "knew few by ther countenance," but rather "remembred much by ther tongs." Instead of criticizing him for poor eye-contact, Hildersham concludes, "So careful was hee in the government of his eies."[93]

What the dinner fare was is not specified, but on one occasion a nobleman delivered to Greenham by messenger some venison specifically for a meal with his friends. It happened, however, to be a time when "the lord threatned some plague to his church, and punishment to the common wealth." So Greenham sent it back with a note of appreciation and this comment: "it is a fitter tym now to fast and pray with mourning then to feast and play with

---

[89] Fol. 6r.
[90] Fol. 10v.
[91] Fol. 12v.
[92] Fol. 30v.
[93] Fol. 27r. Cf., Greenham, "Of the government of the Eyes," *Workes*, 675-8. Greenham regarded eyes as instruments of evil as well as of good. Eyes, he said, "stir up the thoughts of the heart." He quotes St. Jerome who called eyes "the streames or springs of lust." Greenham also refers to the covetous eye, the adulterous eye, the eye of pride, and the eye of idleness.

mirthmaking."[94]

Dinner times at the rectory were not jolly times. Greenham loved to be with his friends, but even then engaged his hyperactive conscience, wondering whether he was doing enough to enhance their salvation or receiving enough "good from them to his salvation."[95] It is difficult, he said, to suffer reproach from enemies, but even worse to observe "the not profiting of his friends."[96] Although Greenham said he was sometimes "merry," he added that he was "affraid of our mirth." Nevertheless he admitted that he remembered best those things that had been impressed on him at a time of "some great joy or mirth."[97] At table his manner was reserved, for he thought it best to be moderate rather than "extraordinary" in display of either joy or sorrow. Such emotion may be shown "privately to a good frind, or before the lord," but, appealing to the example of Joseph meeting his brothers in Pharaoh's court, his advice was "to make our affections as little known in company as may bee."[98] When he spoke of a matter at dinner "hee loved to sift it deeper" and yet more pleasantly and less seriously than in formal settings. If he were interrupted, he would listen, but with the caveat that when the person who had interrupted had finished his point, he would help Greenham remember and resume the earlier discussion.[99]

## VII

The substantial number of references to women in tabletalk indicates another dimension of Greenham's Dry Drayton ministry. There are at least thirty references without indication whether any women were included at dinner. Many are referred to as asking Greenham's counsel on some matter or other, others are included in brief accounts of spiritual episodes. Men are mentioned more often than women in the tabletalk, but there are even more instances where the gender of persons to whom Greenham ministered remains unspecified. A comparison of the references to men and women

---

[94] Fol. 64r.
[95] Fol. 13r.
[96] Fol. 14r.
[97] Fol. 13r. Cf., 51r.
[98] Fol. 23r.
[99] Fols. 33r,v.

indicates no negative bias against women. They appear to be no more
or less troubled, no more or less sinful, than the men in Greenham's
parish. Some are specifically described as "gentlewomen" and
occasionally as godly women. There is one unexplained reference to a
"strange woman";[100] another to one who believed she was with child
by the devil;[101] another to one who thought herself bewitched;[102] and
yet another to one who was so troubled in mind that she had become
the unfortunate victim of seizures.[103] One woman is criticized for
being too absorbed in outward things,[104] and another for false claims
to mystical spirit revelations.[105]

Tabletalk contains a few hints regarding the social status of women
in Dry Drayton. Greenham thought it good procedure for fathers to
give their daughters in marriage, but if the father is no longer living,
"hee said then hee would not have the mother do it." He rather
advised that as a general rule a father in his will should "appoint some
vicegerent to do his duty."[106] Another episode is recorded in which
cryptic reference is made to a woman afflicted in mind, who
"forgetting al womanhood fel down before him," perhaps immodestly.
Greenham turned his face from the woman, and with his back to her,
"fel on his knees and praied" for her.[107] In a reminder that sexual
harassment is not an exclusively twentieth century problem,
Greenham warns against the "viewing, familar speaking, and touching
of a woman" as "a thing most dangerous."[108] In an uncharac-
teristically sanguine assessment he states: "Godly men are not in
danger of grosly wicked woemen."[109] No mention is made of the
danger, or lack thereof, to godly women of grossly wicked men. In
another discussion about remarriage after the death of a spouse, he
directs his comments to a hypothetical male, rather than female,
survivor. He advises that under normal circumstances a one year
interval is appropriate. Remarriage too quickly may offend the friends

---

[100] Fol. 32r.
[101] Fols. 31r, v.
[102] Fol. 47r.
[103] Fol. 15v. In most of these cases, according to the tabletalk, Greenham was
able to bring about healing by means of wise counsel and prayer.
[104] Fol. 5r.
[105] Fol. 18r.
[106] Fol. 49v.
[107] Fol. 17r.
[108] Fol. 59r.
[109] Fol. 62v.

of the departed and imply that "their love was but light, being so soon forgotten...." Besides, "it is almost unnatural to get another body in bed before the former bee rotten in the grave."[110]

From the tabletalk, it becomes apparent that Christian marriage was important to Greenham and that he thoughtfully designed a pastoral approach to it. Nevertheless, in the spirit of the apostle Paul, Greenham seems to regard celibacy as a higher calling. "When one asked him concerning Marriage, whether it were good to Marry, seing sometimes when concupiscence prickt him, hee was much moved to it," Greenham responds with the observation that many marry too hastily, without first determining whether "by praier, fasting, and avoiding al provocations of concupiscence" they might have the "gift of chastity or no." But he adds that if "no," the Lord can use marriage "to his glory and our comfort."[111]

On another occasion, he counseled a man before marriage "to make longer trial of his affections, whither they were of god, or no," for it is easy to be deceived by the "natural delight" of sexual attraction. He adds a brief story about a "certain man" who was moved to marry but who waited, engaged in frequent prayer, and thereby "was delivered" from his sexual drives. So potent was his prayer, however, that when he married later, he "had such a feeblenes in his body that hee cold not use the act of generation."[112] Elsewhere, he admonishes a young man who had "overslipt in love," requiring the couple to confess their sin to the church, indicate sorrow for "offending against god and the church," and seek forgiveness. He also prayed "that this fault might so humble them, that they might the more warilie walk, without offence the residue of their life."[113]

Greenham rarely mentions his own marriage, but on one occasion voices concern "not onely over the salvation, but also over the diet of his wife...." Regarding the latter he said: "Bee moderate in things most which the appetite liketh of most, and check the too much greedines of an earthly thing, and you shal find this to bee a good physick to the body and an wholesome preservation for the soule."[114] When he came home from an out-of-town journey and learned "of

---

[110] Fols. 42r,v.
[111] Fol. 16v.
[112] Fol. 25r.
[113] Fols. 51v, 52r.
[114] Fol. 38r.

some thing not falling out wel in his family, in his absence," he blamed himself for inadequate prayer on their behalf "and so, said hee, was justly punished."[115]

He regarded the public solemnizing of marriage important,[116] and conducted pre-marital counseling in which he asked the couple specifically about their mutual compatibility, whether either party had been "precontracted" to another, whether the marriages had parental consent, and whether they intended to "continue this action publickly and with the prayers of the church to solemnize ther meeting according to the word." When these questions were answered to his satisfaction, he would proceed with counsel regarding the duties of husband and wife, and conclude the session with prayer.[117] He supported the custom of the father giving his daughter in marriage, "both to shew his authority over her and to witnes his consent in bestowing her...."[118]

In a passage on how a man may know "whether his wyfe bee brought him of the lord or no," Greenham enumerates three things: basic compatibility, mutual use of the means of faith without "ungodly incantations" and "beastlike" charms, and mutual concern to promote the cause of God's kingdom rather than marrying "for riches, beauty or such outward things...."[119] The passage ends with counsel that suggests Greenham's belief in a primary procreative purpose for marriage, for he expresses his hope that the couple "desire t'hasten the kingdom of christ by fulfilling as much as in them lyeth some number of the elect...." Hildersham's commentary on this is that "wee see condemned here al marrying with old woemen...wherin ther is no hope of this thing, beecause it is the sowing in a barren ground, without hope of procreation."[120]

## VIII

In his Dry Drayton ministry, Greenham responded not only to spiritual concerns, but also addressed the material needs of the

---

[115] Fol. 24v.
[116] Fol. 30v.
[117] Fols. 43r, v.
[118] Fol. 45r. Cf., 49v and 50r.
[119] Fol. 50v.
[120] Fol. 51r.

community. He regarded the spiritual and material realms as intertwined. Material prosperity has spiritual ramifications according to the tabletalk, which mentions, somewhat mysteriously, "this long prosperity of England" that would likely breed "heresy," or, equally dangerous to spiritual health, "security," or even "some great adversity." Then, in a graphic description of the dangers of wealth worthy of James the apostle, Greenham declares, "yet when prosperity is ful, and growen foggy and fat, so as the bowels of it bee stuft, and strout out as it were with repletion, then must needs follow some rupture, and the abundance of wetch must needs have a vent, to break out into some botch in one place or other."[121]

The tabletalk also makes reference to his compassion for the poor,[122] but it is Samuel Clarke who has left a most interesting account of Greenham's astute economic policies.[123] Life in Dry Drayton was hard for many. Landowners were relatively well-off, but ordinary laborers received about ten pounds in total annual earnings, barely enough for survival even in that distant day and age.[124] Greenham established a reputation for generating means of community assistance to those in need. When diminished supplies raised the price of barley to the inflated sum of ten groats a bushel, Greenham, several centuries before Keynes, stepped in to influence the market artificially, making barley available to the have-nots of the village at half price. In addition, he called a meeting of twenty of the wealthiest landowners in the immediate area and persuaded them to establish a community granary, therein to store grain, every person according to his ability. From this cooperative the poor could buy barley for four groats a bushel, less than half the market price, but with a ceiling established on the amount they could purchase. One

---

[121] Fol. 27r. Cf., James 5:1-6.

[122] Fol. 35v.

[123] *Thirty-Two Divines*, 12-13. Unless otherwise indicated, the quotations in the following paragraphs come from this passage.

[124] Keith Wrightson and David Levine, *Poverty and Piety in an English Village*, (New York, London: Academic Press, 1979) 41,42. On economic conditions in sixteenth century Cambridgeshire villages, see also Margaret Spufford, *Contrasting Communities* (Cambridge: Cambridge University Press, 1974) Part I, and P. J. Bowden, "Agricultural Prices, Farm Profits and Rents," Joan Thirsk, ed., *The Agrarian History of England and Wales* (Cambridge: Cambridge University Press, 1981) IV, 593-695. According to Spufford, the market value of all agricultural foodstuffs rose by 167 percent between 1540 and 1590, with especially sharp rises in 1586-7 and 1590, p. 48.

day a week was designated as distribution day for the poor when they could come and purchase amounts determined by the size of their families: "where there were but two in a Family, they received one peck a week, and so more according to that proportion; only no one Family had above three pecks a week."

Greenham himself was one of the leading contributors to the cooperative. He was a man of some means in the village, for his living of one hundred pounds a year was a good one, and as rector he received in addition the first tenth of the produce from the church-owned lands. He personally kept only two head of livestock, however, so "that the poor might have his straw," and while the going rate for straw was two shillings for one day's threshing, Greenham sold his for only ten pence. So it was, by virtue of Greenham's Christian economics of the visible hand, that the poor were provided for at a time when they "had been well neer famished."

Economic issues were also addressed from the pulpit. In the midst of the dearth of grain there was a tendency at the daily market to scrimp on the size of the bushels they sold, a practice that stoked Greenham's ire. "This Master Greenham Preached much against, and Publikely reproved wheresoever he came." He threatened a personal boycott of the market "for which he came into some trouble." Yet he maintained an external attitude of pious composure. He would ask his servant when he returned from the market about the price of grain, "and if it was dear, he would say, I pray God bring down the price of it; and if it was Cheap, he would heartily bless God for it."

Greenham became known for his charity beyond the limited confines of his Dry Drayton parish. Wherever he encountered need, he would arrange for money to be sent. When he rode into Cambridge past the prison on Castle Hill, the prisoners knew they did not have to beg, "for if he had any money in his Purse, they were sure to have part of it." His generosity sometimes outstripped his means, for when it came time to hire extra help to bring in the harvest, Greenham himself would have to borrow to meet the special expense.

## IX

Greenham's prodigious efforts on behalf of Dry Drayton took its physical toll. Apparently hard work combined with considerable anxiety and lack of adequate rest undermined his health in the 1580s. The tabletalk indicates that he struggled with insomnia, but, predictably, he used nocturnal periods of sleeplessness for prayer and meditation.[125] He suffered from toothaches and a fistula, but managed to turn these ailments into a sermonette on patience and the sanctifying benefits of affliction.[126] There are references to his failing memory and to "infirmities of his stomach," which he gladly bore for they "provoked him" to self-examination.[127]

Were his painful endeavors appreciated? How was Greenham's ministry received in Dry Drayton? Where should it be placed on the success/failure spectrum? Evidently, some of the staunch country folk of Dry Drayton resisted his faithful ministry. Samuel Clarke alludes to the "untractableness and unteachableness of that people amongst whom he had taken such exceeding great paines."[128] Thomas Fuller says that although Dry Drayton was "often watered with Mr. Greenham's tears, and oftener with his prayers and preaching, who moistened the rich with his counsel, the poor with his charity— neither produced proportionable fruitfulness. The generality of his parish remained ignorant and obstinate....Hence the verses, 'Greenham had pastures green, But sheep full lean.'" Fuller also mentions "the little profit of his long pains to so poor and peevish a parish."[129]

Greenham himself, in his surviving sermons, treatises, and tabletalk, does not engage in the lengthy jeremiads about his parishioners that became commonplace among some of his colleagues, but he occasionally laments the religious confusion and even rank secularism left in the wake of the Reformation. He states, for example, that he fears atheism more than papism in the realm, "for many having escaped out of the gulfe of superstition, are now too farre punged and swallowed up of prophanesse, thinking either that there is no God, or else that he is not so fearefull and mercifull, as his threatnings and promises commend him to be."[130]

He also complains about resistance to sermons in Dry Drayton.

---

[125] Fol. 46r.
[126] Fol. 21r.
[127] Fol. 37r.
[128] *Thirty-Two Lives*, 15.
[129] *The Church History of Britain*, III, 147.
[130] "The first portion of grave Counsels," *Workes*, 3. See also REM 524, fols. 9r & 51v.

Greenham does not dwell on this as extensively as Gifford and Dent, but he was obviously frustrated by the luke-warm reception of his preaching and speaks of a "sermon sickness" that commonly afflicted his people. Even though they seemed to be positively affected by the power of the Word during the service, "when once the voyce ceaseth, and they are out of the Church doores, and have acquainted themselves with the aire of the world, they forget what they heard, and wherewith they were moved, and so retire to their former life againe."[131] He was grieved when he saw no fruit from his preaching in people's lives, even "when hee had been most vehement" and thought "that now if ever, mens harts would bee moved."[132] With more than a touch of cynicism, he mentions to a parishioner whose wife had died, "I feared god would bury something from you, because I saw you often bury mine instructions made unto you."[133] He was most disappointed in the "not profiting" of his friends for whom he had the highest expectations, "that is, such as hee thought the joy, crown, and glory of his ministery." [134] He experienced at least mild depression, complaining of regularly falling from the pinnacle of joy to "dulnes and deadnes."[135] At times he apparently felt overwhelmed by the workload, even in little Dry Drayton, for he reflects on the need for two pastors, one "to attend the sick," the other "to teach the whole."[136] He seems also to have considered leaving the ministry, for although he had entered it "with the consent of the most godly and learned brethren," he had done so with the understanding that "if the lord would vouchsafe him a blessing therin, hee would continue in that calling, but if the lord denying his grace and blessing would seme to refuse him, hee would publickly in the congregation to the glory of god and shaming of himself confes his unhability and unwoorthines of the place and so depart."[137]

In the midst of his disappointments, he tried to retain perspective by adopting a long range view, taking his cue from the local farmers who looked for the harvest long after sowing the seed.[138] If only one

---

[131] "The first portion of grave Counsels," ibid., 36.
[132] REM 524, fol. 14v.
[133] Fols. 27v, 28r.
[134] Fol. 14r.
[135] Fol. 14v , 20v.
[136] Fol. 26r
[137] Fol. 67v.
[138] Fol. 7v.

in ten profited from his ministry, he estimates that he still had "the winings that christ had."[139] Moreover, he found fulfillment in his pastoral work. To one who apologized for taking too much of his time, he replies that because it was time spent in "weldoing," it was his joy to be of help; "for this caus I live," he exclaims.[140] In fact, Greenham *never* complains about the reception of his pastoral counsel. His disillusionment centers on preaching. He undoubtedly experienced what Richard Baxter did a few decades later. Baxter wrote:

> I have found by experience, that an ignorant sot that hath
> been an unprofitable hearer so long, hath got more knowledge
> and remorse of conscience in half an hours close discourse,
> then they did from ten year's publike preaching.[141]

To characterize his Dry Drayton ministry as a "failure" seems overdrawn.[142] Greenham's tenure there was undoubtedly difficult, but probably not that unusual considering the complaints of Dent, Gifford, and others cited above, about the widespread difficulties of ministering to that generation. And if there was failure, who failed? Nicholas Bownd writes, "Many do wrongfully complaine, that their minister is unprofitable to them, hee doeth them no good, they cannot conceave him. (I doe not say, but that the complaintes of some are just,) yet let them consider whether some great part of the fault be not in themselves," since they come to church unprepared and hopelessly ignorant of the Scriptures.[143]

At least some of the evidence for his "failed" ministry comes from Greenham himself, a less than reliable source for an objective assessment. Perhaps his evaluation was colored by natural modesty or godly self-effacement. It would not have been very "puritan" of him to

---

[139] Fol. 14r. Cf., fol. 2r.
[140] Fol. 7v.
[141] *The Reformed Pastor* (London, 1656) 357.
[142] Keith Wrightson and David Levine, *Poverty and Piety in an English Village* (New York & London: Academic Press, 1979) 161. Cf., Margaret Spufford, *Contrasting Communities*, 327. Spufford's evidence for Greenham's "lack of influence" is based on a very small sample of wills—only eight during Greenham's tenure. On the questionable evidential value of wills in general, see Duffy, *The Stripping of the Altars*, 504ff.
[143] *Doctrine of the Sabbath*, 200.

brag about his successes. Negative assessments from the pastors themselves were endemic in Greenham's day. Not much later, George Herbert observed that the "Countrey Parson is generally sad," because "he meets continually with two most sad spectacles, Sin, and Miserie: God dishonoured every day; and man afflicted."[144] Herbert could well have been describing Richard Greenham or any number of his contemporaries, or, for that matter, many a twentieth century pastor as well. When Greenham writes about "sermon sickness," or "lack of fruit," or the "not profiting" of his parishioners, this can hardly be taken as legitimate evidence for a failed ministry. Likewise, his parishioners' complaints that the word Greenham preached was not the true word because so few were brought to obedience "by so long preaching of it,"[145] should not be accepted as grounds for belief in Greenham's failure, but rather as a witness to the wisdom of a preacher many centuries earlier who declared, "There is nothing new under the sun."[146]

---

[144] *The Country Parson* (London, 1675) 113.
[145] "A third portion...of an hundred grave counsels," *Workes*, 54.
[146] Ecclesiastes 1:9-10.

# 3

# CONTROVERSY AND POLITICS

## I

Richard Greenham loved peace and pursued it. His tabletalk consistently reveals a pastor with an irenic temperament whose first instinct in tense situations was to smooth troubled waters. The admiring author of the tabletalk says that Greenham used no bitter words, but "gentle and curteous speaches"; he exercised exemplary patience with his enemies; he "labored to retain love" toward those who disagreed with him.[1] Both Samuel Clarke and Henry Holland also emphasize that a defining feature of the man and his ministry was his desire for peace. "In his holy Ministerie, hee was ever carefull to avoide all occasions of offence," writes Holland.[2] Clarke commends Greenham for his restraining influence against schism in the church, and says that one of the aims of his training of young ministers was "to Provoke them highly to Prize, and preciously to esteem the peace of the Church, and People of God."[3]

Although he was a lover of peace, Greenham was also a realist acutely aware of the divisive consequences of sin, not only in the world at large, but within the church of God on earth. The church here is not yet what she ought to be. Her members may be forgiven sinners, but they are sinful still, capable of fomenting all manner of discord in the body of Christ. Greenham believed controversy in the church was inevitable, and, in the mystery of God's providence, sometimes a surprising means for the promotion of truth and the advancement of the gospel.

---

[1] REM 524, fols. 12v, 25v, 34v.
[2] "The Preface to the Reader," in all editions of Greenham's *Workes*.
[3] *Thirty-two Lives*, 14-15.

What then, shall we blot out controversies? That were to teach the spirit of God wisedome....God hath ordained there should be contentions, and not onely permitteth them, but saith, they must be....It is a dreame of idle braines, that any good can be received without controversies...without the barking of some dog or other. It is not so in evill things: they are received with silence....[4]

In Greenham's God-ordained catch-22, controversy in the church is a means of good; the absence of controversy a possible symptom of evil. Greenham believed in a sovereign God who is both able and willing to avert all evil or turn it into blessing.

## II

The Church of England was conceived and born in controversy. Henry VIII's marriage problems led to stormy controversy with the Vatican. After he separated the church in England from Roman jurisdiction, controversy began about the tempo and extent of reform, and continued during the reign of Edward VI. Under Mary, who completely reversed the protestant direction of the church, the turmoil intensified. Even those with strong protestant sympathies, like the Marian exiles, fought among each other. When Elizabeth came to the throne shortly before Greenham entered Cambridge, fresh attempts for more serious reform could again be initiated. But she resisted "radical reform" and in the 1560s tensions escalated, for by this time a substantial number of English protestant exiles had returned from continental centers of reformation with spiritual appetites whetted for full and fast reformation of the Church of England. The Act of Uniformity, adopted by parliament in 1559, prompted virtually no end of discussion and controversy. Among its disputed liturgical provisions was the requirement that the clerical vestments prescribed in the early years of King Edward VI be reinstated.

Already in Edward's reign this requirement had fueled controversy, for the vestments were regarded by some as a popish hangover from medieval times. The first phase of the vestments controversy began in

---

[4] "Of injuries, offences and controversies," *Workes*, 728.

1550 when John Hooper initially refused to don the garb prescribed for him as newly appointed Bishop of Gloucester. He eventually relented, but only after a fierce debate with some of his colleagues. Vestments were the least of the problems faced by protestants under Mary, but in the 1560s the second chapter of the vestments controversy began. The dispute reached a boiling point by the middle of the decade, and it continued to simmer throughout the rest of the century and into the next. Indeed, the vestments controversy had much greater significance than first meets the eye. It led directly to the Presbyterian movement, and even to more radical ideas about the proper relationship of the church to the civil order. It was also in the midst of this controversy that the term "puritan" was first used as a term of a derision for those radicals who refused the vestments in the name of an appeal to the *purity* of the New Testament church and the "best reformed churches" on the continent.[5]

The vestments battle was raging in Cambridge precisely while Greenham was there preparing for the ministry. At St. John's College in the mid-1560s William Fulke, later Master of Pembroke, refused to conform.[6] How did Greenham respond to this issue? Was he a conformist or non-conformist? Was he a "puritan" regarding vestments? If so, what variety? Did he follow in the footsteps of another Pembroke man, Thomas Sampson, whom Strype calls the "original Elizabethan nonconformist," or did he adopt a stance closer to that of the more moderate Matthew Hutton, master of Pembroke during the height of the controversy? The evidence suggests that Greenham did not become a serious participant in the debate until the 1570s in Dry Drayton, although his views were undoubtedly shaped earlier while he was in Cambridge. In those preordination years he could deal with the matter at arm's length as an academic rather than personal issue. Once instituted as rector of Dry Drayton, however, that luxury was no longer available. Then it became a question of practical obedience to the legally prescribed ordinal.

Dry Drayton lies within the diocese of Ely, whose bishop during Greenham's first decade in the parish was Richard Cox.[7] Consecrated

---

[5] John H. Primus, *The Vestments Controversy* (Kampen: J. H. Kok, 1960).
[6] See "Troubles at St. John's," Ch. VI in Harry Porter, *Reformation and Reaction in Tudor Cambridge*, 119-35.
[7] On Cox see DNB, and Felicity Heal, *The Bishops of Ely And Their Diocese During The Reformation Period: 1515-1600* (Ph.D. diss., Cambridge University,

in December of 1559, Cox was one of Archbishop Matthew Parker's first appointees under Elizabeth. These were days of confusion, flux, and tension in most English parishes. It was not an easy time to be bishop, but Cox was a capable leader and was no stranger to ecclesiastical turmoil. He had been involved in an earlier liturgical skirmish while an exile in Germany during the Marian interlude. Cox was leader of the pro-Prayer Book faction against the anti-Prayer Book party headed by John Knox in the famous "troubles" at Frankfort.[8] As a result of his continental experience, he had sympathy for many aspects of the puritan vision but not for puritan politics. He strongly supported the puritans' concern for a better preaching ministry, and appreciated their attempts to establish godly spirituality in the parishes, but he did not like non-conformity and he despised presbyterianism.

In August of 1571, Bishop Cox required from his diocesan clergy subscription to an oath of support for the Book of Common Prayer, the use of the vestments, and the Thirty-Nine Articles of the Church of England.[9] The vestments statement is as follows: "that the apparell ordeyned by law and commanded by the prince to the ecclesiasticall ministers ys not wicked, but tollerable and to be used obedientlie for order and cumlines only." It is a statement befitting an ecclesiastical diplomat, carefully formulated in moderate language. Cox does not ask or expect enthusiastic approval of vestments, but only agreement that they are "not wicked," that they are at least "tollerable," and that "for order and cumlines only" they should be used obediently. The oath received 108 subscribers; Greenham's name is conspicuously absent. On the other hand, in the following decade, neither does his name appear among the eleven clerics from the diocese of Ely who wrote to Archbishop Whitgift protesting the requirement of vestments, or among the seven who petitioned the Privy Council asking that they be released or excepted from subscription.[10]

---

1972) 104ff.
[8] *A Brief Discourse of the Troubles begun at Frankfort*, ed. Edward Arber (London: Elliot Stock, 1908). Cf., Christina H. Garrett, *The Marian Exiles* (Cambridge: University Press, 1938) 134-6.
[9] EDR, B/2/6, 198-202.
[10] *Second Parte of a Register*, I, 227-9. Greenham's patron, John Hutton, one of the Ely gentry who supported godly, preaching ministers, is one of the eleven who wrote to Whitgift. When Whitgift succeeded Grindal as archbishop in 1583, he

Greenham's tabletalk contains a substantial number of references to ceremonies in general and several to vestments in particular. From these statements it is apparent that he was a vestments skeptic who nonetheless insisted on keeping liturgical matters in their proper place on the scale of relative importance. On one occasion, when someone asked his advice regarding "outward things" Greenham replyed: "If you first wil confer with mee and establish yorself in things concerning faith and repentance, then ask mee and I wil advise you freely for your outward estate." He adds a well-balanced and judicious (albeit somewhat garbled) comment that he would "not for al the world wish or advice" the wearing of surplice and cap, but "would counsaile you generaly to bee wel grounded ere to leav them, lest that you shaking them of[f] rather of light affection then sound of judgement, afterward take them againe to your shame and the offence of others."[11] When he addresses the argument that refusal to obey church law regarding vestments is likely to lead to disrespect for other laws, his comments are ambivalent to the point of incomprehension, but he does not close the door to selective ecclesiastical disobedience.[12] On another occasion, there is no reported comment from Greenham at all. The entry simply reads, "A woman seing a good minister wear a surplice said the man had Jacobs voyce but Esaus garment." Perhaps the reference to a "good" minister wearing a surplice indicated some degree of tolerance.[13]

His position on vestments is developed most extensively in a lengthy letter to Bishop Cox, dated 1573, in which he outlines a position sufficiently ambiguous to keep the authorities from his door without abandoning his conscientious objection.[14] The crafty equivocation that characterizes the letter is apparent already in the opening words: "I have hanged long betweene hope and feare...." He had hoped that his "playne and simple walking in my calling" would have disarmed the bishop sufficiently to avert his disapproval of Greenham's liturgical waywardness, but he harbored fears that he had become the object of the bishop's suspicion and that this might

---

applied stronger pressure for conformity.
[11] REM 524, fols. 8v, 9r. Cf., *Workes*, 44.
[12] Ibid., fols. 47v. 48r.
[13] Ibid., fol. 59v.
[14] "The Apologie or aunswere of Maister Grenham, Minister of Dreaton, unto the Bishop of Ely, being commaunded to subscribe, and to use the Romish habite, with allowance of the com. booke," *A parte of a register*, I, 86-93.

hinder him from his important ministerial responsibilities. He expresses appreciation for the bishop's patience "in this long bearing with me," and for requiring only a letter of explanation rather than the inconvenience of a personal appearance in Ely. Appealing to an authority higher than the bishop, Greenham argues that the real issue in the vestments dispute is one of "the inward intente of the minde," whereof God alone is the witness. He states that he cannot in good conscience wear the apparel nor subscribe to it, and then resorts to blatant toadyism with a plea of reluctance to argue the matter since he is only a "poore Countryman," while the bishop is "a man of such authoritie." He can only claim faithfulness "in preaching Christ crucified unto my selfe and Country people," even though he is unable fully to conform and subscribe to the new rites. He promises that he will nevertheless "by all meanes seeke peace and pursue it," adding wistfully, "if I can finde it." On the other hand, he thinks it would be wrong to do "for living sake" (i.e., to keep his clerical position) what he originally declined to do for his conscience's sake. "He that buildeth not in conscience," Greenham declares, "buyldeth in hell."

Having made the appeal to principle, he proceeds to develop a situation ethic for liturgical practice which opens up the possibility of a purely external conformity legitimized "in respect of person, time, place, maner, and ende of doing." For example, in spite of personal reservations, conformity may be defended out of respect for the honorable people who brought these practices into the church, and in consideration of the times in which they did their work. "Unto what mortall man did the Church ever owe more then unto Maister Luther," he exclaims, who nevertheless failed to radically purge the church of medieval leftovers. Luther was a chosen instrument of God, but "*Lutherus non viditomnia* Luther did not see all things." Greenham, in other words, implies that revelation is progressive, so that as time passes it becomes clearer what full reformation entails. Taking the relativities of time and place into account, he concedes willingness to use certain ceremonies "so farre forth as I might not hurt my conscience, or give offence to others." And he promises not to condemn others who use the ceremonies even if they are "repugnant to the expresse worde of God."

In answer to a leading question from the bishop about following the advice of a number of highly respected reformers—Bucer, Martyr, Bullinger, Beza, and Gualter—to be tolerant of certain abuses, Greenham gives a long, convoluted answer, ending up with personal conscience again. His own conscience, however, was emitting mixed signals, for he was obviously torn between conscientious scruples about the vestments, and conscientious obedience to established earthly authority. Finally, he affirms his loyalty to Prince and Church as well as to Truth, declaring that "if through errour I have any whit offended I wil be alwayes readie, by the worde of God, to bee reformed." He closes the lengthy letter with a benedictory prayer: "The God of peace beate downe Sathan underneath our feete, take away all offences, and graunt by the working of his spirite, that wee may bee of one accorde in his Christe, Amen."

There is no record of a response from Cox, but it appears that he and Greenham remained on good terms. Later, on at least two occasions, Cox entrusted Greenham with special assignments involving the twin threats of Catholicism and the Family of Love within the diocese.[15]

## III

Greenham's statements on other disputed ceremonies in the church also indicate personal reservations combined with concern for peace and obedience. He fears that capitulation to one ceremony will lead to more, for there is a "natural logique" that reasons, "if this may bee used [then] that may bee used...as an old woman did, who seing the minister baptise children with a cros, thought that shee might cros herself, when shee came to pray."[16] Greenham himself did not use the sign of the cross in baptism, for he regarded baptism itself to be a such a sign and thought it unnecessary to add another, for "it is against gods ordinance to make a double seal to one thing.[17] Elsewhere, he expounds for two pages on the perils of using the sign in baptism.[18] He calls it a "superfluous additament," and warns against burdening the gospel "with too great a multitude of ceremonies," for this is to confuse law and gospel. "Besides, Baptism

---

[15] See EDR, D/2/10, fol. 195v, and below, 70ff.
[16] REM 524, fol. 25r.
[17] Ibid., fol. 29v.
[18] Ibid., fols. 55v, 56r.

it self is sufficiently a significative sign of the cros, even as the gospel is sermo crucis, so baptism is signum crucis." The church should not ordain two signs "seing the lord in wisdome contenteth himself with one...."

Greenham was also opposed to the display of the cross in churches and shrines. "Let us labour to have Christ crucified in our hearts, by the ministerie of the word, ever preparing our selves in truth to beare the crosse of Christ...."[19]

In an interesting comment regarding stained glass windows in the church, he shifts the attention away from the legitimacy of stained glass itself to the proper procedure to be used when dealing with such issues. This is not a matter for the minister alone to decide. His role is to teach, not destroy. He must gain popular consent, guiding consciences to do the right, for "in a minister ther should bee wisdome; and love mixed with zeal" and he must conduct himself in such a way that testifies to his use of "sound, discreet, and loving means."[20] In another place, he demonstrates his political astuteness when he advises a minister who felt called to preach against the "many corruptions, and abuses in the church," not to do so on the first occasion, but rather "preach faith and repentance from sin." Then later, "when god shal have given you some power, and credit in their consciences...you may more safely do this." To address such controversial issues too quickly may result in an aborted ministry, being "cut of[f] from the place by others, and so never have free acces again."[21]

Greenham's comments on holy days are also somewhat ambivalent. He fears that observance of the many traditional holy days runs the danger of driving the "true use of the sabboth out of the dores of the church,"[22] and yet suggests using them as fasting days, "both beecaus wee might then do it with lest suspicion, or offence of others, and beecaus then wee may redeem the tyme in resting from our callings."[23]

The same ambivalence characterizes his observations about using the Magnificat and Nunc Dimittis after the Old and New Testament

[19] "Of divers Christian instructions," *Workes*, 319.
[20] REM 524, fols. 36v, 37r.
[21] Ibid., fols. 39v, 40r.
[22] Ibid., fol. 24r.
[23] Ibid., fol. 13v.

readings as prescribed by the Book of Common Prayer. He said he himself did not use them, for he regarded them as easily corrupted by "custome and continuance," and yet he thought they were initially established "in the wisdome of the spirit," for they convey the gospel message of redemption. Mary and Simeon are indeed "most holy witnesses of our redemtion in christ," and their songs were "first brought into the church for a more continual remembrance, of those benefits, which wee have in christ: howsoever now custome without conscience hath rather made them odious, then conscience without custome doth continew unto them that pure use, which becommeth spiritual thanksgiving."[24] Beyond this, Greenham is virtually silent about the officially authorized Prayer Book. He apparently used it, probably with some modifications. Colleagues of his, with similar liturgical scruples, produced a "puritan prayer book" called, *A booke of the Forme of common prayers*, drawn essentially from Knox's Genevan service-book and Book of Common Order.[25] This alternative prayer book was presented to Parliament for approval in 1584 but was not accepted. Its use, however, was widespread, and it is likely that Greenham used it as well.

The tabletalk presents Greenham's approach to ceremonies as eminently rational. In things commanded and forbidden, he would ask for reasons, and "if it were good hee would yeeld to it" and otherwise "hee would gainsay it" but with a tried and proved reason. Ceremonies that are not of the essence of religion but are "lesser adjuncts" such as "sitting, standing, kneeling, walking, at the receiving of the sacrament," are to be distinguished from "substantial ceremonies" like the sacraments themselves. With regard to the lesser adjuncts, "hee would not withstand or condemn any but leav them to ther own reason, seing very good men do soe dissagree in them" and even "desire a reformation." In the essentials of worship it is important to be "strickt and holy," but no commonwealth in Christian history has demanded "uniformity in every particular." Things established by law must be "very sound and profitable."[26]

---

[24] Ibid., fol. 44r.
[25] Walter H. Frere and Francis Procter, *A New History of the Book of Common Prayer* (London: Macmillan and Co., 1902) 132. On puritan worship in the sixteenth century, see Patrick Collinson, *The Elizabethan Puritan Movement*, 356-71.
[26] REM 524, fols. 54v, 55r.

So, did he conform or did he not? Greenham's position on disputed liturgical issues remains somewhat murky, even after piecing together the many comments sprinkled throughout the sources. His attempt to find a middle way results in apparent, perhaps deliberate, ambivalence. He seems to have been a sort of conforming non-conformist. In this respect, his views are quite similar to those of Martin Bucer, who had helped to shape the thought and practice of so many in Cambridge. Bucer was quoted by those on either side of the liturgical question, usually with equal legitimacy. He was personally opposed to the use of vestments and other remnants of medieval ceremony in the church, but he nonetheless counseled conformity when the alternative would be removal from the pulpit where the indispensable Word is preached.

Greenham shared Bucer's concern for the Word of God and its faithful proclamation, and also for the inviolable conscience, which generated a keen sense of responsibility not only to one's own convictions but also to established authority and the need for peace in the church. Ultimately his profound respect for authority and good order overruled his liturgical misgivings. These misgivings arose from his basic principle regarding liturgical ceremonies: "that if they have not their warrant from the word of the Lord they are like to be used without fruit; and in danger to be turned into hurtful superstition."[27] This seems to put Greenham on the side of the more radical reformers, but, upon close examination, it is apparent that even this forthright statement is worded in such a way as to allow some practical maneuvering, especially through phrases like, "they are like to be used," and "in danger" of superstition. He warns of the dangers, but does not close the door to discretionary use. In his concern for obedience and good order, Greenham gives advice designed for maximum flexibility. He states that "just obedience" may be given an "unjust commandement," as long as "it bee in things meerly outward," and then comments on the dispute over sitting or kneeling for the Eucharist: "As for such things, Let us do as much as wee can with the peace of the church lest wee make the remedy of the evil wors then the evil it self."[28] This approach of "pragmatic

---

[27] "Of ceremonies, things indifferent...," *Workes*, 652.
[28] REM 524, fol. 10v.

compromise" formed the core of his cooperative Puritanism.[29]

## IV

The liturgical controversy exposed some sharply differing points of view within the Church of England about more important issues such as the meaning of adiaphora, freedom of conscience, use of Scripture, the role of the church, and the tempo and extent of reform. Above all, the controversy over liturgical ceremonies raised the fundamental issue of authority: authority of conscience, Scripture, church, and state. Questions of Christian liberty and obedience to external authority loom large in the origins of Puritanism, just as they did in the origins of the Reformation on the continent.[30]

It became increasingly clear to those who did not wish to conform to the vestments rubric, that fundamental changes in church government might resolve the matter. If a church polity were adopted in which parity of the clergy and more local autonomy were fundamental principles, the dissenting pastors might well experience the liberty they craved. Thomas Cartwright, another Cambridge compatriot of Greenham in the 1560s, fired the opening salvo for presbyterianism in a series of lectures delivered in Cambridge in 1570, a few months before Greenham took up his work in Dry Drayton. Cartwright called for a radical restructuring of church government after the model of the early New Testament church portrayed in the book of Acts. This reconstruction would be based on the principles of clerical parity and shared authority, thus eliminating clerical hierarchy. Two years later, John Field and Thomas Wilcox published an even more inflammatory critique of the church in *An Admonition to the Parliament*, which was essentially a strident call for total administrative overhaul with presbyterianism as the goal. Cartwright and John Whitgift, a Pembroke alumnus, debated the issue in print for much of the rest of the decade.[31]

The 1580s brought an even bolder presbyterian development, the

---

[29] Patrick Collinson, *The Elizabethan Puritan Movement*, 384.

[30] Cf., John S. Coolidge, *The Pauline Renaissance in England* (Oxford: Clarendon Press, 1970) 39ff.

[31] Donald J. McGinn, *The Admonition Controversy* (New Brunswick: Rutgers University Press, 1949). See also Peter Lake, *Anglicans and Puritans?* (London: Unwin Hyman, 1988).

classis movement, which went beyond the call for change to change itself.[32] Here and there throughout the land, groups of like-minded clergy organized into ministerial conferences which functioned somewhat like presbyteries or classes within the Church of England. They were an outgrowth of the earlier "prophesyings" of the 1560s and 70s, informal conferences of godly pastors devoted especially to the study of Scripture and the practice of preaching. These conferences were initially unopposed by church and civil authorities. The Queen, however, became suspicious of the movement, regarding it as a potentially subversive effort to undermine the established seats of power in church and state. This led to her famous dispute with Archbishop Grindall (another Pembroke alumnus) when he refused to carry out her order to suppress the prophesyings, and even challenged the extent of her authority over ecclesiastical affairs. Whitgift became Grindal's successor in 1583, and immediately adopted a policy of much stronger pressure for conformity, and of complete suppression of the underground presbyterian movement.

Greenham's attitude toward these developments is difficult to discern, for he maintained a low profile when it came to national church affairs. John Strype, however, preserves two letters written in July and August of 1570 in support of Cartwright and addressed to William Cecil, Chancellor of Cambridge University.[33] The letters defend and extol Cartwright's piety, sound doctrine, and overall good intentions. Some twenty-five names are listed as signatories, Greenham's among them. Strype also reports that a presbyterian classis was organized at Cambridge, and that it met "at tymes of Commencement, and Sturbridge fayre," apparently because these occasions could be used to camoflauge the purpose of the meetings. Greenham is mentioned as a member of this Cambridge group, along with William Whitaker, Cartwright, John Knewstub, Walter Travers, Laurence Chaderton, William Perkins, and others. They appear to have been a loosely organized group marked by strong convictions about the need for preaching ministers and for church governmental

---

[32] Patrick Collinson, *The Elizabethan Puritan Movement*, 131-45, 168-76, 222-239; and Roland G. Usher, *The Presbyterian Movement in the Reign of Queen Elizabeth* (London: Royal Historical Society, 1905).

[33] *Annals of the Reformation* (Oxford: Clarendon Press, 1824) I, ii, 376; and II, ii, 412-17.

changes in a presbyterian direction.[34]

Perhaps Greenham was a member, but he was not a ringleader. In his writings, he never criticizes the Church of England as such, and one looks in vain for any presbyterian propaganda. He might spring to the defense of a faithful and respected colleague in danger of deposition, as he did for Cartwright, but Greenham would also urge the judicious weighing of the relative importance of church government and the gospel. "Many meddle and stirre much about a new Church government," he writes, "which are sensles and barren in the doctrine of new birth: but alas, what though a man know many things, and yet know not himselfe to be a new creature in Jesus Christ?"[35] He also warns against preoccupation with future hopes at the expense of dealing with the realities of the present. "It is often the policie of Sathan to make us travell in some good thing to come, when more fitly wee might be occupied in good things present."[36]

Strype admires Greenham's circumspection in the church government controversy. He records a story he heard from George Downham of Christ's College, who was at one time a presbyterian sympathizer, but who, "after mature study," returned to hearty support of episcopacy. According to Strype, Downham once heard Greenham, in a sermon at Cambridge, rebuke young scholars, who, "before they had studied the grounds of theology, would over-busy themselves in matters of discipline." Greenham likened this to building the roof of a house before laying its foundations.[37] The story is consistent with Samuel Clarke's comment about Greenham's restraining influence on impatient young rebels in Cambridge, keeping "not a few from errors and schism," and urging them to operate within the confines of the law out of concern for the peace of the church.[38]

Even though Robert Brown had been one of his student interns, Greenham was later fiercely critical of the Brownish separatists. He longed for church unity and abhorred schism. In severest terms he warns of God's judgment upon the schismatic: "the Lord shall destroy

---

[34] Strype, *The Life and Acts of John Whitgift* (Oxford: Clarendon Press, 1822) II, 6-7. Cf. Roland G. Usler, *The Presbyterian Movement in the Reign of Queen Elizabeth* (London: Royal Historical Society, 1905) xxix, xli.

[35] "Another or second portion of...grave Counsels," *Workes*, 48.

[36] Ibid.

[37] *Annals*, III, i, 719-20.

[38] *Thirty-two Divines*, 14-15.

him and he shall either grow prophane or worldly, or he shall be cut
off by death, or beare some other token of Gods wrath."[39] In the
spirit of Bucer and Calvin, Greenham makes a distinction between
essentials and accidentals in the church, arguing that where the
essentials are present, there exists the true church even if some of the
accidentals are wanting.[40] Christians should not "flie the Church"
even where pure worship is lacking, but rather exercise "prayer and
patience" for better things to come.[41] The Brownists were guilty of
misplaced zeal, focussing on the sins of others rather than their own.
Greenham writes often about the spiritual danger of casting the first
stone, of ignoring the beam in one's own eye while dealing with the
splinter in others, an attitude with considerable ecumenical
implications. He also expresses concern about the Brownists' lack of
respect for constituted authority, thus reflecting one of the most
significant differences between cooperative and separatist Puritanism.
The Brownists, he writes, "rush into an open reprehension of men
that are mightie in authority, as though no regard of place, time and
persons were to be had.[42] He implies that the separatists need a better
sense of history, which would help them avoid quick and absolutist
judgements.

Greenham's irenic instincts were coupled with a conservative view
of authority. He constantly emphasized obedience to authorities of
both church and state. In tones reminscent of Luther and Calvin, he
insists that even ungodly rulers are to be tolerated. "For, though
Princes doe not their duties, yet wee must not therefore rebel against
them: and though we be persecuted of rulers without a cause, yet we
must stand in awe of Gods word," which declares that those who
strike with the sword shall perish by the sword. Ungodly rulers need
not be feared, for they can hurt the body only, not the soul. So no
matter how evil he may be, curse not the King, says Greenham, for
even evil kings are ordained instruments of God, should be respected
as such, and must be faithfully obeyed. "If then either our Princes
shall be ungodly, or their under officers unfaithfull, we must not
thereupon grudge to pay tribute, to give taske, and to yeeld subsidie,"
for even corrupt government has a divine purpose. It is "the hand of

---

[39] "The first portion of grave Counsels," ibid., 37.
[40] Ibid.
[41] "Of the Church," ibid, 648.
[42] "Of Zeale," *Workes*, 258.

Gods wrath" justly layed upon the people for some sin.[43]

By means of these general references to princes and kings, Greenham avoids possible charges of disloyalty to Elizabeth. He does not wish to imply that the problem of ungodly rulers pertains in England; he is dealing with the issue in the abstract. Never does Greenham speak negatively of the Queen. On the contrary, "He much rejoyced in and Praised God for the happy government of Queen Elizabeth, and for the blessed calm and peace which the Church and People of God enjoyed under the same, speaking often of it, both publickly and privately, as he had occasion, endeavouring to stirre up the hearts of all men (as much as in him lay) to Praise God with him for it, and to pray also for the continuance thereof." Clarke relates that just the day before Greenham died, he was troubled about the failure of many who were not sufficiently thankful "for those wonderfull and happy deliverances" from "Popish Adversaries" which the Queen had accomplished, probably a reference to the recent defeat of the Spanish Armada.[44] Greenham's *Workes* reflect his awareness of the international political situation, especially the French and Spanish threats to the kingdom which constantly occupied the Queen's attention. At one point he calls for prayer on the nation's behalf. "The Commonwealth also, being subject to privie conspiracie, and forraine war whereby it might be overthrowne; these, if men be lovers of their countrie, will teach them what need they have to pray."[45]

These dual concerns—for the peace of the church and obedience to authority—made Greenham a stabilizing puritan rather than a revolutionary in Elizabethan England. The only revolution Greenham promoted was in the lives of his parishioners. He labored diligently for the reformation of Dry Drayton without becoming deeply involved in reformation battles at the national level. He was ultimately more interested in personal piety than ecclesiastical politics. He had passionate protestant convictions but they were combined with deeply conservative instincts about peace and good order. Such a combination does not generate a spirit of revolution. On the national level of church and state, therefore, Greenham's Puritanism was more

---

[43] "Meditations on the 119 Psalm," *Workes*, 577-78.
[44] Samuel Clarke, *Thirty-two Lives*, 14.
[45] "Meditations on the 119 Psalm," *Workes*, 561.

conservative than transformative.[46]

V

The liturgical and church government controversies were intramural battles within the Church of England. But above and beyond them, the wars of the church were fought on other fronts as well. These in fact were larger and ultimately more significant battles, which had shaping, perspectival affect on the controversies within the church. Both Greenham's theology and politics were significantly influenced by the controversies between the church and forces threatening it from the outside. In Greenham's *Workes*, these external forces are mentioned much more frequently than are the liturgical and church governmental matters. They constituted threats on the right and the left; Greenham, along with the Church of England in general, carefully positioned himself in the center. The two threats were "papism" on the right, and the "Family of Love" on the left, evil forces mentioned over and over again in his writings. It is over against these religious alternatives that Greenham defined himself as an English protestant. Those most keenly aware of the threats from the outside tended not to allow internal liturgical and governmental squabbles to divide them. Since these threats constituted a foe common to both those with puritan leanings and all others in the Church of England, they had a unifying impact upon the church.

Greenham entered Cambridge to train for the ministry only a few short months after the death of the Catholic Queen Mary. Her five-year reign had been a total disaster for committed protestants. She strove to stamp out every protestant element that had been introduced in the latter years of her father's tenure and during the brief term of her half-brother, Edward. Her reign was regarded as a monstrous evil by those with protestant sympathies. Recognizing that they were in mortal danger, many fled to safe places of exile on the continent. Of those who remained, many died for their convictions about biblical authority, the way of salvation, and the proper worship of God.

Whenever these matters surface in Greenham's writings, so does

---

[46] Cf., Patrick Collinson, *English Puritanism*, 31.

mention of the Roman threat. Scripture alone as religious authority over against the authority of human beings, institutions, and traditions; salvation by divine grace alone over against salvation earned through human effort; justification by faith alone over against works righteousness; the priesthood of all believers over against a special mediatorial class; and Word centered worship over against sacramental worship—these are bedrock protestant doctrines that appear regularly in Greenham's writings. Even concern about vestments and church government were discussed and understood against the backdrop of the break with Rome. The radicals' opposition to vestments was a by-product of opposition to remnants of papism, and the call for presbyterianism had, at the very least, overtones suggesting that this was a more "protestant" system of government. Considering the early period in which Greenham's convictions were formed and brought to maturity in Cambridge, it is not surprising that the Roman threat was so much in the foreground of his thought. His antipathy to Rome accounts, at least in part, for his ultimate loyalty to the Church of England and to Elizabeth, the protestant Queen. Sixteenth century Puritanism was much more anti-Roman Catholic than anti-anglican. Popery was the insidious evil that had to be fully removed—root, trunk and branch—from the realm.

There was a second threat equally toxic for Greenham. In fact, he mentions it more frequently than papism in his writings. This was the sect called "Family of Love," a utopian cult especially prominent in East Anglia.[47] Greenham refers to the movement literally hundreds of times in his *Workes*, in part because he became personally involved in official investigations of the sect. It was founded on the continent by Heinrich Niclaes, a German mercer, who had become disillusioned with the institutional church. Niclaes was constantly frustrated in his attempts to find a community of Christians in which the love of Christ was fully reflected and adequately practiced. In typical cultic fashion, he finally declared himself to be a new prophet to whom God had revealed the true pattern for the salvation of humankind. Niclaes

---

[47] See Christopher Marsh, *The Family of Love in English Society 1550-1630* (Cambridge: University Press, 1994); Felicity Heal, "The Family of Love and the Diocese of Ely," in *Schism, Heresy, and Religious Protest* (Studies in Church History, 1972) vol. 9, 213-22; Alistair Hamilton, *The Family of Love* (Cambridge: James Clarke and Co., 1981); and Jean D. Moss, "The Family of Love and English Critics," *The Sixteenth Century Journal*, VI, I, April 1975, 35-52.

laid claim to a special, personal, indwelling of the Spirit of love, and to special revelations from this Spirit. He attracted some followers in the low countries where the first communities of "familists" were organized around 1540. From there they spread, first to France, and eventually to England where the movement grew rapidly, especially after Christopher Vitels translated some of Niclaes's writings into English. Vitels was active in East Anglia as early as the 1550s, and the movement seems to have grown rapidly, especially in the 1570s, for by the end of that decade the civil government had become alarmed and the Queen's Privy Council decided to investigate.[48] Precisely during the first decade of Greenham's ministry in Dry Drayton, therefore, the Family of Love was busily at work right in his own diocese of Ely, especially in the towns of Balsham and Wisbech, a little to the north of Cambridge.

Political and ecclesiastical leaders regarded the familists not only as heretical, but also as a subversive threat to good order in the commonwealth. Because of their emphasis on inner illumination by the Spirit, they were suspected of having antinomian tendencies. In one of his direct revelations from God, Niclaes was informed that the last judgment was under way. To prepare for it, he mapped out a special plan for salvation. His followers formed "houses of love," where a stringent devotional discipline was maintained, leading to the ultimate goal of total appropriation of God's love—"Godded with God" in Niclaes's terms. When this level of spirituality was reached, mortal sin no longer had to be feared. Moral perfectability, in other words, was attainable in this life. These beliefs and practices convinced leaders in the Church of England that the familists were guilty of an Arian christology and a Pelagian view of sin, grace, and good works.

Several anti-familist tracts appeared in the 1570s, with titles that reveal fear and revulsion bordering on hysteria. *The Displaying of an horrible secte of grosse and wicked Heretiques* was authored by John Rogers; *A Confutation of Monstrous and horrible heresies* by Richard Greenham's friend and colleague, John Knewstub. Rogers lists fifty-three specific charges of heresy.[49] Knewstub alleged that Niclaes "turneth religion upside downe, and buildeth heaven heere

---

[48] *APC*, XII, 231-32, 269.
[49] Fols. Hiii-Jii.

upon earth, maketh God man: and man, God; heaven, hell; and hel, heaven." Niclaes's opinions are described as "venom and poyson," which will inflict eternal death on anyone infected thereby.[50] As Christopher Marsh has suggested, perhaps the intensity of puritan reaction against the familists can be explained by the puritans' own uncertainty about their status with the government in the "crisis" years of the 1570s and 80s. They needed a scapegoat, and the Family of Love provided a timely one.[51]

The Privy Council entered the fray in 1580 when it was discovered that the heresy had even infiltrated the Queen's Yeomen of the Guard. The Council sent a letter to Bishop Cox of Ely expressing deep concern about the familists, especially about their "maintaining erroneous doctrines and using private conventicles contrarie to her Majesties lawes." It was the Queen's good pleasure that Cox and all the other bishops in the realm "take good care to the suppressing and punishing of them." To that end, the Council appointed four assistants to help Bishop Cox in the investigation. One of the four was Richard Greenham.[52]

This special commission dutifully performed its task, and the bishop reported to the Privy Council the results of the investigation. The report is preserved in Gonville and Caius MS. 53/40, "a book of affairs relating to Richard Cox, Bp. of Ely." This manuscript also contains a lengthier report of a similar investigation of the "familye of love abiding at Wysbytch" by another committee, this one made up of the bishop; his Chancellor, Dr. Bridgewater; William Fulke, Master of Pembroke; Roger Goad, Provost of King's; and again, Richard Greenham. Their investigation took place on 3-5 October 1580, when about a dozen persons "vehemently suspected to be followers of H. N." were interrogated.[53] Cox, who died in 1581, was becoming very frail, and it is evident that Greenham played a prominent role for the prosecution. The final report includes a section entitled, "Other Artycles dyvised by mr. Greeneham exhibited and subscribed as before eodem die." These articles, seven in all, constitute a miniature confession of orthodox Christianity over against the beliefs of the

---

[50] Fol. *4.
[51] *The Family of Love in English Society*, 113-24.
[52] APC, XII, 232-3.
[53] Fols. 126v-131r.

familists.[54]

First, against the Arianism and docetism of the familists, Greenham asserts that Christ suffered not only mental and spiritual torture on the cross, but physical "torments of his body" as well, "so that his sweate was droppes of bloode tryckling downe to the grounde." He did not feign forsakenness by God, but truly and naturally felt it, and finally "truly and naturally dyed." The second article is an implicit protest against the familists' works righteousness and perfectionism. Greenham proclaims salvation by faith in Christ only, "not by love onlye," and also asserts that sin and its ravages remain in humankind "untill we be onclothed of this our naturall flesh and bodely dwelling place." Article three affirms the orthodox doctrine of the trinity in almost Athanasian terms, again in contradiction of the familists' Arianism. God is a "divine substaunce and nature" existing in three persons: "we beleeve the father to be god, the sonne to be god, and the holy gost to be god," and these three are "coeternall and coequall, so that in all thinges, the trynity in unytie, and unitie in trynitie is to be worshipped." The fourth article seems to be formulated against papism more than familism and contains an interesting reference to the universal scope of Christ's redemptive work. It speaks of the complete sufficiency of Christ's sacrifice to satisfy "for all the synnes of the whole worlde both originall and actuall." This is affirmed over against the "sacryfices of the masses" in which the priests claimed to repeat the original offering of Christ. Such presumptuous claims are "blasphemous fables and dangerous deceipts." In article five, Greenham again professes a truly human Christ who was, nevertheless, without sin. However, those who are baptized and "borne againe in Christ" continue to struggle with sin, "and if wee say that we have no synne we deceave our selves and the truth is not in us.[55]

The familists' quest for perfection on earth is again addressed in the sixth article. Greenham's response is especially significant for it reveals his churchly, non-sectarian Puritanism. Puritans, like the familists, were sometimes criticized for their emphasis on a "purity" which their detractors thought unattainable in this world. In article

---

[54] Fols. 128r&v.

[55] In one of his sermons Greenham says against the familists that Christians should not "imagine any spiritual Christ to be within" them, "Of the latter or second effect of Christ," *Workes*, 373.

six, Greenham articulates a more moderate, Augustinian, anti-donatist position about the admixture of good and evil in the visible church. There "the evell be ever myngled with the good," he writes, "and somtyme the evell have chiefe authorytie in the ministration of the word and Sacraments," but even when it does, if those sacraments are administered in Christ's name and by his commission and authority, "we maie use the ministerye, both in hearing the worde of god, and in the receaving of the Sacraments." The effectiveness of Christ's ordinance is not removed by human wickedness, "nor the grace of god and his gyftes dyminished." The sacraments operate "effectually because of Christes instytution and promyse although they be administered by evell men."[56] In his preface to Knewstub's book against the Family of Love, Chancellor William Cecil suggests that the familists constitute the "true succession of those ancient Catharists and Puritans who thought themselves not to sinne...." From such "Puritanism" Greenham clearly dissociates himself.

A brief article seven concludes Greenham's testimony. Those who "presume to saye that every man shalbe saved by the lawe or sect which he professeth" are "accursed," he declares. "For holye scriptures doe sett out unto us only the name Jesus Christ, wherein men must be saved."

Greenham's thought and ministry were defined largely on these two battlefronts: the papists on the right and the familists on the left. At times he uses the law/gospel distinction to characterize their respective weaknesses—legalism on the one hand and antinomianism on the other. If the one was guilty of a spirit-quenching institutionalism, the other was equally guilty of a rudderless libertinism which undermined the good order of traditional regulations and established institutions. If one was dominated by ceremony, the other was destructive of the indispensable means of grace: the true preaching of the word, and proper administration of the sacraments. In Greenham's words: "Thus we see how we sayle betweene two rocks, and betweene two flats, and therefore need the sterne of God his spirit and government of the word to sayle aright.[57]

---

[56] Even Thomas Cartwright, in his debate with Whitgift, denied the validity of sacraments administered by non-preaching ministers, Peter Lake, *Anglicans and Puritans?*, 38.

[57] "Of the latter or second effect of Christ his crosses," *Workes*, 374.

Greenham's basic position as theologian and pastor was not formed in the context of debates between conformists and non-conformists in the Church of England. For the most part, he rose above the battles over liturgical requirements and church governmental changes. With respect to those issues, his Puritanism was very tepid—in Fuller's terms, "mild and moderate," rather than "fierce and fiery."[58] He was ultimately more concerned about practical godliness than he was about liturgy and polity. Like the majority of his colleagues in the Church of England, he was simply a devout, evangelical protestant who positioned himself between the unsavory alternatives of papism on the right and the familists on the left. His ministry in Dry Drayton was conducted in antipathy to those two institutional threats to Reformation Protestantism. His polemic against both Roman Catholicism and the Family of Love, as well as his exceptional pastoral counselling and faithful gospel proclamation, resonate with strong protestant theological convictions. He did not create a theology, but he reflects one, and it is to an elucidation of the central principles of his thought that we now turn.

---

[58] Quoted in Patrick Collinson, *English Puritanism*, 20.

# 4

# THEOLOGICAL LANDMARKS: GOD AND HIS WORD

## I

The puritans have been examined historically, sociologically, psychologically, politically, and, certainly not least of all, economically. Max Weber, Christopher Hill, Michael Walzer, and others have contributed prodigious and provocative studies of how Puritanism shaped the modern, secular world. Without denying the importance of these works, A. G. Dickens writes, "When we have finished our efforts to modernize and secularize Puritanism, it remains an obstinately religious phenomenon, and its common characteristics must be sought in its religious teachings."[1] Dewey Wallace has also stated the need to study Puritanism as a theological movement,[2] recognizing that ultimately the engine that gave it its power and made it an historical force to be reckoned with was not its economics, but its theology; not its view of work, but its faith in God.

Perhaps Richard Greenham seems an unlikely source for a study of puritan theology, for his strengths lay particularly in "the cure of troubled souls." He was by no means a systematic theologian like his friend and contemporary, William Perkins, but a practicing pastor whose collected writings are noteworthy for their *lack* of system.

---

[1] Arthur G. Dickens, *The English Reformation* (London: B. T. Batsford LTD, 1964) 319.
[2] *Puritans and Predestination* (Chapel Hill: University of North Carolina Press, 1982) vii.

Nevertheless, in the religious landscape of Greenham's *Workes*, there appear regularly certain theological themes which constitute the central landmarks of his faith. He does not consciously articulate these for purposes of argument or analysis; they simply arise naturally in the course of the development of his practical theology. In their parish work, the puritans placed preaching at the center, and it is apparent that the godly preachers of the sixteenth century were well grounded in Christian doctrine. In this chapter, Greenham's two basic landmarks will be discussed: *God* and the *Word of God*. These appear so regularly and become so conspicuous that they qualify as the two most fundamental elements, or "prolegomena" of his belief system. In close connection with these topics, Greenham's concept of the *knowledge* of God and the Word, and his hermeneutical use of *law and gospel,* will also be considered.

## II

The reader of Greenham's *Workes* is ushered into a universe many light-years away from the secularized, western world of the twentieth century. Greenham's world is one in which the presence of God is absolutely the defining factor. The sovereign God "is everywhere; if we run from him, we run as in a circle, the further we run from one side, the neerer we run to another, and still we are in the Lord, his compasse."[3] This was the core of his faith. All else, whether predestination, justification, sanctification, covenant, law, or grace, flows from this basic and overwhelming conviction of the presence and power of God. The *coram deo* theme of both Luther and Calvin is equally strong in Greenham. Every moment of every day humankind stands "before the face of the Lord,"[4] he declares. "To be perswaded of Gods presence in our thoughts, words and labours, is a pure rule of Christianitie. In every place we are before God...."[5] In all of life, therefore, the godly are engaged in worship. "We are said to be alwaies in Gods presence in the time of God his worship....And sure it is, that the more we are in his presence, whiles we are in any holy exercise, the more shall we be in his worship even in our ordinarie

---

[3] "Of Godlinesse, "*Workes,* 690.
[4] "Of Gods worship," ibid., 801.
[5] "Another or second portion...of grave Counsels," ibid., 46.

callings."[6] Life has a single, comprehensive purpose: the glory and praise of God. "For this is the end of our creation: this is the end of our redemption, this is the end of our sanctification, this is the end of all our praying, and obtaining, even plentifullly to praise the name of our good God."[7] By glorifying God, human beings realize their own glory. When "our chiefest case is to glorifie God," then "wee indeed doe seeke our owne glorie."[8] Greenham's catechism begins with a question about humankind's desire for blessedness, but the answer is centered in God. The true way of blessedness is: "To know God to bee my Father in Jesus Christ, by the revelation of the spirit according to his word, & therfore to serve him according to his will, and to set forth his glorie...."[9]

Although Greenham's God is a loving Father, he is also wholly other, utterly free, sovereign, and non-contingent. The boundary between God and humanity is profoundly important. His human creatures need to be ever aware that "wee are still be men, and God alone is God."[10] This boundary is implicit everywhere in Greenham's writings, and he deals with it explicitly in a treatise on the fear of God. This fear arises from human awareness of the distance and difference between God and humanity. It is a reverent fear generated by the knowledge of human finitude and divine freedom. It is a healthy and creative fear for it leads to awareness of sin and God's wrath upon it. Such fear does not immobilize but quickens the godly. "It is good to be stricken with feare," he writes, for fear leads directly to humility, faith, and moral diligence.[11]

Greenham was overawed by the power of God. He marvels at the "great power" of God's "very nostrels," for he exhales consuming fire from them. God's "little finger" brought about the plagues in Egypt. "If he be so mightie when he toucheth us but with his finger, how terrible is he if he strikes us with his arme?"[12] In his treatise on the resurrection, Greenham cites many examples of God's power in the Scriptures—the flood, the Exodus, the dividing of the waters of the

---

[6] "A third portion...of an hundred grave counsels," ibid., 60.
[7] "Meditations on the 119 Psalm," ibid., 600. Cf., William Perkins, *Works* (London: J. Legatt, 1616-18) I, 747.
[8] "Another or second portion," *Workes*, 47.
[9] "A short form of catechising," ibid., 71.
[10] "The first portion of grave Counsels," ibid., 6.
[11] "A Treatise of Gods feare," ibid., 195-8; "Of Feare," ibid., 682-3.
[12] "A treatise of Gods feare," ibid., 198.

Red Sea, the wilderness miracles, Daniel and the fiery furnace, Jonah
and the whale—but God's power displayed in the divine works of
creation and resurrection is unsurpassed. The God who is the
fountain of fire, hail, thunderbolts, "lice and fleas," hosts of angels,
indeed all of creation, is also the God of the resurrection. Since he
had the power to create the world out of nothing, surely he has
sufficient power to raise the dead.[13]

Much has been made of the puritans' fear of the devil and his
awesome power, but when the question is raised about the relative
power of God and Satan, Greenham needs no time to ponder. Sin and
evil are realities to be dealt with, but the devil "doth all by constraint
and restraint under the Lord." Even all human affliction is, therefore,
contained within the power of God "in whose hands are both the
entrance, the continuance, and the issues of our sufferings."[14] This
thought does not lead Greenham to question God's goodness and
mercy, but paradoxically, to greater confidence and assurance. God is
all powerful. Satan, sin, and affliction remain within the scope of that
power. Hence, for the believer, "there is nothing doth drawe out more
assurance from God, as when he seeth that throughly and confidently,
yet with all humilitie we depend upon his promise, providence, and
power."[15]

Enamored though he was with the power of God, Greenham
avoids abstractions. He does not raise speculative questions about
whether God could create a world so large he couldn't move it, but
confines his ruminations to the Scriptures. God's power is exercised
within the parameters of his revealed love and justice. Greenham
writes, "the power of God is able to perform whatsoever the word
doth shew, or justice doth desire to be done." The almightiness of
God means that he has the power "to performe that with might which
he doth promise," and to bring to pass "that which he threateneth."
God "can do whatsoever he will doe," but "he cannot faile in his
trueth, he cannot alter the covenant gone out of his mouth...."[16] In
his catechism, Greenham relates God's almightiness directly to his
providential care. He is almighty in the absolutely certain
preservation of all that he has made. This is a doctrine that

[13] "A Treatise of the Resurrection," ibid., 178-186.
[14] "The first portion of grave Counsels," ibid., 2.
[15] "A third portion...of an hundred grave counsels," ibid., 66.
[16] Ibid., 184.

"ministreth...four notable comforts." These include assurance of the protective care of God's "good Angels"; confidence that neither the devil nor wicked people can bring harm to the godly "but when, and as farre forth as God doth give them leave"; certainty that creation has been designed for humanity's "profitable and convenient use"; and, finally, trust that "though I suffer by Sathan, or want of the creatures, yet all this shall turne to my good in the ende."[17]

Greenham rarely expounds on the trinitarian existence of God, but assumes it, frequently alluding to this or that person of the Trinity. The credo he developed in his response to the Family of Love includes a formal statement with Athanasian overtones.

> We doe acknowledg god to be a divine substaunce and nature, and not only Wysedome, righteousnes, mercy, etc. we acknowledge this divine substaunce, to be distinct into three persons the father the sonne and the holy gost, we beleeve the father to be god, the sonne to be god, and the holy gost to be god. And in this trynitie that none is afore or after other, none greater, or lesse than other, but that whole three be coeternall and coequall, so that in all thinges, the trynity in unytie, and unitie in trynitie is to be worshipped.[18]

Elsewhere in his writings, the point at which Greenham deals explicitly with trinitarian doctrine is in his counsel on good order. "Order must be had in all things," he writes, "especially in heavenly things." He then proceeds to speak of trinitarian order in God, but one that appears to have more epistemological than ontological importance.

> We shall see an order even in God himselfe: in the Trinitie, though all the persons bee equall, yet there is an established order of the second person, of the third person, though not of essence which is indivisible, yet for better order, of teaching of us to come to the knowledge of God.[19]

---

[17] "A short form of catechising," ibid., 82.
[18] Gonville and Caius MS 53/30, fol. 128r.
[19] "Of Order how necessary in all things," ibid., 833.

The Trinity is the avenue by which we know God and without which God remains obscure and ineffable. Furthermore, from this trinitarian order flows a necessity for order in human life and activity. A deed done confusedly "is as good as not done." Greenham describes hell as a place of no order. God, on the other hand, is perfect, trinitarian order.[20]

Greenham's Christology is essentially Chalcedonian without the adverbial technicalities. In his catechism, perhaps in reaction to the suspected Arianism of the Family of Love, he underscores his commitment to the eternal oneness of Christ and the Father with an appeal to the historic anti-Arian statement in the Nicene Creed. Christ is the "onely begotten Sonne of God...God of God, Light of Light, verie God of very God, begotten not made, beeing of one substance with the Father, by whom all things were made."[21] Christ's full humanity is affirmed as well, for God's righteousness requires that the same nature that sinned should pay for sin. Therefore, he was born of a woman "as others bee, and subject to all infirmities of man, sinne onely excepted." His sinlessness was necessary not only to make it possible for him to bear the sins of mankind, but also so that "Godhead and Manhood" could be "joyned together" in the one person of Christ. The doctrine of his full humanity leads to the assurance that "Christ is fit to suffer the punishment of my sinne: and being man himselfe, is also meete to bee more pitifull and mercifull unto men." Greenham's catechism also includes questions and answers about the offices of Christ: prophet, priest, and king. As prophet he is the "onely" teacher of the Church; as priest he offers himself as a sacrifice for sin, functions as mediator, and brings assurance that "I also am a Priest"; and as king he rules by his word and spirit, and guarantees victory over "the flesh, the world, the divell, death, and hell."

In terms of relative emphasis on Christ as Saviour and Christ as Lord, Greenham reflects Luther more than Calvin. His emphasis is on justification through the cross of Christ, rather than on his Lordship over the world and sanctifying role in the Church. Even in response to the question: "Why call you him Lord?" Greenham answers in

---

[20] Ibid.

[21] "A short forme of catechising," ibid., 82. All of the quotations that follow in this paragraph are from the catechism, pp. 82 and 83.

terms of sacrifice rather than victory: "Because not with gold nor silver, but with his precious bloud hee hath purchased us to bee a peculiar people to himselfe." He does refer to Christ at one point as "the author and finisher of holines,"[22] but such statements are relatively rare.

The doctrine of the Holy Spirit receives enormous emphasis throughout Greenham's *Workes*. The entire Bible, Greenham declares, is centered in the Holy Spirit. "All the doctrine of the Scriptures may be referred to these two heads. First, how wee may be prepared to receive the spirit of God. Secondly, how the spirit may be retained when as wee have once received it."[23] The totality of Christian faith and life is contingent upon the work of the Holy Spirit. Without it, "the word worketh not," prayers are powerless, sacraments are "small and sillie," and other worship orders and exercises are unprofitable. Furthermore, the gospel of grace with its message of Christ, redemption and justification falls on deaf ears "unless God give us of his good spirit, to profit by the same."[24] The Holy Spirit is the "most excellent" gift, without which "surely we belong not to God."[25]

Greenham does not speculate about the nature and being of the Holy Spirit, but concentrates completely on his work in the believer and in the Church. Here the Spirit's teaching function is most prominent.[26] The Spirit is, first of all, the teacher of sin, "who raiseth up in us a great and general astonishment by reason of all those great and enormous sinnes that we have committed." He prompts a "speciall griefe for speciall sinnes." Secondly, the Spirit arouses in the godly a profound mistrust of self, especially of one's own understanding and reason. He teaches that human judgment is unreliable, that "our reason is unreasonable," thus prompting an attitude of humility. Thirdly, the Spirit plays a central role in the

---

[22] "The first portion of grave Counsels, "*Workes*, 31.

[23] "The first Sermon, of Quenching the Spirit," ibid., 241. These are the opening words of a sermon on 1 Thessalonians 5:19, "Quench not the spirit." That this was a special emphasis in his ministry is also reflected in the fact that this was Greenham's first published work, published as a separate item along with a few letters and short treatises, edited by Richard Bradocke, (London, 1598).

[24] Ibid.

[25] "A treatise of sending the Holy Ghost," ibid., 223.

[26] See, for example, "Meditations on the 119 Psalm," ibid., 405, where the Holy Spirit is mentioned six times in half a page as teacher, instructor, and enlightener.

justification of the sinner, for he opens the door to the grace and mercy of God, and opens eyes to the meaning of Christ's suffering. He brings about the gifts of joy and peace in human hearts that know "our sinnes are forgiven us, and God is at once with us." Finally, the Holy Spirit is the source of "the life and nimblenes that is in us to doe good." By the Spirit's work, the Christian is "not onely reclaimed from evill, but also applied and framed to that which is good." The believer's understanding, judgment, will, and reason are all transformed. The Spirit brings "the life of God" into believers who then "do live accordingly, bringing forth the fruits of the spirit."[27]

Greenham's teaching about the Holy Spirit is predominantly devotional and experiential in character. It is a practical pneumatology with a strong theological base, for it arises from his emphasis on the centrality of God and from his trinitarian understanding of God. The doctrine of the triune God is foundational for Greenham's theology and ministry; the doctrine of the Holy Spirit is crucial to the believer's experience of God.[28]

## III

While the fundamental reality in Greenham's universe is the triune God, there is a secondary reality that is bound up with the primary. It constitutes the indispensable, visible link between God and humanity. It is central and foundational as well, for all one says or thinks or knows about God is dependent upon its existence. This reality is the Word of God, normally conceived of by Greenham as the written Word. Rarely does he allude to Jesus as the Word, while references to the inscripturated Word appear on every page of his *Workes*. It is the main theme of his longest single treatise: "Meditations on the 119 Psalm." Greenham epitomizes the Reformation's passion for the Bible. God is transcendent and invisible. He has come near in Christ, but Christ is now also the ascended Lord. Human beings need something to keep in touch with the divine. For the medieval church, the sacraments provided the tactile means of contact, but for the Reformers the Bible was the apprehensible link with God.

---

[27] "The first Sermon, of Quenching the Spirit," ibid., 242-4.
[28] Cf., G. Nuttall, *The Holy Spirit in Puritan Faith and Experience* (Oxford: Basil Blackwell, 1946).

Human beings are absolutely dependent upon that Word, for God remains unknown and unseen without it. It is "the glasse wherein alone whilest we are in this life we see the face of the Lord," and the "conduit" through which all God's mercies flow to humankind.[29] Greenham joins the two realities, God and Word, in an indissoluble unity. He writes, "No man can knowe his owne heart but by God and by the word, which is of the same nature that God is." It is, therefore, "more deare than heaven and earth," the greatest treasure God has given to humankind. God and his Word are so bound together, that love for the Word becomes the test of love for God. "Let us examine," he writes, "if the reading, hearing, and meditating of Gods word bee as sweete unto us, as our very life....The great delight in Gods word overshadoweth all worldly pleasures."

It is through the Word that believers participate in the life of God. Like God himself, the Word "wil stick with us to the end," and will "save us from all evils, accompany us in all dangers, recover us in all infirmities, pitie and relieve us in all miseries."[30] Since the Word and God become virtually synonymous in Greenham's thought, he ascribes God's purity to the Word. At the end of a particularly colorful paragraph on this theme, he writes, "Thus we see how exact, how pure, how comfortable, how everlasting the word is."[31]

Since the Word is "of the same nature that god is," it shares in and radiates the awesome power of God. The Word is the instrument of his power and the basis for the creation's stability. In an eloquent statement on creation, Greenham argues that the earth, because of its finitude, is intrinsically "very fickle and readie to fall." Why then does it give the appearance of solidity and stability? It is "because of the word wherein God hath commaunded it so to be," says Greenham. By his Word, "The Lord gave bounds to the Sea the which it should not passe." The great flood violated those boundaries but only by the Lord's command, and now the waters are contained again because "God hath so appointed it" by his Word.[32]

His devout commitment to the Word inspires Greenham to breathtaking bursts of eloquence. At one point he offers in a lengthy paragraph what must be the largest number of metaphors for

---

[29] "Meditations on the 119 Psalm," *Workes*, 524, 490.
[30] Ibid., 550. Cf., J. S. Coolidge, *The Pauline Renaissance*, 145.
[31] "Meditations on the 119 Psalm," *Workes*, 550.
[32] Ibid., 443.

Scripture ever assembled, thirty-seven in all!

> The word of God is reverenced with many titles, it is the
> revealed will of God; the librarie of the holy Ghost; the cubit
> of the Sanctuarie; the Lantern of Israel...; the spirituall
> Manna; Christ his Aphorismes; the wisedome of the crosse;
> the Lord his legacie; the touchstone of error; the key of the
> sheepfold; the mystery of godlinesse; the oldest way of life and
> truth...; the fulness of knowledge; the Schoolemaster of
> mankind; the beacon of the soule; the seede of new birth; the
> mouth of the Lord Jehovah; the two-edged sword; the acts
> and statutes of the highest Parliament; the mint of the
> Church; the lode-starre of the faithfull pilgrim; the signet of
> God his right hand; the Lambes book; the watch-bel; the
> glasse of our life; the scepter of his kingdom; the arch of the
> truth; the breath of the Holy Ghost; God his Oracle; the
> Epistle of God to the world; the inestimable pearle; the
> tenour of our freehold; the covenant of promise; the Court-
> roule of his fines and amercements; the well of the water of
> life; the Lord his treasure; the lightning and thunder of the
> most High.[33]

As the believer's supreme authority, the Bible is not susceptible to
rational proof, and yet, in a paragraph reminiscent of Calvin's
arguments for the authenticity of Scripture, Greenham presents nine
reasons for its "excellencie." These include such characteristics as
form and style, fulfilled prophecies, its preservation over many
centuries, its realistic assessment of sinful humanity, and the
willingness of martyrs to die for it.[34]

Given the dominance of the Holy Spirit in Greenham's thought, it
is not surprising to find him emphasizing a most intimate relationship
between Word and Spirit as well. The Bible, he declares, "is the
Librarie of the holy Ghost."[35] He is the primary author, and since he
"conceived" it, understanding of that Word is dependent upon the
Holy Spirit. "There is a hearing of the letter," which is empty and

---

[33] "Of good workes," ibid., 826.
[34] "Of Gods promises," ibid., 756. Cf., John Calvin, *Institutes,* I, viii.
[35] "Of Gods promises, excellencie, and truth of Gods word," ibid., 756.

futile, but there is also "an hearing of the Spirit," when the Word comes with the gifts of insight and understanding.[36] The intimate relationship of Word and Spirit is reflected throughout Greenham's writings especially in the recurring formula: "the holy Ghost here telleth us..."

The interrelationship of Word and Spirit was the subject of considerable theological discussion in the sixteenth century. Greenham enters that discussion when he considers whether Word or Spirit has primacy in the creation of faith in human hearts. His position is that "we first receive the spirit; howbeit to feele our faith we must necessarily receive the word." He uses the metaphor of smoke and fire to illustrate the relationship. Smoke shows there is fire hidden in the ashes; "yet there was fire before the smoke came." Similarly, the Word makes faith known, but the Spirit of God was present first.[37]

## IV

For knowledge of God, the believer is absolutely dependent upon the Word applied to the heart by the illuminating Holy Spirit. This constitutes the core of Greenham's epistemology. There is no other way of knowing God, no medieval or humanist "natural theology" by which human beings can gain even a modicum of knowledge of the divine through reason unenlightened by the Scriptures and the Holy Spirit. Because human minds are also victims of the fall, we are to "mistrust our reason." Indeed, the mysteries of God "are revealed unto them that renounce their owne reason." Human reason plays a role in the initial comprehension of the Word of God, yet that Word must not be placed in the understanding alone, but also "in the heart and affections."[38] The "seat of faith is not the braine, but in the heart, and the head is not the place to keep the promises of God, but the heart is the chest to lay them up in."[39] It is only this genuine heart knowledge that will lead to zeal, the most advanced stage of faith. On Greenham's spiritual thermometer, zeal is near the boiling point. It is the opposite of lukewarm faith. He writes, "zeal is hot, & cannot long

---

[36] "Meditations on the 119 Psalm," ibid., 517.
[37] "The first portion of grave Counsels," ibid., 12. Cf., REM 524, fol. 45r.
[38] Ibid., 519.
[39] "Of the heavenly purchase in three Sermons," Workes, 294.

be holden in." But even zeal, Greenham emphasizes, is grounded in knowledge, another indicator that knowledge is never, for him, an end in itself, or sufficient by itself for the Christian life.[40]

Greenham's definition of knowledge is reminiscent of Calvin's:

> By knowledge we may understand, not the knowledge of the letter floting in the braine, and flowing even at the tongues end (which indeed is not worthie the name of knowledge:) but the true understanding of the word taught by the spirit, which entreth the heart, and worketh on the affections, frameth to obedience, and assureth of everlasting life.

Such knowledge, he says, cannot be found in "prophane writings," but only in the Word of God approached with a pure heart.[41] Greenham emphasizes over and over again that the heart is the seat of the Christian religion. He rebukes the ancient and medieval philosophers who said "that the minde was the seat of knowledge, yet they could never see, that the heart is the seat of the Christian religion." Since the "seate for divinitie" is the heart, "doe not place it in our braine," he pleads. Since knowledge is a matter of the heart, the Christian faith is accessible to all. Even "the simple man of the countrie," who submits his heart to God, "shall afterward attaine to great knowledge."[42]

The strong ethical dimension of Greenham's thought that will be considered later surfaces already at this point in his view of knowledge. True knowledge grounded in the heart will inevitably lead to obedience. In his lengthy meditation on Psalm 119, Greenham repeatedly alludes to the radical difference between knowledge and ignorance, between the light of truth and the darkness of falsehood. This genuine, God-fearing knowledge is never separated from obedience. "Knowledge of the word" and the "obedience of the same" are always mentioned in the same breath. An oft-recurring phrase in Greenham's *Workes* is: "the obedience of true knowledge."[43]

In part through this existential approach to knowledge, Greenham

---

[40] "Of Zeale," ibid., 255-259; cf., 829-31.
[41] "Meditations on Proverbs 14," ibid., 624; and REM 524, fols. 35r and 63v. Cf., John Calvin, *Institutes*, III, vi, 4.
[42] "Meditations on the 119 Psalm," ibid., 518.
[43] Ibid., 465, 473-74.

avoided the protestant scholasticism that developed in the second half of the sixteenth century, characterized by emphasis on deductive reasoning based on Aristotelian metaphysics, reliance on reason in theological development, abstract and speculative thought about God, and logical progression of all theology from the eternal decrees of God.[44] By the end of the century, English theologians were drawing heavily on continental protestant scholastics such as Theodore Beza, Francis Junius, and Jerome Zanchius, but in the works of Greenham, none of the scholastic characteristics mentioned above is to be found. Greenham frequently employs Ramist logic, but this alone hardly qualifies as scholasticism, especially since Ramism was deliberately anti-Aristotelian.[45] His friend and younger contemporary, William Perkins, was influenced by Beza and Zanchius, but even Perkins defined theology as "the science of living blessedly forever," hardly a scholastic definition.[46] Greenham nowhere defines "theology," but his entire approach would fit nicely within Perkins's definition. Greenham emphasized that unapplied doctrine is a waste of time, and states that all the applications of doctrine are covered in the following five points: "1. To teach and establish true opinions. 2. Or to confute false opinions. 3. Or to correct evil manners. 4. Or to frame good manners. 5. Or to comfort withal."[47]

In his reflections on truth, Greenham emphasizes orthopraxis at least as much as orthodoxy. He speaks of "the truth of our actions in stedfastnesse of life," and laments the inconsistency of word and deed in Christian life. What we "protest in word, we spoyle in our workes." The "Amen in our mouthes is drowned by the blood of our actions crying so loude before the Lord." When this occurs, "there is no truth in our lives." Those who claim to have the "truth of religion," but do not reflect that truth in both word and deed "cannot be said to have the truth" after all. Some talk piously about religion "a whole dinner

---

[44] Dewey Wallace, *Puritans and Predestination*, 57. Cf., Brian G. Armstrong, *Calvinism and the Amyraut Heresy* (Madison: University of Wisconsin Press, 1969) 31-8, 127-40, and Gordon S. Wakefield, *Puritan Devotion* (London: Epworth Press, 1957) 111-29.

[45] John P. Donnelly, *Calvinism and Scholasticism in Vermigli's Doctrine of Man and Grace* (Leiden: E. J. Brill, 1976) 193.

[46] *A Golden Chaine*, fol. A. 1. Cf., Richard A. Muller, "Perkins' A Golden Chaine: Predestinarian System or Schematized Ordo Salutis?" *The Sixteenth Century Journal,* IX, 1 (1978) 69-81.

[47] "Of Prophecie and Preaching," *Workes,* 772.

time, or halfe a day," but their lives "falsifie whatever they have said."

Although he rarely alludes to Christ as the Word of God, in his comments on truth Greenham draws on John 14:6. Christ is "the trueth it selfe," he concludes. What is crucial for Christian faith and life, therefore, is that thoughts, hearts, words, and actions conform to Christ the truth. From him comes "sinceritie of heart, simplicitie of speech, and constancie of life." When these are not in conformity with the supreme standard, then "hearts are false, and they being false, our tongues are out of rule, and our outward life can never be true."[48] For Greenham, knowing the truth is more than an intellectual enterprize. He expresses the ultimate goal of the Christian faith in terms of *being* true to Christ the Truth.

Because of the misgivings Greenham harbors about human reason under the conditions of the fall, he equivocates about the place of reason and the importance of the life of the mind. On the one hand, he voices suspicion of learning. It is the work of fallen humankind, and Jesus himself promised to destroy the wisdom of the wise. The apostle Paul also called human learning and wisdom into question in his first epistle to the Corinthians. Greenham writes, "The crosse of Christ is the marke we shoote at, without the which all authoritie, learning and knowledge is accursed of God."[49] Supernatural things transcend rational knowledge. In a discussion of angels Greenham writes, "we are rather to pray for the experience of their ministerie unto us, than either to describe, or prescribe it."[50]

On the other hand, he often appeals to human reason, especially in his polemic against the Family of Love, which was regarded as dangerously mystical in its view of the relationship between humanity and God. Mysticism was regarded as a threat by the reformers because it was likely to lead to social disorder. Again, it is primarily the Word of God that becomes the antidote to mysticism. The Holy Spirit does not speak to the believer apart from that Word. In one of his aphorisms Greenham writes, "Where the Scripture hath not a mouth, we ought not to have eares."[51] Greenham was very suspicious of those who claimed to have received special revelation by means of visions. Believers should be "mooved" by the Word, not by visions. Granted,

---

[48] "Of Truth and errors, sincerity and contempt of the word," ibid., 817-21.
[49] "On the first effect of Christs crosse," ibid., 367.
[50] "The first portion of grave Counsels," ibid., 3.
[51] "Another or second portion...of grave Counsels," ibid., 46.

visions were once "ordinary and Preaching extraordinary," but in the sixteenth century "preaching is ordinary and visions extraordinary." Reading and hearing the Word demand single-minded effort. Greenham lists eight requirements for the appropriation of Scripture: diligence, wisdom, preparation, meditation, conference, faith, practice, and prayer. "The three first goe before reading and preaching. The foure next come after them. The last must goe before, and with them, and come after them."[52]

The Word comes in intelligible, inscripturated form, and faithful preaching of it requires study and intellectual insight. Greenham, therefore, applauds institutions of learning for their contributions to the advancement of the faith. He is aware of the crucial role played by the universities in the English Reformation and refers to ancient Samuel as the "first builder of Colledges" in an attempt to establish biblical authority for the existence of schools. The universities, he writes, are "the Lebanon of the Lorde, from which timber must be fetched to build the Temple," i.e., the protestant church in England. Never reticent about multiplying metaphors, Greenham adds that the schools are "conduits, to derive water into the whole land," and "polished Saphires to garnish the house of the Lord."[53]

In academic preparation for the ministry, Greenham sets the study of "divinitie" above philosophy, another signal of his suspicion of medieval developments within the schools. "Concerning our studie," he writes, "it may be that a speciall working of God is in us, that Philosophie is made unto us so unsavorie, and Divinitie so sweet." In Christian learning, "generall precepts, which may make for the truth" are to be gathered, but the "foolish quiddities" of philosophy should be avoided.[54] "Wee must learn a Logick of the holy Ghost," he says in the context of a warning against following the example of the learned ungodly. In fact, to go "against the holy Ghost doe even destroy Logike," for fallen human beings are liars while God is perfect truth itself.

Greenham recognized that the Word of God has come down through the centuries by means of a process of transmission and translation. The biblical quotations from Greenham's *Workes* appear

---

[52] "A direction for the reading of the Scriptures," ibid., 173.
[53] "Of Knowledge and Ignorance," ibid, 734.
[54] "A third portion likewise of an hundred grave counsels," ibid., 68.

to be from the Geneva Bible although they are not always reproduced word for word, especially when the text or passage is used in the body of a sermon or treatise. On these occasions he is either quoting from memory, or the scribe or editor did not record the quotation accurately. Citations from the Old Testament are at least as numerous as those from the New. He shows some preference for the historical books over the prophets of the Old Testament, although Isaiah and Jeremiah are the individual books quoted most frequently. In the collection of seventeen sermons, ten are based on New Testament passages and seven on the Old. Psalms and Proverbs are favorite books of Greenham judging from their prominence in his *Workes*. The single largest treatise is his "Meditations on the 119th Psalm" in which he devotes 228 pages to brief homilies on most of the 176 verses in the Psalm. Four of the seventeen collected sermons are on texts from Proverbs.

## V

Greenham's hermeneutical method is inconsistent. At times, an embryonic historical critical approach surfaces, in which Greenham recognizes that the reader of Scripture must "marke the scope and drift of the writer ..., compare the things that goe before, with the things that follow after ..., conferre one place with another, the olde Testament with the new, the allegorie with the plaine speeches." When this is done perfect harmony will be found in the Scriptures "and therefore we have the trueth in these last dayes."[55] At other times Greenham simply adopts a "mirror" approach to biblical history.[56] Frequently in his treatises and sermons, the distance between the world of the Bible and sixteenth century England collapses, time is levelled, and the trials and tribulations of the Church of England become one with those depicted in the Old Testament. England becomes the mirror image of ancient Israel. The biblical drama of covenant, exodus, captivity, and return is being played out yet again in sixteenth century England, and heros of faith like Abraham and Moses, Joshua and Samuel, David and Elijah

---

[55] "A treatise of sending the Holy Ghost," ibid., 219.
[56] Cf., Nancy L. Beaty, *The Craft of Dying: A Study in the Literary Tradition of the Ars Moriendi in England* (New Haven and London: Yale University Press, 1970) 121.

become models for the reformation church without reference to historical conditions or distinctions.

The principal hermeneutical key Greenham uses to unlock the Scriptures, however, is the dialectic of law and gospel.[57] Later in English Puritanism the doctrine of the covenant would replace law and gospel as the governing theme of the Bible, but for Greenham, the law/gospel doctrine is decidedly more prominent than the covenant.[58] References to it abound throughout his writings, but it is explained and elaborated most fully in his catechism.

Greenham's "A Short Forme of Catechising" is especially important among his writings because it is the most systematic statement of his theology and provides the best insights regarding the conceptual framework of his thought. As the gerund in the title indicates, his catechism was not an exercise in abstract theology, but was intended for regular use, especially for the instruction of the youth whom Greenham apparently catechised each Thursday and again on Sunday afternoon. The Book of Common Prayer encouraged instruction in the creed, decalogue, and Lord's Prayer and included a short catechism as well. Alexander Nowell's catechism was another early classic and received official status in the Church of England, but it was very long—160 pages in the 1572 Latin edition—and not very practical for ordinary parish purposes.[59] This is probably one reason why so many practicing puritan pastors, Greenham among them, produced their own much shorter versions. Of the writing of catechisms there was virtually no end in the latter half of the sixteenth century. Henry S. Bennett confidently estimates that "at least a hundred catechisms" appeared during Elizabeth's reign.[60] They

---

[57] What follows on this topic is a revised version of my article, "Lutheran Law and Gospel in the Early Puritan Theology of Richard Greenham," *Lutheran Quarterly*, Vol. VIII, No. 3, ( Autumn, 1994): 287-98.

[58] Thomas Cartwright in his catechism first distinguishes law and gospel, and then equates them respectively with the covenant of works and the covenant of grace, Albert Peel and Leland Carlson, *Cartwrightiana* (London: Allen and Unwin, 1951) 159.

[59] Nowell's *Catechism* (Cambridge: Parker Society, 1853) includes both the original Latin version and the English translation.

[60] *English Books and Readers 1558-1603* (Cambridge, 1965) 147. Andrew Maunsell lists some eighty-eight items under "Catechismes" in the 1595 edition of his catalogue. Some of these are duplications and others of questionable status as true catechisms, but at least sixty of them are clearly unofficial catechisms produced between 1560 and 1595, *The First Part of the Catalogue of English printed Bookes* (London, 1595). For a typology of Elizabethan catechisms, see Peter F.

demonstrate the eagerness of the puritans to instruct the people in Reformation doctrine, and their role in shaping English protestant religious consciousness is not to be underestimated. They were intended for use in the home as well as in the church, thereby playing a very important part in the protestant domestication of religion in which the family was regarded as a little church.[61]

The opening question and answer of Greenham's catechism, so important for setting the stage for the rest of the exposition, are as follows:

> *Whereas all men desire to bee blessed, and the most men are deceived in seeking blessedness, tell mee which is the true way thereunto?* To know God to bee my Father in Jesus Christ, by the revelation of the spirit according to his word, & therfore to serve him according to his will, and to set forth his glorie; believing that I shall want nothing that is good for mee in this life, and that I shall enjoy everlasting blessednes in the world to come.[62]

This is followed by the epistemological question: "*How know you this?*" The answer opens the door to the rest of the catechism: "By the working of the holie Ghost, and by the meanes of Gods word." The reference to God's Word is followed by a page of questions and answers on the complete sufficiency of the Scriptures, their fundamental purpose ("That wee might have pure rules of his worship, and sure grounds of our salvation"), the inability of sinful human beings to produce such information, the importance of reading the Scriptures both privately and publicly, and the need for preaching. ("*Why must preaching be joyned with reading?* Because it is the most principall and proper meanes to beget Faith in us.") Then follows the question with the law and gospel response: "*Which be the*

---

Jensen, *The Life of Faith in the Teaching of Elizabethan Protestants* (Ph. D diss. Oxford University, 1979) Ch. 5.

[61] Lawrence Stone, *The Family, Sex and Marriage in England 1500-1800* (1977) 140-2. One of the first and most popular catechisms was written by John More, but usually attributed to Edward Dering: *A briefe and necessary Catechism or Instruction*, which appeared in 1572 and went through at least eighteen subsequent editions. The full title suggests strongly the household use of catechisms in Elizabethan England.

[62] "A Short Forme of Catechising," *Workes*, 71.

*principall parts of Gods word?*" Greenham's answer: "The Law and the Gospell."[63] Obviously, in Greenham's view, law and gospel constitute the whole of the Scriptures.

He defines the law and the gospel as follows: The law "is that part of the Word that commaundeth all good, and forbiddeth all evill," while the gospel "is that part of the word which containeth the free promises of God made unto us in Jesus Christ, without any respect of our deservings." After presenting these definitions, Greenham again raises the question of Scripture's purpose, that is, what must be learned from the "whole word of God." Its purpose is two-fold, he says. "First, to make a right and sound entrance to our salvation," and second, "how to encrease, and continue in the same unto the ende." With regard to the first of these, Greenham enumerates the three things that are "required for our right and sound entrance to our salvation" in language reminiscent of the three parts of the Heidelberg Catechism.

1. First, to know and to be perswaded of the greatnes of our sinnes, and the miserie due to the same.
2. Secondly, to know and be perswaded, how we may be delivered from them.
3. Thirdly, to know and bee perswaded what thankes wee owe to God for our deliverance.[64]

The law, according to Greenham, functions almost exclusively with respect to the first of these, that is, as a teacher of sin. Sin is revealed by the Holy Spirit "leading us into the true understanding of the Law, and a due examination of ourselves thereby." Then follow eight pages of detailed analysis of the law in the form of the ten commandments.[65] Here Greenham's catechism differs markedly from the "Heidelberger," where the ten commandments are considered much later in connection with the third item about thanks to God for deliverance. For Greenham, the ten commandments do not serve as the rule of gratitude, but as a menacing whip driving people to Christ. The law demands perfect obedience, and since human beings are

---

[63] Ibid., 72.
[64] Ibid. Cf., *Heidelberg Catechism*, LD 1, Q&A 2.
[65] "A Short Forme of Catechising," *Workes*, 73-80.

fallen and cannot obey the law "neither in all nor in any one point," they stand condemned. Lawbreakers are subject to "the curse of God, and death, with manifold miseries both of body or soule" in this life, and will receive "everlasting death and damnation both of bodie and soule in the world to come." Greenham sums up the use of the law in these words: "The use is, to bring us to a sound perswasion and feeling of our sinnes, because they have deserved so grievous punishment, as either the death of the sonne of God, or hell fire." The truth that comes through the law is realized first in God's children, "because it bringeth them to be truely humbled in themselves for their sinnes, and then sendeth them to Christ, in whome it is fully fulfilled," and second in "The wicked; because it declareth to them their just confusion, when to the ende they either presume or despaire." In either case, the function of the law is to condemn all who "commit sinne and lye in it." In Greenham's catechism, there is no "third use" of the law as the means of Christian gratitude.

The gospel, on the other hand, "worketh in us a true and lively faith in Jesus Christ, whereby wee lay holde of the free remission of our sinnes in him, and the true repentance of them." It proclaims a "Mediatour and Deliverer" who is "very man" and "true God" and who calls people to faith. The author of this faith is the Holy Spirit, who uses the means of the gospel to bring faith into being. This gospel is "declared unto us in the holy Scriptures, but the Church of God hath gathered out of them a certaine summe thereof."[66] Greenham is here referring to the Apostles' Creed to which he subsequently devotes six pages of commentary. Believing these articles of faith "all doe come to this ende, that being justified by faith, I am righteous in Christ before God."[67]

Greenham then discusses the "four fruits" of faith, one of which includes another reference to the law. "I get strength to fight against my outward sinnes, to subdue my inward corruption, to doe outward good workes, and to delight in the law of God in the inward man." Here he speaks more positively than earlier about "delight in the law" in the context of faith in the gospel. This, however, is law in a different form. It is the law "in the inward man," that is, engraved

---

[66] Ibid., 81.
[67] Ibid., 86.

upon the heart, rather than the external law expounded earlier. Furthermore, as Greenham proceeds to elaborate on the meaning and necessity of good works, the written law hardly functions at all. Good works proceed from repentance which is "a turning of ourselves to God, whereby wee crucifie and kill the corruption of our nature, and reforme ourselves in the inward man, according to Gods will." To crucify the corruption of our nature is essentially to have sorrow for sin, to hate it, and to flee from it. Once again it is emphasized that this response to sin is prompted by "the threatenings of the Law, and the feare of Gods judgements," but the actual reformation of self can be brought about "onely by the promises of the Gospel, whereby we feele the fruit of the rising again in Christ." In other words, even in the context of the Christian life, the law and the gospel continue to function in diametrically opposite ways, the law still threatening punishment, and the gospel bringing about the fruit of good works. Greenham states that when we are raised up into a new life, we have a "law written in our hearts," but he does not at this point and in this context speak of the law written in the Old Testament. He does say, however, as he proceeds to define the "properties" of good works, that "they be such as God hath commanded in his Law." And yet, within a few lines he again declares that it is the function of the law to bring the sinner to "the knowledge of our sinnes, and feeling of our miseries," and of the gospel to "worke and increase Faith in us."[68]

This sharp contrast between law and gospel is conveniently summed up by Greenham in his catechism when he distinguishes between penitence and repentance. "Penitence is a sorrow for sinne, wrought by the Law: Repentance is recovering our selves from sinne, wrought by the Gospell." He goes on to ask, "*Is there such difference betweene the Law and the Gospel?*"

Yea: for the Law differeth from the Gospell in foure things.
1. First the Law revealeth sinne, rebuketh us for it, and leaveth us in it: but the Gospell doth reveale unto us Remission of sinnes, bringeth us to CHRIST, and freeth us from the punishment belonging unto sinne.
2. The Law commandeth to do good, and giveth no strength: but the Gospell inableth us to do good, the holy Ghost

---

[68] Ibid., 86-88.

writing the law in our hearts, & assuring us of the promise.

3. The Law is the ministerie of wrath, and condemnation and death; but the Gospell is the ministerie of grace, justification, and life.

4. In many points the Law may be conceived by reason; but the Gospell in all points is farre above the reach of mans reason.

Law and gospel only agree in this, he writes, "that they bee both of God, and declare one kinde of righteousnesse, though they differ in offering it unto us."[69]

The law/gospel motif appears and reappears again and again throughout Greenham's *Workes*. "The law indeede reveales sinne," he writes, but "the Gospell cures sinne, the law woundeth...the Gospell healeth...." And again, "The exhortations of the law kill, the exhortations of the Gospell quicken."[70] He criticises the "mixture of the Lawe and the Gospell,"[71] contrasts the "shadow" of the law" with the "bright sun of the Gospell," and asserts that the commandments "cannot comfort us" for they are "a killing letter." The gospel, on the other hand, "bringeth peace and comfort."[72] Hence the "ministerie of the Gospell is better than the ministerie of the law."[73] In his tabletalk he even relates the story of a woman who dies, apparently of shock or extreme dismay, after hearing the law proclaimed.[74]

He uses law and gospel as typological categories for his preaching, and expresses concern about the proper balance of the two.[75] He concludes that both must be proclaimed, for in isolation from the law, the gospel is not the gospel. He writes, "it is very requisite that we first have the law preached unto us, that we may have a lively feeling of our sinnes," for "we cannot be moved lively with the promises of Christ, except we first by the law...see the full measure of punishment that our sins have deserved."[76] Yet preachers should "not so presse the Law, that we suppresse the Gospell in mens

---

[69] Ibid., 88.
[70] "Of Christian Warfare," *Workes*, 309.
[71] "Of the latter or second effect of Christ his crosse," ibid., 374.
[72] "Meditations on the 119 Psalm," ibid., 481-86.
[73] "The summe of the Epistle to the Hebrewes," ibid., 627.
[74] REM 524, fol. 61v.
[75] Ibid., fol. 7v.
[76] "Of flying ill company, Idolatry, and Sweareing," *Workes*, 334.

consciences."[77] The needs and circumstances of the parishioners will help determine where the preacher's emphasis should lie. If they are "alreadie humbled," they "must have the promises." If they are mired in sinful ignorance or have "fallen by securitie," then "the Law rather than the Gospell is to be urged."[78] At another point he speaks of law and gospel as the two hands of God. "God hath two hands: in the one he holdeth a hammer to breake the proud in pieces, and to bray them into powder; in the other hand he hath a horne, to powre Gods blessings upon the humble."[79]

Greenham was not the only early English reformer to use the law/gospel dialectic. William Tyndale, who studied in Wittenberg, emphasized it strongly as did John Frith. It appears in Nowell's catechism, as well as in the important early catechisms of Thomas Becon and John Ponet. It can be found in virtually all of the early, unofficial Elizabethan catechisms produced by puritan pastors. In all of these, the law is expounded first, before the exposition of the gospel in the Apostles' Creed, quite unlike Calvin's Genevan Catechism and the Reformed Heidelberger, where the order is first Creed, then decalogue. The English reformers typically used the law in its decalogue form as a teacher of sin, rather than as a gracious guide to the Christian life. But in none of these contemporary catechisms is the law/gospel dialectic used with such prominence and force as it is in the writings of Greenham. He emphasizes it to the extent that it becomes a defining feature of his thought.

It apparently never occurred to him that this strong emphasis on the distinction between law and gospel might, logically or theologically, militate against the development of his sanctification theology. Indeed, for Greenham and other early English reformers, the one did not work against the other. However much these reformers used the law/gospel distinction, they also from the beginning retained a strong ethical dimension in their theology. This is true also of Greenham. As we shall see in the next chapter, Greenham's emphasis on the sanctified Christian life is another of the salient features of his thought. He managed to combine a Lutheran emphasis on law and gospel with a Reformed emphasis on the

---

[77] "Of Prophecie and Preaching," ibid., 772. Cf., REM 524, fol. 60r.
[78] "A third portion likewise of an hundred grave counsels," *Workes,* 59.
[79]    "Another or second portion of an hundred and one and fifty grave Counsels," ibid., 50.

sanctified life. Perhaps this combination was a result, in part, of his two-fold polemic against Rome and the Family of Love. He sought to avoid, on the one hand, the legalism of Rome, and on the other, the suspected antinomianism of the familists.

The two most fundamental themes in Greenham's thought are God and the Word of God. Other themes may be even more obvious, such as his emphasis on a godly life, but none is more basic. In his treatment of these doctrines his theology is Reformation theology, combining Luther's law/gospel dialectic with Calvin's heavy concern for ethical obligation, and reflecting their mutual emphasis on the sovereignty, power, and love of God, their view of Scripture and the knowledge of God, and their rejection of abstract, speculative scholasticism. Greenham's doctrines of God and the Word of God are reminders that what has come to be called "Puritanism" in sixteenth century England was theologically simply "protestant" or "reformational" or "evangelical," sharing broadly with all of English Protestantism the riches of the continental Reformation as a whole.

# 5

# SANCTIFICATION BY FAITH

## I

Throughout the history of the church, concern for the moral life has been a *sine qua non* of the Christian faith. Christians are expected to live godly lives, and "godliness" is a word that traces back to the Bible itself. The Christian Scriptures can be read as a lengthy account, or many accounts, of the moral failures and successes of the people of God. Magnificent examples of piety also abound in the early and medieval as well as modern periods of church history, and, since followers of Christ are not immune to the fall, the slippery slide into moral carelessness has always been regarded as a constant threat.

In the context of the sixteenth century Reformation, charges and counter-charges of licentious behaviour were common. The Reformers believed "papists" were immoral, but were themselves initially attacked as antinomian by their Roman foes. The doctrines of sin and grace as Luther formulated and emphasized them, and especially his doctrine of justification by faith alone, were regarded as inimical to the pursuit of godliness. Calvin, sensitive to that charge, carved out a larger place in his theology for Christian piety and the sanctified life. Total depravity, unconditional election, and irresistible grace do not seem to be doctrines that naturally lead to moral pursuit, but the Swiss and Rhineland reformers managed to combine these doctrines with a passionate concern for good works. There was in the Reformation century itself, a "pietist movement" that antedates the better known one of the eighteenth century.[1]

English reformers contributed substantially to that movement.

---

[1] Cf., Charles E. Hambrick-Stowe, *The Practice of Piety* (Chapel Hill: University of North Carolina Press, 1982); Fred E. Stoeffler, *The Rise of Evangelical Pietism* (Leiden: E. J. Brill, 1965).

The emphasis on godly living was omnipresent in English Protestantism from the very beginning. It was not deliberately manufactured later to counter any perceived weaknesses in Calvinian theology.[2] Some of the earliest English reformers–Tyndale, Cranmer, Hooper, Latimer, Rogers, Ridley, Bradford (most of them Cambridge men)–were all noted for their emphasis on a piety marked by a strong sense of God's majesty and sovereignty, a deep conviction about human rebellion and sin, an earnest concern to bring quiet assurance to consciences deeply troubled about sin, and a heavy emphasis on the sanctified life. They would likely have promoted such piety even without a boost from the Rhineland in the person of Martin Bucer, who taught at Cambridge from April, 1549 until his death in February, 1551, but he lent his great influence to the advancement of practical piety as well.

These English reformers knew that Christian piety does not come automatically. It has to be deliberately cultivated in a disciplined manner through an ardent devotional life that brings about a greater sense of union with God. Both private and public exercises of worship were aimed at bringing about greater godliness, not out of a self-indulgent concern for personal salvation, but for the glory of God.[3] This emphasis was not peculiarly "puritan," at least not in its origins, but piety comes in various shapes and sizes and with diverse emphases and expressions. English Puritanism brought the impulse for piety to an advanced level of development and raised it to new heights of literary expression.

## II

Richard Greenham is a superb example of the emphasis on piety in the English Reformed tradition. Godliness is at the core of his Christianity. He emphasized sanctification by faith even more than justification by faith. He writes, "All that is to be desired of a man is this, that he be vertuous, godly, and truly religious."[4] His passion for godliness flows from his belief in God and experience of God's forgiving grace. Hand in hand with his overpowering sense of the

---

[2] Contra Perry Miller, see below, p. 126.
[3] Contra Stoeffler, *The Rise of Evangelical Pietism*, 55.
[4] "Of a Good name," *Workes*, 259.

reality of God and his presence everywhere, was an equally
overwhelming emphasis on the need to be like God. God and the
pursuit of godliness are correlatives in his thought. God is not
glorified without godliness, and his people are not godly without God.
Consequently, doctrinal instruction is regularly accompanied by
practical admonition in Greenham's writings. Doctrine is affective;
head and heart are not divided; theology and piety are intertwined.
Perkins's definition of theology as the "science of living blessedly
forever" accurately describes Greenham's approach. The science of
living blessedly is theology because it is absolutely God-centered.
Living blessedly is living like God. It is God-like-ness. Greenham
asserts that God gives "a taste of heaven and of his goodnesse" to
those who follow him.[5] True godliness is actually the goodness of God
reflected in his children. The indwelling God is the source of
Christian faith and life. Consequently, good works are "testifications"
of God's indwelling presence.[6] The    purpose    of    godliness    is
"edification," a word that appears frequently in Greenham's *Workes*.
There is "no similitude in the Scriptures used more often than the
similitude of building, which often is Englished by this word
*Edifying*," he writes.[7] The entire aim and purpose of the Christian life,
therefore, can be summed up in this single word. Here Greenham
echos the central theme of the classic letter from the Marian exiles to
Queen Elizabeth in the preface to the Genevan Bible.[8] The English
exiles, like Israel of old, had returned for the purpose of rebuilding
the temple. Godly preachers like Richard Greenham were busily
engaged in this reconstruction, which begins with personal
edification. In New Testament terms it is the "building up of our
selves" to become "temples of the holy Ghost."[9] This personal
sanctification is such an inescapable and indispensable part of biblical
faith because "we are the temples wherein the Lord will vouchsafe to
dwell."[10] As God is clean, pure, and holy, so must be those who are
the habitations of God in the Spirit. Greenham's piety was far more

---

[5] "Of Godlinesse," ibid., 689.
[6] "A short direction for one troubled in minde," ibid., 880.
[7] "Of the heavenly purchase," ibid., 297. Cf., "Meditations on the 119 Psalm,"
ibid., 375. On the prominence of edification in puritan thought, see Coolidge, *The
Pauline Renaissance*, 27 ff., and 47 ff.
[8] See above, pp. 16-17.
[9] "Of the heavenly purchase," *Workes*, 297-8.
[10] "Of Regeneration and Sanctification," ibid., 804.

than an egocentric warm glow of personal experience. He explicitly warns against reliance on subjective feelings: "Oh brother bee of good comfort, we hold Christ by faith, and not by feeling."[11] He emphasizes heavily a believer's experience of God, but the accent is finally on God more than on personal experience. Again, the goal is always *God*-liness. This theocentrism also keeps Greenham's piety from degenerating into sheer moralism. His emphasis is not on good works as ends in themselves or as the result of purely human endeavor, but on good works as the result of the living God indwelling the faithful. It is a God-centered, God-initiated sanctification: "God sanctifieth us, when he maketh us partakers of his holinesse...."[12]

With great consistency, Greenham's admonitions to specific good works are theologically based. The virtue of patience, for example, can only be cultivated by centering in God. Indeed, his cooperative Puritanism is related to his emphasis on waiting for God to provide for the reformation of the church: "how much more will the Lorde governe and preserve it now under the kingdome of Jesus Christ, if peaceably we waite, untill the arme of the Lord be revealed unto us."[13] The antidote to a complaining spirit is to be found through "faith in Gods mercies, and in the benefits which Christ hath by his death purchased unto us." Those who are "thoroughly grounded" in the providence of God, "will withstand all occasions of murmering."[14] Other Christian virtues are similarly rooted in God. The gift of humility comes with a recognition of God's grace and a realization that all things are freely given by him.[15] The spirit of mercy to others is joined to God's mercy, for "if there be no mercie in us, with what face can we come to the Lord, and say, give us a kingdome, let they kingdome come, if we denie our brethren the gift of so much as of a peece of bread?"[16] Neighbor love is grounded in God's love through Christ. Even a proper diet is theologically controlled, for the godly must so eat that they may be "made thereby more fit either to speake or heare the praises of God with more cheerfulnes and reverence."[17]

---

[11] "The first portion of grave Counsels," ibid., 12.
[12] "Meditations on the 119 Psalm," ibid., 592.
[13] "A third portion...of an hundred grave counsels," ibid., 61.
[14] "Of murmering," ibid., 251-2; cf., 758.
[15] "Of Humilitie," ibid., 268-70; cf., 712.
[16] "Of Gods wrath, Justice, and Mercie," ibid., 699, 700.
[17] "The first portion of grave Counsels," ibid., 10.

For Greenham, good works are always prompted, enabled, and measured by God.

Justification and sanctification, faith and works, are, therefore, bound together through common authorship. Justification is not represented as God's work, and sanctification as a human endeavor; both are the work of God in which believers participate by faith. Greenham explains the intricate connections between justification and sanctification as follows:

> For as God sanctifieth us, when he maketh us partakers of his holinesse, and we sanctifie him when we shew him to be holie: so God is said to justifie us, when we are approved just before God; and we justifie God, when we testifie that he is just. In like maner faith justifieth us, in that it acquiteth us before God from our sinnes for Christ his sake, in whom we beleeve: workes justifie us, in as much as they witnesse to us, and to men, that we are justified by faith in God, whereof our sanctification is a pledge.[18]

In other words, it is by good workes, i.e., sanctification, that believers declare and make known their justification. In this sense, the New Testament book of James speaks of "justification by works." Good works are "apples of the tree of faith."[19] Greenham does not explicitly refer to a "practical syllogism," but he does mention good works as a test of salvation: "yet our workes doe witness for us, that we are the children of God, because we are guided by the spirit...."[20] Legalism and works righteousness are avoided by his deemphasis on the role of the law in good works[21] and by his repeated emphasis on good works as the result of the "spirit of God" operative in the Christian's life. Good works are the "effects of grace," and "the fruits of God his spirit." Good works are "no cause why we are good," but "we are accounted good" by faith in Christ, and "therefore we are good." We are not "good in respect of our workes, but our workes are

---

[18] "Meditations on the 119 Psalm," ibid., 592. Cf., William P. Stephens, *The Holy Spirit in the Theology of Martin Bucer* (Cambridge: University Press, 1970) 53.

[19] "Of good workes, and our obedience to Gods word," *Workes*, 827.

[20] "A short direction for one troubled in minde," ibid., 874.

[21] See the discussion of law and gospel above, pp. 93ff.,

good in respect of us justified before by faith."[22]

"Whosoever is joyned to Christ for his justification, must also be joyned to him for his sanctification," Greenham writes.[23] Being "joyned to Christ" is the key. This is not accomplished through mere human striving. In Greenham's trinitarian approach to sanctification, God is the author, Christ is the model, and the Holy Spirit is the energizer. It is by the Holy Spirit that believers are joined to Christ.

## III

Greenham's emphasis on the Holy Spirit in his doctrine of God has already been considered.[24] In trinitarian economics generally, it is God the Holy Spirit who is most frequently associated with the work of sanctification. It is not surprising, therefore, to find references to the Holy Spirit liberally sprinkled among Greenham's sermons, treatises, and meditations on the godly life. Human beings are to be built up into temples of the Holy Spirit. It is the Holy Spirit who teaches the way of godliness, brings the godly into union with Christ, and empowers believers for righteous living. The Holy Spirit also makes the "means of godliness" effectual in believers' lives, for "without this spirit of God, no holy exercise can have his full effect," neither Word, nor prayer, nor sacraments, which "seeme small and sillie things in our eyes" without the work of the Spirit. All of the orders and exercises God has provided as means of grace and faith "are unprofitable to man," unless the Spirit is "present to convey them into our hearts, there to seale up the fruit of them."[25] Greenham emphasizes heavily the teaching function of the Holy Spirit. He is the one who teaches believers all of those familiar aspects of the faith–gospel, law, sin, grace, and righteousness.[26]

The "first worke of the spirit" is to arouse the conviction of sin. He creates "a great and generall astonishment" at the enormity of human sinfulness. Human capacities frequently exalted are exposed as fallen and frail. The Spirit reveals, for example, that "reason is

---

[22] "Meditations on the 119 Psalm," ibid., 593.
[23] "Of Feare," ibid., 682. Cf., "A third portion...of an hundred grave counsels," ibid., 61.
[24] See above, pp. 83ff.
[25] "Of Quenching the Spirit," *Workes*, 241.
[26] "Meditations on the 119 Psalm," ibid., 429-31, 453, 462, 474-5, 601, 607.

unreasonable"; it is even "hurtfull unto us, a great enemie to faith, and a great patrone of infidelitie and unbeleefe." The Spirit "draweth us into the presence of God," where it becomes evident that human "strength is weaknes in respect of him."[27] This disclosure of sinfulness is only the initial and introductory work of the Spirit. On the positive side, the Holy Spirit applies the whole of salvation to believers' lives. He brings the peace and joy of justification and the forgiveness of sin. But above all, his is the work of sanctification. "If the blood of Christ hath washed us from the guiltines of sinne; then the holy Ghost hath purged us from the filthiness of sinne."[28] It is the Holy Spirit who creates "the life and nimblenes that is in us to do good." He enables the "performance of those things, which are pleasing unto God," so that the Christian believer finds herself not only reclaimed from evil, "but also applied and framed to that which is good." The Spirit enlightens the understanding, empowering it to penetrate the mysteries of godliness; he reforms judgment, enabling true discernment between false and true religion; and he directs attention and affection to the things that are above, to the heavenly world.[29] Greenham sums up the work of the Spirit in four categories. First, he "seazeth upon a man" and destroys "evil affections, noysome lusts, and other stubble"; secondly, he purges and purifies, "that we may be a cleane and holy vessell and temple for him to rest and dwell in"; thirdly, he is a "shining lampe" giving light upon the way of faith; and finally, he "doth set us on heat, & inflameth us with a zeale of gods glorie, with a care of our dutie, and with a love of all mankinde." Thus the Holy Spirit enables believers to "walke in that good way which leadeth unto life, and to doe all those good workes which may glorifie God, or be commodious unto men."[30]

In an unusual and somewhat surprising passage, Greenham argues that there are two sorts of workings of the Holy Spirit. There is an "inferiour working which may be lost; and a more effectuall working of the spirit which can never be taken away from them that have it." The "inferiour working" can be seen in Jesus's parable of the sower, for here he speaks of those who heard and seemed to accept the Word initially, but did not follow through with a godly life. Undoubtedly,

---

[27] "Of Quenching the Spirit," ibid., 242-3.
[28] "Another or second portion of...grave Counsels," ibid., 49. Cf., 803.
[29] "Of Quenching the Spirit," ibid., 243-4. Cf., 681.
[30] Ibid., 244.

says Greenham, the Spirit of God was at work in them for they received the Word, even gladly, and believed what they had received. Their faith, however, was temporary; after a short time it vanished and the Spirit departed from them, victims either of the "pleasures and profits of this life," or the "fierie heate of persecution." Also, in Hebrews 6, the author speaks of those who receive the Holy Spirit, are apparently enlightened and even taste "the power of the life to come," and yet fall away as a result of the quenching of that Spirit in them.[31]

The second, more effectual work of the Spirit can never be taken away. It involves not a superficial exposure to the Word, but a "deepe taste" of it by which redemption is effected. Greenham argues that these two workings of the Spirit–ineffectual and effectual–should not be surprising to his rural Dry Drayton auditors, for God works the same way in agriculture. Some kernels of corn are sown but never germinate, some trees are planted and never take root, others blossom but do not bring forth fruit. Since this occurs in nature, something similar can be expected in the realm of the Spirit.[32]

These different workings of the Holy Spirit lead Greenham to reflect on the distinctions between the godly and the wicked, between those in whom the Spirit "lasteth but for a time," and those with whom the Spirit abideth forever. One difference is found in the measure of enlightenment and insight into the Word. "Certaine it is, that both the godly and wicked are inlightened," he writes, but the knowledge and insight of the godly is "certaine and distinct," enabling them to apply both law and gospel–threatenings and promises–to their lives. The knowledge of the ungodly on the other hand, is "confused, generall, & uncertaine," so that they are unable to make use of the superficial knowledge they possess. There is also a difference in "affections." Certainly, "the wicked doe desire the helpe and the favour of God," but only because they seek relief from grief and pain. The godly delight in God even without the pleasures of this life, in the midst of grief, pain, and suffering. The ungodly may grieve when they sin, but only because they fear punishment. The godly grieve for sin because they know they have offended God. There is also a striking difference between those with the "inferiour working"

---

[31] Ibid., 245.
[32] Ibid.

of the Spirit and those with the effectual working with regard to their love for God. Both may speak of their love for God, but "one of sinceritie, the other for wages." King Saul loved God, but only because he had received a kingdom; Judas loved God, but only because he was chosen to be an Apostle and "carried the bagge." True children of God in whom the Spirit has worked effectually, love God in himself without regard for reward. They love him even when he afflicts them. Finally, those who have an inferiour working of the Spirit do not truly appreciate the gifts and graces of God in their lives, but rather "take all glorie to themselves." In those who have the effectual working, there is true thankfulness for all mercies received.[33]

This distinction between the "inferiour" and "effectual" working of the Holy Spirit may well have left his parishioners uncertain and uneasy. Significantly, Greenham later states the distinction in a different, and perhaps more appropriate, way. He distinguishes between the gift of the Holy Spirit himself, and the "graces" of the Spirit. One may be "deprived indeede for a time of the graces of the sanctifying spirit, but not of the Holy Ghost wherewith he was sanctified...."[34]

## IV

The triune God is the author of sanctification, but the actual process and deliberate cultivation of godliness are worked out in human lives. Consequently, Greenham's doctrine of sanctification presupposes certain anthropological views. Greenham brings the heart and conscience, for example, to center stage. Although he does not define precisely what he means by the "heart," he seems to conceive of it as the spiritual center of human existence and as the unique point of contact between the Holy Spirit and humanity. The human heart he says, "is Gods owne part" and must therefore be totally dedicated to the Lord and his service.[35] It is the source of spiritual nourishment "for the hart is a spring and hath spouts to send out as a conduit" through which all spiritual needs are supplied.[36] The first man, Adam, was "corrupted in his heart" and ever since his fall "our

---

[33] Ibid., 246-7.
[34] "Rules concerning the power and priviledges of Gods word," ibid., 868.
[35] "The first portion of grave Counsels," ibid., 17.
[36] "Of the Exercises of Religion," ibid., 675.

heart is a wandering thing." Greenham quotes Jeremiah who urges, "wash thine heart,"[37] and discusses the meaning of "circumcized hearts." The foreskin is a biblical metaphor used as a reference for "whatsoever groweth within us, which is an impediment to us in doing good."[38] To circumcize the heart, then, is to remove all obstacles to godliness. Superficial treatments that fail to address the problem of spiritually diseased hearts are doomed to failure. "Applie the plaster to any place save to the heart, and it will doe no good," Greenham declares.[39]

He teaches that "whosoever would have sound happinesse, must have a sound heart," which has several special characteristics: universal obedience to the full scope of God's will; a continual increase in godliness; a constant and careful use of all the means to godliness; the performance of these means "as in Gods presence" without concern for human approval; and the patient acceptance of admonition and reproof for the purpose of greater godliness. It is not enough, he says, to go to sermon, sacrament, and prayer out of custom, for "God doth require more than this: hee calleth for the heart in all of these."[40]

As the spiritual center of human existence, the heart is also the locus of conscience, that mysterious receiver and transmitter of divine signals to human beings. References to conscience appear frequently in Greenham's *Workes*, but he theorizes about it only very briefly. He defines it as follows:

> Conscience is a sensible feeling of Gods judgements grounded upon the word, nourished by the consideration of the latter day, stirring up our hearts to the approoving of our doings both before God and men.[41]

Upon reading this definition one suspects that Greenham limits conscience to believers only. Such indeed is the case, for he goes on to say explicitly that conscience "is an effect of faith, faith therefore as the cause must go before; where no faith is, there is no knowledge;

---

[37] "Where is taught how wee must narrowly watch over our hearts," ibid., 704.
[38] Ibid., 706.
[39] "Of hypocrisie and hardnesse of hart," ibid., 719.
[40] "Meditations on the 119 Psalm," ibid., 387-9. Cf., 619 on the pure heart.
[41] "Of Conscience," ibid., 832.

where there is no knowledge, there is no conscience." Those without faith may refer to their conscience, but "they might better say, this is mine opinion, this is my fancie." Conscience plays a vital role in the godly, sanctified life, for "it is placed in the heart, to the stirring up of us, and summoning of us to approove those things which we know before God."[42] He says little more about the meaning of conscience except in isolated passages in which he gives counsel for afflicted ones. He emphasizes that since conscience is "a tender peece, we must beware how we offer any violence to it." It stands as a "thousand witnesses" against sin and proclaims and reinforces the conviction of death as the sure penalty for sin.[43] To be afflicted by a tormented conscience is a "weight most grievous, and burthen intolerable." Peace of conscience, on the other hand, is both a blessed gift and a virtue to be pursued. "Care of a good conscience, breedeth comfort in holinesse; and pleasure in holinesse, breedes assurance of blessednesse."[44]

Another anthropological insight that surfaces in Greenham's sanctification theology is the intimate relationship of body and soul. Given the strongly platonic motif in continental reformers' views of body and soul, Greenham's greater emphasis on their unity, and especially his affirmation of the body, are quite remarkable. The body, he says, is not the enemy of the soul, but is needed for such spiritual activities as repentance and sanctification. If anything, the soul is the enemy of the body, for sin issues from the soul, so that "there is never any corrupt action in the bodie, but there hath been first a corrupt motion and sinful affection in the soule." Greenham criticizes those who "doe much inveigh against the body, crying out, that it is the enemy of the soule," when they ought to be extolling the body as the "friend of the soule."[45] The body is a gift from the Lord; "the Lords loving hand is upon your body," so it is to be dedicated to his service.[46] It is essential for the worship of God, for by using ears, tongues, hands and knees, "God requireth the body to worship him as well as the soule."[47] Administration of the sacraments would be

---

[42] Ibid.
[43] "Of Conscience," ibid., 650.
[44] "A Sweet comfort for an afflicted Conscience," ibid., 98.
[45] "The first portion of grave Counsels," ibid., 26.
[46] "Another or second portion of...grave Counsels," ibid., 50.
[47] "Of Gods worship," ibid., 801.

inconceivable without bodies, and he adds provocatively that the fruit of the sacrament "must appeare as well in the bodie, as in the soule," that is, sacraments have consequences for human behaviour. He again unites body and soul when he asserts that "as God hath made both for his glory in this life, so hath he appointed to glorifie both in the life to come."

Demonstrating surprisingly progressive psychological insight, Greenham argues that since it is the soul that corrupts the body (and not vice versa), the treatment for bodily afflictions should begin with the soul.

> This generall doctrine then may be gathered, that what disease or affliction soever commeth to a mans body, for what cause soever, yea though it be for the triall of faith; yet the way to come out of it, is to looke to our soules, and to cleanse them: for if they be once purified, then the bodie will be easily cured.[48]

This is not a sixteenth century version of faith-healing, but an expression of Greenham's conviction that a godly life is apt to have positive benefits for physical welfare. Moderation "in those things which thine appetite liketh best" will be not only "good physicke" for the body, but also "a wholesome preservative" for the soul.[49]

Consistent with his affirmation of a close harmony between body and soul, Greenham emphasizes that the process of sanctification involves both. The understanding, memory and affection–all capacities of the soul in his view–must be renewed, but in sanctification God also communicates new holiness to the body in the receipt of "new eyes, new eares, new tongues, new hands, and new feete." He writes eloquently about sanctified seeing, hearing, speaking, doing, and walking, making sharp distinctions between "papism" and protestantism along the way. English eyes once "lusted after popish pomps" and were "ravished with delight in the creatures of God," but the Reformation has brought renewed vision of the beauty of the creator, and the eyes become "teachers of the soule thereby." Likewise the ears, once "carried away with the vaine

---

[48] "Meditations on the 119 Psalm," ibid., 440.
[49] "Of the Ministerie," ibid., 743. Cf., 34.

chaunting of Papists," have been fashioned anew and are attuned to "the word," to "gracious speeches," and to "chast communication." Tongues which once prayed "ignorantly, vainly, and superstitiously," are now enabled to speak the truth and pray sincerely to God. Hands lifted up in the past to false gods of Catholicism can now be stretched out to the true God, and used to show his love and power in "relieving the needie, in giving of alms, in helping the afflicted." And finally, the feet that once ran to serve the idols of "huntings, bearebaitings, and enterludes on the Sabbath day," and were so "swift and nimble in dauncing," have been turned to "runne to the Church of God, to the hearing of the word, to offer pure prayers, to receive the Sacraments." Those renewed feet must also "now carrie us to prisons, to sick persons, to the house of mourning," so that they may be used to the glory of God and the good of our neighbors.[50]

## V

The sanctification process involving the work of the Holy Spirit in the hearts, consciences, souls, and bodies of believers, begins with the personal conviction of sin. This is the initial task of the Holy Spirit as indicated above. Although godliness is grounded in God, for Greenham the first step toward godliness is the recognition of estrangement from God. Emphasis on sin is powerful in Greenham's *Workes*. It is not an end in itself, but leads to a deeper appreciation for God's grace. The utter devastation wrought by sin illumines the grace and mercy of God. "The way to see the length, depth, breadth and height of Gods mercies, is first with shame and sorrow to see the length, depth, breadth and height of our owne sinne."[51]

Since the fall, this world has been in rebellion against its creator. It is filled with spiritual powers hostile to God. Greenham distinguishes between "the world as it is by creation" ruled by God, and the world as it is now ruled by "the Divell" who is called "the prince of the world."[52] His extensive meditations on Psalm 119 also reflect a world created by God and originally governed by his laws, but now gone to "the divell," who is mentioned on nearly every page.

---

[50] "Of the latter or second effect of Christ his crosses," ibid., 372-3.
[51] "The first portion of grave Counsels," ibid., 25.
[52] "Of Christian warfare," ibid., 310.

Satan first appeared as a "sillie serpent," but now goes around as a "roring Lion."[53] The world, in fact, is still in a process of degeneration–or at least it was in the sixteenth century, for Greenham assumes the secularization theory. He says, "our times are worse, than the time wherein the Prophet lived, and wee are easier and readier to take harm by evill example than he was...."[54] He speaks vividly of the "rage of sinne in these dayes," and of how "Satan daily bewitcheth us in Pagainisme, Atheisme, Machevillisme," and "Anabaptisme." The devil is a "spirituall and more secret adversarie, felt before he be seene, at hand before we be aware of him," and yet, "lesse feared then before he was."[55] Greenham's universe was also inhabited by witches. He alludes to them infrequently, yet mentions these servants of Satan, who "carry out the will of the divell,"[56] often enough to indicate that he takes them seriously. The ultimate seduction takes place when witches lead the unsuspecting to believe that the Devil and his servants do not really exist. Greenham warns that "it is a policie of the divell to perswade us there is no divell, as it is the policie of wizards to perswade us that there are no witches."[57]

But for all his emphasis on the reality and power of the devil and his cohorts, at the end of the day, Greenham places his trust in a God who reigns supreme. The devil is to be feared, but not too much "seeing he hath but a derived power, and therefore a limited power," a power that Christ has overcome.[58] Neither should the threat of witches be overdrawn, for they "cannot hurt, further than the Lord wil...."[59] Through faith in God, believers will discover that although witches may "prevaile in pettie and little things, yet when they come to great points, they can doe nothing."[60] Greenham surprisingly discourages flight from the devil, but rather recommends an offensive strategy. He states that "Satan must not be fled from (for that will embolden him) but he must be resisted by the word, and by prayer, and by the power of Christ."[61] Genuine faith can easily overcome the

---

[53] Ibid., 313. Cf., "Of divers names applyed to the Divell in Scripture," ibid., 845.
[54] "Meditations on the 119 Psalm," ibid., 493.
[55] "The first portion of grave Counsels," ibid., 43.
[56] "Meditations on the 119 Psalm," ibid., 468.
[57] "Of Christian warfare," ibid., 313.
[58] "The first portion of grave Counsels," ibid., 43.
[59] "Of Witchcraft and unbeliefe," ibid., 822.
[60] "Of Christian warfare," ibid., 314.
[61] "A third portion...of an hundred grave counsels," ibid., 66.

power of Satan, for just "one sparke of pure zeal doth fire out the divell."[62]

A fallen world in the partially limited grip of the devil forms the backdrop to the greatest obstacle in the way to godliness: personal sin. Greenham does not take refuge in the excuse that "the devil made me do it." In his vision of godliness, the human sin for which humankind is finally and utterly responsible must be overcome. References to human sinfulness in Greenham's writings appear with relentless persistency, sometimes in long passages of inspired eloquence. In one particularly lengthy and graphic description, he outlines the many indications of the enormity of human wickedness.[63] In another passage, he speaks of a "chain of sinnes, for he that yeeldeth to one, draweth on another; grant a little one, and a great one will follow." His description of sinners often follows the order of the ten commandments, which function principally as the revelation of sin and the whip to drive sinners to Christ. He speaks, for example, of the sin evident in "profane persons, in abusers of the name of God, in breakers of the Sabbath, in disobedient persons, murderers, adulterers, theeves, and backbiters."[64] But at its worst and at its depth, sin is not overt and obvious, but internal and hidden. "Oh great corruption of our hearts! Oh bottomles pit of hypocrisie," he cries.[65] Frequently, he seeks to unmask this hypocrisy by exposing the pharisaical pretense of sinners, who are "painted sepulchres and dishes clean without, but foule within."[66] God will not be decieved. Neither will he overlook "small" sins, for before the Lord "no sinne will be counted little." The love of God is violated even by what we consider to be the least of sins.[67]

The presence of sin in a universe created by a God of infinite goodness is a mystery that Greenham probes very briefly in a passage with Augustinian overtones, where he argues that programmed goodness is not goodness at all.

Violent good things and constrained deserve no prayse, and

---

[62] Ibid., 55.
[63] "Of sinne, and how to abstaine from the least, and of iniquitie, and the punishments thereof," ibid., 788-94.
[64] "Meditations on the 119 Psalm," ibid., 536.
[65] Ibid., 543.
[66] Ibid., 542.
[67] "Meditations on Prov. 14," ibid., 626.

therefore the Lord suffered Adam to bee able to sinne, that
not sinning when he might have sinned, hee might truly be
rewarded; and not to have sinned when there was in him no
abilitie to sinne, was worth no commendation.[68]

He follows with an equally brief and somewhat cryptic theodicy.
God is not the author of sin, he argues, for although he is the "cause
of every action in man," it is "our owne corruption" for which we are
completely responsible that is "the cause of the sinne of the action."[69]
The serpent in the garden was "the first instrument" of sin. In its
devious approach and destructive results, sin retains serpentine
characteristics. "For first it windeth round about us, as though it
would embrace us, but in the end...with the tayle it doth sting us."[70]

His account of the immediate aftermath of the fall in Genesis
demonstrates not only Greenham's considerable rhetorical skill, but
also psychological insight into human behaviour. Conscience pricked,
Adam hides behind a scanty bit of foliage, but "not content with a few
leaves," he goes into a thicket of woods. God finds him, brings him
out "into the plaine," and asks him "substantiall questions."
Whereupon Adam changes strategy. Realizing he cannot hide himself
any longer, he nevertheless continues the attempt to hide his sin and
"shifteth it off to Eve." The Holy Spirit gives this account in Genesis,
says Greenham, to teach us that it is most difficult "nakedly to uncase
thy sinnes before God." Rather, when caught in the midst of sin, it is
human nature "either to denie it to be a sin," or to "denie our selves
to have sinned in that sinne," or to "quarrell and wrangle" about the
nature of sin.[71] Such masquerading is contrary to true godliness,
which is achieved only through full admission and confession of sin.
Paradoxically, to obtain righteousness the sinner must acknowledge
himself "voide of all righteousness, and full of unrighteousness."[72]
Greenham's unyielding emphasis on sin reaches its rhetorical heights
in the following turgid prose: "For the scum thereof is almost
continually boyling and walloping in us, foming out such filthy froth
and stinking savor" that "the body of sinne shall never be from us so

---

[68] "Of Seeking God," ibid., 851.
[69] Ibid.
[70] "A third portion...of an hundred grave counsels," ibid., 63.
[71] "The first portion of grave Counsels," ibid., 32.
[72] "The markes of a righteous man," ibid., 119.

long as we live." Since the original fall into sin, human history has become "a stie of sinne and sinkehole of iniquitie."[73]

## VI

Acknowledgement of sin is the first step to true godliness, but psychological complications could arise from such verbal battering about the filthy froth boiling and walloping within. The problem of "afflicted consciences" had to be addressed in the Christian journey of sanctification. Richard Greenham rose to the occasion. In the Cambridge area he became known as the chief physician specializing in afflicted consciences and wounded spirits. Henry Holland believed so at any rate, and he made sure that Greenham's skills in this area were adequately exhibited in his *Workes*.[74] The treatises, sermons, and wise counsels contain impressive insights into the human psyche and reveal keen pastoral sensitivity to mental anguish.

The sin emphasis, Greenham acknowledges, is the culprit, for afflicted consciences are "ever accompanied with the accusation of sinne." This results in inner pain and misery that makes physical ailments pale by comparison. A person may be "sickke, reproched, impoverished, imprisoned, and banished," but still have a clear conscience.

But when the spirit is wounded, there is still a guiltinesse of sinne, and when a mans spirit is troubled, he suspecteth all his waies, he feareth all his sinnes, he knowes not what sinne to begin with, it breedes such hurlyburlies in him, that when it is day he wisheth for night; when it is night he would have it day...his dreames are fearfull to him, his sleepe oft times forsaketh him: if he speaketh he is little eased: if he keepeth silence, he boyleth in disquietnesse of heart: the light doth not comfort him, the darknesse doth terrifie him.[75]

In his prescription for treating these agonies of the afflicted conscience, Greenham recommends a two-step, law/gospel remedy,

[73] "A second Treatise of the same argument," ibid., 113.
[74] See "Preface To The Reader."
[75] "A Sweet comfort for an afflicted Conscience," *Workes*, 97-8.

which he describes with the use of medical and surgical metaphors. Sin is the culprit, so it must be fully exposed by applying the law which is like "a burning iron" to "pearce our consciences." This will "cleanse the wound of the soule by sharpe threatnings, least that a skin pulled over the conscience for a while, we leave the rotten corruption uncured underneath."[76] But the law alone will lead to "a bottomlesse sea of sorrowes,"[77] so after purging "the sore by the vinegar of the Law," the "oyle of the Gospell" must be quickly applied.[78] Faithful meditation on the "sweete promises" centering in Christ and his cross will result in personal assurance of pardon. When "grounded in the doctrine of Christs death and resurrection," peace of conscience is assured.[79] Union with Christ is the ultimate balm for afflicted consciences. When God's children are one with Christ, they need no longer fear divine wrath against their sins, for their "judgement day was when Christ was judged," and the day of his resurrection was the day of their redemption.[80]

Greenham marks the pathway to peace and assurance with doctrinal rather than ethical signposts. The painfulness of an afflicted conscience cannot be assuaged by reflection on one's own good works, but only by meditation upon the death and resurrection of Jesus Christ. Theodore Beza's practical syllogism, which uses ethical reflection to assuage election anxiety, does not appear in Greenham, in part because of the sharp distinction he makes between the functions of law and gospel.[81] The practical syllogism calls for measurement of the Christian life by the standard of the law. Greenham uses the law almost exclusively as teacher of sin, then sets it aside and moves on to the gospel. "When the law accuseth thee because thou hast not observed it, send it to Christ, and say: there is a man that hath fulfilled the law: to him I cleave....I have nothing to do with thee, I have another law of libertie, which through Christ hath set me free."[82] Once the introspective self-examination of sin by the mirror of the law is accomplished, Greenham's emphasis is entirely extrospective, away from self and toward Christ. Only the

---

[76] Ibid., 101.
[77] Ibid., 105.
[78] Ibid., 109.
[79] Ibid., 105.
[80] "A third portion...of an hundred grave counsels," ibid., 63. Cf., 368.
[81] See above, pp. 95ff.
[82] "A second Treatise of the same argument," *Workes*, 114.

gospel, the good news of God's grace in Christ, can soothe the troubled conscience and bring personal assurance. Peace of conscience, which results, leads to godliness, for when grounded in the doctrines of the cross and resurrection, believers will gain strength for "sanctification and righteousness."[83] This strength comes not by way of the law, but the gospel. "The Law commandeth to do good, and giveth no strength: but the Gospell inableth us to do good, the holy Ghost writing the law in our hearts, & assuring us of the promise."[84] The godly are enabled to overcome the pleasures of this world by faith in Christ and his Word "that feareth us from doing any thing against his will."[85] The new life, or as Greenham calls it, the "reformation of our selves," is energized "by the promises of the Gospell, whereby we feele the fruit of the rising againe of Christ."[86]

Invariably, the last word delivered by Richard Greenham is not sin, but grace. Virtually every treatise and sermon includes the gospel of God's grace, which is inevitably victorious over sin and leads to deep, rich, meaningful joy in the Christian life.[87] The sinner is assured that "no sinne is so great, but in Christ it is pardonable."[88] The ultimate balm for the afflicted conscience is the ransom for sin and the "perfect deliverance beyond all expectation" graciously given by God through Christ.[89]

## VII

Union with Christ in the process of sanctification is the theme of one of the sermons included in Greenham's *Workes*. It is based on Galatians 6:15: *For in Christ Jesus neither circumcision availeth any thing, nor uncircumcision, but a new creature.* It describes in detail what it means to be new creatures of true godliness.[90] The sermon begins with reflections on the crucifixion and resurrection of

---

[83] "A Sweet comfort for an afflicted Conscience," ibid., 105.
[84] "A short forme of catechising," ibid., 88.
[85] Ibid., 89.
[86] Ibid., 87.
[87] See, for example, the conclusions of the eleventh, twelfth, and sixteenth sermons, ibid., 314, 328, & 368.
[88] "The first portion of grave Counsels," ibid., 6.
[89] Ibid., 33.
[90] "Of the latter or second effect of Christ his crosses...and by what means men are made new creatures," ibid., 370-8.

Christ, linking the crucifixion with the death of sin in those who by faith are joined to Christ, and the resurrection with the newness of life that follows. He writes, "it is the power of his resurrection that raiseth us to newnes of life." Christ arose "to impute righteousnes unto us, so also to worke in us righteousnesse and holinesse." Sharing in the crucifixion of Christ and having one's sins forgiven is only half the story; becoming new, godly creatures in Christ is the rest of it. It is not enough to be freed from the guilt and corruption of sin; believers must also "bee made partakers of that holinesse which floweth from Christ."[91]

New creaturehood means to have those virtues restored that were originally given in the perfect creation: "whatsoever wee lost in the first creation, we must receive in the second; and whatsoever we have been deprived of by Adam, we have it restored in Christ." Adam was created in God's image, "not in substance but in qualities," and those who have now become new creatures in Christ are again "made partakers of the godly nature" and have been renewed so as "in holy qualities to resemble the Creatour." Again, Greenham emphasizes the close relationship between God and godliness, creation and sanctification, theology and personal renewal, Adam and Christ. In Adam humanity was created with wisdom, righteousness, holiness, and perfect felicity. These were either destroyed or distorted in the fall, but in Christ they have all been renewed. Henceforth, "we must not live as we were wont, but our lives must be changed to the obedience of the word, which wee must testifie in thought, word and deede." Christ himself "must be our holinesse, that is, our flesh must be so crucified in his flesh, and his holinesse must so be communicated unto us" that a complete transformation of life and conduct is experienced.[92]

## VIII

Greenham's dark fears of the "divelish vermine of the Familie of love" kept him from the moralistic perfectionism sometimes associated with the term "Puritanism." Spiritual renewal and holiness do not occur in one dramatic moment, but develop more gradually,

---

[91] Ibid., 370.
[92] Ibid., 370-1.

he argues. Redemption is a second birth that begins anew the natural growth processes of human life. Just as "in the naturall birth children are not at the first old men...even so in the spirituall birth we grow from strength to strength, from measure to measure, untill wee come to perfection."[93] This ultimate perfection, however, is not realized in this world, but in the next. The true godliness believers are to pursue in this life, is not "an absolute unspottedness," Greenham says with candor. Such perfectionism is not only unbiblical, but even spiritually and psychologically harmful. He advises that the godly should "not seeke to be more righteous" than they can be, because a naive quest for the holy grail of perfection will only lead to further despair.[94] The redeemed in this life continue to have "relicks" of sin.[95] He offers this surprising, non-puritan-sounding advice: "we must neither be too righteous, nor too sinfull."[96] In one of his many warnings against perfectionism, he refers to the medieval Cathari, and adds a parenthetical aside: "such as were indeed the Puritanes in the Primitive Church."[97] Avoid the extremes, he says, "for vertue is a meane betweene two extremes." The Anabaptists, Family of Love, and the "true Puritanes" are "too righteous."[98] At another point he declares that the willful intention to do what is right is more important than the actual result, for a righteous will is graciously accepted by God. "God judgeth," he says, "according to purpose, not performance, according to affect, not effect."[99] Greenham's views on a gradual sanctification toward perfection are summed up eloquently in his sermon on renewal in Christ.

Neither do I dreame of being cleane without sinne, or of any imagined perfection in this life; but I require that we should not wittingly and willingly lye in sinne; and though we cannot come to perfection, yet to strive to come to perfection. For we are said to be new creatures not in being perfitly renewed, but in that we are in renewing, and finding the remnants of sinne withstanding the worke of new birth, wee looke for

[93] Ibid., 371.
[94] "A Sweet comfort for an afflicted Conscience," ibid., 104.
[95] "Of Feare," ibid., 682.
[96] "Of the latter or second effect of Christ his crosses," ibid., 373.
[97] "Of Justification," ibid., 848.
[98] "Of Conscience," ibid., 832.
[99] "Of Conscience," ibid., 650.

Christ a Redeemer to make an end of sinne in us.[100]

## IX

Throughout his sanctification theology, Greenham's call for godliness is invariably a call for personal, rather than social or cultural, holiness. When he uses the word "reformed," it usually has personal reference as, for example, in his comment that "our heart is reformed but in part,"[101] or when he laments that the time God has given "wherein we might reforme ourselves, wee have abused in being so little reformed."[102] He does issue an occasional warning, however, that in the pursuit of personal godliness, day to day occupations should not be neglected. "You are in earth to follow your calling," he writes, "you are not yet in heaven." Even Adam in the state of perfection had earthly work assigned by God. This proves that our "outward" callings were not the result of sin, "but were ordained before sin."[103] Moreover, the Word of God "not only instructs us in things concerning our salvation," but also teaches about the "things of this life."[104]

Greenham reflects the ambivalence of someone who believes that the cosmos ultimately belongs to God and is under his sovereign direction, and yet realizes that the world is a sinful place where godly life is extremely difficult. All created things are good, for God made them, but they are not necessarily all good for us, "unlesse by knowledge and faith we be able to use them according to the ordinance of God."[105] Greenham frequently alludes to the intrinsic goodness of God's creation and therefore defends "a temperate and moderate use of Gods creatures," i.e., created things.[106] He states that "too much austeritie is not commended, for why then should there bee such divers tastes in meates: And wine was given not only to quench the thirst, but also to make the hearts of men glad...therefore the children of Israel were commaunded to eate and to bee merrie

---

[100] "Of the latter or second effect of Christ his crosses," ibid., 373.
[101] "Meditations on the 119 Psalm," ibid., 528.
[102] Ibid., 532.
[103] "Another or second portion of...grave Counsels," ibid., 50. Cf., William Perkins, "A Treatise of the Vocations, or Callings of men," *Works*, I, 747-79.
[104] "Another or second portion of...grave Counsels," *Workes*, 52.
[105] Ibid.
[106] "A Treatise of Fasting," ibid., 214.

before the Lord."[107] At the same time, he recommends a standard of moderation in the possession of worldly goods. Riches "are no signes of Gods favour," and neither is the want of them a sign of his displeasure. Greenham repeats biblical warnings about riches. They are not wrong in themselves, but "are evil commonly in either getting, or in keeping, or in using, or in loving them."[108] In an aphoristic warning against materialism, he writes: "They that be in the hell of things fleshly, cannot see the heaven of things spirituall."[109] And in another: "earthly riches doe deceive our hearts, when heavenly riches doe not delight us."[110] A "carefull seeking" of spiritual things brings a "godly neglect" of material things.[111] "The more one tasteth of heavenly things, the lesse is his joy in earthly things."[112] If God sends riches, he does so to test the recipient's thankfulness, faithfulness, and willingness to use them on behalf of the needy neighbor.[113] But ultimately, there is another kind of riches God's people are to pursue: the riches of godliness, for "godliness is the greatest riches before God and Angels in heaven."[114]

# X

The ambivalence Greenham demonstrates in his thoughts about material goods and spiritual things is also evident in his comments on the present and future dimensions of the Kingdom of God. There is a sense in which "Christ his kingdome is now,"[115] but Greenham's ultimate hope is in another world, one that human beings cannot build but God will certainly establish. Christ's kingdom is present in this world wherever there is obedient faith generated by the Holy Spirit, who is the continuing presence of God in the universe. This kingdom consists in "the graces of the spirit" in the lives of believers. An intimate relationship exists between the present and future kingdom; there is no hope for entering the kingdom in the hereafter

---

[107] "Of Prosperity and Adversity," ibid., 769. Cf., Calvin, *Institutes*, III, 10.
[108] "Of Riches and their abuse," ibid., 783.
[109] "Another or second portion of...grave Counsels," ibid., 46.
[110] "The first portion of grave Counsels," ibid., 29.
[111] Ibid., 4,7.
[112] Ibid., 19.
[113] "Of Riches and their abuse," ibid., 784.
[114] "The first portion of grave Counsels," ibid., 30.
[115] "A Treatise of sending the Holy Ghost," ibid., 221.

without entering it here below.[116]

The godly life in this world ends with death. Just as it was so important for Greenham to live well, so also the godly must die well. In his "Treatise of the Resurrection" he reflects on differing attitudes toward death, some fearing it too much, others too little.[117] It is not morbid but "wholesome" for a Christian to meditate on death. It will be good, after all, to "be gleaned from those miserable calamities" of this sinful world. Departure from it will be like "a returning from exile" and a "deliverie out of prison."[118] Although he affirms a meaningful place for God's people in this world, Greenham finally puts his anchor down in the world to come. "Paradise is our native countrie, and we in this world be as exiles and as strangers," he writes.[119] The godly have no "long abiding place" but are pilgrims here. In this world they have "fewe friends and many enemies," namely personal corruption, the vanities of the world, the evil example of the wicked, and that "great enemie of mankinde the divell."[120] None of these will be present in the new creation, which Greenham describes with hope and longing.

> As farre as the spirit is above the flesh, God above men, Heaven above the earth, Eternitie above frailtie; so farre is the new creation above the olde: for the one is but mortall and corrupt seede that shall perish: but the other is of immortall seede, and from Heaven, a great worke of God which shall abide forever.[121]

So Greenham reaches the apotheosis of sanctification. Although he expresses deep longing for the world to come, his emphasis on godliness in this world brings about a link between the two. Obedient faith demonstrates that God is active here, and his kingdom, though in shadow form, is already present. Greenham had a vision of a holy,

---

[116] "Of the heavenly purchase in three Sermons," ibid., 288-9.

[117] Ibid., 178-86. Cf., Nancy L. Beaty, *The Craft of Dying: A Study in the Literary Tradition of the Ars Moriendi in England,* 108-56. See also William Perkins, "A Salve for a Sicke Man," *Works,* I, 495-7; 503-4.

[118] "A Treatise of the Resurrection," *Workes,* 179.

[119] "Of our generall and speciall calling," ibid., 645. Cf., Charles Hambrick-Stowe, *The Practice of Piety,* 54 ff.

[120] "Meditations on the 119 Psalm," *Workes,* 405-6.

[121] "Another or second portion of...grave Counsels," ibid., 46.

godly, sanctified life which, on a personal level at least, brought something of heaven to earth. That life is nothing less than the life of God himself. For the call to godliness was the bold call to be like God in whose image humanity was created. Let God be God, and let His people be godly.

# 6

# THE DOCTRINE OF MEANS

## I

In one of his most celebrated essays, Perry Miller drills to the "marrow of puritan divinity."[1] He concludes that at the core of Puritanism is the doctrine of the covenant. This was the special puritan contribution to the legacy of Calvinism, for although this doctrine may have been present in earlier continental Calvinism, it was the puritans in old and new England who gave the covenant sharper definition and made it the centerpiece of their theology. It had a very useful function, serving as an anodyne for the negative side effects of the absolute sovereignty of God and predestinarian understanding of salvation. These familiar Calvinistic doctrines tend to diminish human effort and responsibility, says Miller, and the doctrine of the covenant was used to shore up the anthropological side of the divine/human relationship. Since a covenant involves reciprocal responsibilities, it counters the one-sided, fatalistic implications of predestination, and gives to humankind an active and meaningful role in redemption. The covenant doctrine makes demands on human beings, implying that humans are sentient creatures capable of responding to the sovereign God.

It would be difficult to use Richard Greenham in support of the Miller thesis.[2] The covenant doctrine is present in Greenham's thought, but does not occupy a central, controlling position. When it appears, it is usually with emphasis on the loving promises of God, rather than on the obligations of human beings. Nor does Greenham deal at any length with predestination. He occasionally mentions

---

[1] "The Marrow of Puritan Divinity," in *Errand into The Wilderness* (Cambridge, Massachusetts: Belknap Press, 1956) Ch. III, 48-98.
[2] The thesis itself has been effectively challenged; see George Marsden, "Perry Miller's Rehabilitation of the Puritans: A Critique," *Church History*, vol. 39, (March 1970) 91-105.

election, but it does not appear to be for him a problematic doctrine that threatens to turn vital, moral beings into lifeless, irresponsible pawns. On the contrary, he writes: "Election is a great spurre to good workes." And he adds, "if thou art elected, thou art also elected to the means to faith, and the fruites of it, else thou art not elected."[3]

*The means to faith*—this is a doctrine that *does* occupy a central position in Greenham's practical divinity. That God does not work by remote control but uses human, historical means is a pervasive, virtually omnipresent theme in Greenham's *Workes*. Not one of his treatises omits some reference to the doctrine of means, and it appears frequently in many of them. It obviously had a vital function in his preaching and pastoral ministry. Younger contemporaries like William Perkins and Richard Rogers also emphasized the doctrine of means, but Greenham was one of the first to give it preeminence.[4] Moreover, for Greenham it was not a doctrine artificially contrived in order to carve out a place for human responsibility in a system otherwise dominated by the sovereignty of God. Rather, it issued quite naturally from his doctrine of God as one who normally works through creaturely agency. God's eternal promises are realized and secured in temporal ways. Hence, these promises "doe not make such as feare him to be carelesse, but carefull to use the means."[5] In the doctrine of means, the realms of grace and nature intersect

In his design for creation, God provides earthly goods for human beings to use for their sustenance. Failure to use them is a covert way of tempting God and violating nature. Greenham cites as one of two ways to break the first commandment, "a negligent and carelesse use of the meanes to serve God his providence."[6] He writes, "If wee have lawfull meanes to get our living wee must use them," but always with a keen sense of dependence upon the God who provides them.[7] Greenham warns against the danger of transferring faith from God to the means. Trust in God, he says, not the means. The Lord exercises sovereign jurisdiction over them. And yet, Greenham speaks of a self-imposed "limitation" on God's power. "We graunt the Lord useth

---

[3] "Of Workes," *Workes*, 838.
[4] Simon K. H. Chan, *The Puritan Meditative Tradition* (Ph.D. diss., Cambridge University, 1986) 11.
[5] "Of Prayer and Meditation," *Workes*, 777.
[6] "A shorte forme of catechising," ibid., 74.
[7] "Of the Exercises of Religion," ibid., 674. Cf., 316-7, 844-5.

meanes, but so as he intendeth and remitteth them by his own limitation and power."[8] Greenham suggests that there is a chain of interdependence in the universe that ultimately links this world to God.

> Man in want sueth to the creatures, the creatures not able to supplie it complaine to the earth, the earth seeketh to the heavens, the heavens crave help from God as the last refuge, whereunto we flie immediately; God as the author, from whom our helpe commeth, heareth the heavens, the heavens answer the earth, the earth relieveth the creatures, the creatures minister unto man.[9]

Given this interconnectedness of the physical and spiritual realms, it is to be expected that God would provide means not only for humanity's material needs, but for spiritual sustenance also. Morevoer, even when a believer is using spiritual means, his physical capacities are also involved. Human hands are best used when they are receiving the sacrament; the eyes when reading the Word, the feet when they carry believers to church for public worship, the ears when they are engaged in hearing the sermon. Since these activities are essentially God's way of providing for our salvation and not simply human inventions, the grace of God remains inviolate. Neglect the means to your peril, he says, but at the same time, "wholly referre the blessing of the meanes to the grace of God." Christians may not trust the means by "neglecting to pray for the grace of God in them: which is but a preposterous zeale of such as are not rightly instructed in the way of their salvation."[10] Neither must the means be separated from godliness itself. He accuses the papists and familists of doing so; the papists by concentrating solely on means without godliness, the family of love on godliness without means.

> Seeing the Lord hath joyned together the meanes of godlines and godlines it selfe, let us not separate them, either with the superstitious Papists, resting in the worke wrought...neither

---

[8] "A third portion...of an hundred grave counsels," ibid., 59.
[9] Ibid.
[10] "The first portion of grave Counsels," ibid., 15.

with frantike heretikes despise the meanes, as though without them we could live in obedience to God, or love to our brethren.[11]

"Every day must have a dayes increase in godlinesse," he writes, and to that end the means must be diligently and deliberately pursued.[12] Greenham alludes to the "painful use" of the means, for just as athletes engage in physical exercises that force them through thresholds of pain, so the use of the means is part of a spiritual regimen that demands total, painful dedication.[13] The discipline required when using the means is evident in a set of Greenham's statements dealing with self-examination. He first confesses, "I have not so loved the meanes...as I should doe." He goes on: "My prayers are more monkish than powerfull." And again: "Great hypocrisie of heart, and vaineglory of speech hath overtaken me." He pledges to more faithfully use the means, and to avoid "customable" praying and "vaine-glorious" speaking.[14]

What exactly are the means God has provided for faith and spiritual growth? Throughout his *Workes*, Greenham emphasizes three means which he evidently regards as primary: preaching the Word, prayer, and the sacraments. In his catechism, however, when he raises the question: *"What meanes hath God ordained to worke and increase Faith in us?"* he responds with a list of five: the Word (or "The Gospell"), prayer, sacraments, discipline, and affliction.[15] Typically, he refers to these as "means to faith" or "means of godliness," not as "means of grace." Among these, preaching the Word has a special, primary place, for it is the Word that actually *initiates* faith, while the others, in conjunction with the Word, *confirm* faith, causing it to grow and flourish. Accordingly, in the analysis that follows, the indispensable practice of preaching the Word, will be considered at much greater length than the four secondary means.

---

[11] "Of godlines and by what meanes we must draw neere to God," ibid., 689.
[12] Ibid., cf., 70.
[13] Ibid., 29.
[14] "A third portion...of an hundred grave counsels," ibid., 68.
[15] "A short forme of catechising," ibid., 88.

## II

There can be no doubt which of the five means is most emphasized by Greenham. The relentless manner in which he drives home his own sense of utter dependency on the Gospel, or as he more frequently calls it, the *Word*, is almost breathtaking. Not only is the "meanes of Gods word," mentioned already in the second answer of his catechism, but it appears regularly in each and every treatise, sermon, and meditation. The "Meditations on the 119 Psalm" are a three hundred page encomium of the Word of God. The Word of God receives such praise and emphasis because, as indicated above, there is absolutely no other way to come to the knowledge of God and of the way of salvation.[16] Among the means, it is in a class by itself, for it is the one God has given "to beget and breede" faith. In a passage in which Greenham deals with the "six notes of salvation," the Word is at the center of each.[17] That Word is God's revealed will, made up of the books of the Old and New Testaments, in which God has included all that is necessary to know for redemption. Since it is God's Word, no one may add to it or subtract from it. Through it, and it alone, humankind may come to know God as Father in Jesus Christ, true service and worship of God according to his will, the way of everlasting blessedness, and the sure grounds of salvation. All who are able must, therefore, immerse themselves in the reading of the Word. Greenham acknowledges the obstacle of illiteracy in his catechism when he asks, *"What if men cannot read?"* He answers simply, "Then they must use the helpe of others that can reade."[18]

The Scriptures are to be read not only privately, but also "publikely in the Church." Reading is not enough, however. The Word must be preached. English Puritanism's total commitment to preaching is one of the defining elements of the movement. The sharp criticism of non-preaching parish priests ("dumb dogges that cannot barke"),[19] the intense concern about provisions for a trained and learned ministry, the incredible confidence that through faithful preaching the nation could and would be reformed—all of this has

---

[16] See Ch. 4, where Greenham's doctrine of the Word is discussed. Here the emphasis will be on the practical use of the Word.
[17] "Notes of salvation," ibid., 172.
[18] "A shorte forme of catechising," 72. See above, p. 32 for literacy estimates.
[19] William Perkins, *Workes*, I, 55 and III, 24.

been thoroughly described and discussed by others.[20] This emphasis on preaching was not a narrowly puritan concern, but was the English counterpart of a protestant emphasis on the continent. The dominance of the pulpit over the altar, or at the very least, the equality of the two, was part of the legacy of Luther, Calvin, and all the other reformers. In this context, it is not startling to read in Greenham's catechism that preaching is the "most principall and proper meanes to beget Faith in us."[21] Elsewhere he says, "And where this ordinarie meanes of salvation faileth, the people for the most part perish."[22]

Reading the Word and preaching it "being of God joyned together in the worke of our salvation, may not be severed asunder."[23] For Greenham, however, *preaching* is the principal means of faith. Thomas Cartwright's memorable statement about the advantage of preaching over reading fits Greenham perfectly: "As the fire stirred giveth more heat, so the word as it were blown by preaching flameth more in the hearers than when it is read."[24] John Geree characterized the puritan's view of reading and preaching in these words: "The word read he esteemed of more authority, but the word preacht of more efficacie."[25] Greenham would have affirmed the second clause, but possibly not the first. For him the preached Word also comes with divine authority.

Greenham lists eight properties of reverent and faithful reading and hearing of the Word: diligence, wisdom, preparation, meditation, conference, faith, practice, and prayer.[26] To insure that the Word is heard with the heart as well as the ear, four special requirements must be observed: careful preparation;[27] willingness to hear the entire Word, not just "parcels" of it; diligence in continual hearing; and the desire to practice what is preached. "We must learn then to draw our

---

[20] See especially Irvonwy Morgan, *The Godly Preachers of the Elizabethan Church* (London: Epworth Press, 1965), and Paul S. Seaver, *The Puritan Lectureships* (Stanford: University Press, 1970).

[21] *Workes*, 72.

[22] "A direction for the reading of the Scriptures," ibid., 173.

[23] Ibid.

[24] Quoted in Richard Hooker, *Laws*, 2:96.

[25] *The Character of an old English Puritane* (London, 1646) 2.

[26] "A direction for the reading of the Scriptures," *Workes*, 173.

[27] Disciplined preparation for hearing the Word was especially important to Greenham. See "Of hearing Gods word," ibid., 834 ff. Cf., Charles Hambrick-Stowe, *The Practice of Piety*, 202-3.

hearts up to our eares, that so one sound may pearce both at once."
The law must be heard as well as the gospel, for the "Sonne of God
hath not alwaies a streame of milke and hony running out of his
mouth, but sometime a two-edged sword."[28] Ultimately, however, the
godly life is generated "by the promises of the Gospell, whereby we
feele the fruit of the rising againe of Christ."[29]

Theologically, Greenham connected preaching with the doctrine
of calling. It constitutes the "outward call" directed toward believers
and unbelievers alike. In and through the preached Word, the Holy
Spirit works in the human heart with an "effectual call" equivalent to
regeneration.[30] Preaching is indispensable for without it the effectual
call does not occur. This conviction accounts for the urgency of
Greenham's pleas to go to sermon as well as for the frequency of his
own preaching. It explains also, in part, his concern for Sabbath-
keeping, for at the heart of it was the public gathering to hear the
preached Word. Not everyone will profit from every sermon, but there
will be critical moments when preaching strikes home with meaning
and force. Preaching the Word involves the suspenseful uncertainty of
Russian roulette, "because we know not who is the man, what is the
time, where is the place, which is the sermon that God hath
appointed to work on us." Consequently, he urges his parishioners to
"runne to every sermon" available.[31]

Greenham's convictions about the centrality of the preached
Word as the means of faith and godliness were formed in the context
of his bipolar polemic against the familists and papists. On the one
hand, he warns against gullible and uncritical acceptance of
theophanous revelations from God. There was a time when visions
were the "ordinary" means of divine communcation and preaching
was "extraordinarie," but now the situation is reversed. In the current
epoch, God normally communicates by means of his Word. Therefore
seek sermons, he says, not visions.[32] On the other hand, with
Catholicism in mind, he rails against the tradition in which the
sacraments "have beene more accompted of than the word, & hearing

---

[28] "Of hearing Gods word," *Workes,* 709-10.
[29] "A short forme of catechising," ibid., 87.
[30] "Of Regeneration and Sanctification," ibid., 804.
[31] "A third portion...of an hundred grave counsels," ibid., 64.
[32] Ibid., 41.

of it preached."[33] The sacraments are important for Greenham—they are another of the five means—but they must be closely linked to the Word. Otherwise, the church lapses into superstitious sacramentalism.

As a result of Greenham's heavy emphasis on the preached Word as the primary means of faith and godliness, the *preacher* moves into the liturgical spotlight. In Greenham's theology of means the preacher himself becomes a channel of grace. This in fact may be the Achilles heel in the doctrine of means: its enormous reliance on human agency. Paradoxically, the puritans placed a heavy burden of virtually divine responsibility on those whom they regarded as sinful, irresponsible human beings. Theoretically, the reformation of the church and nation of England was said to depend on God's grace alone, but practically, it relied on the preaching ability of ordinary mortals. This ability required not only innate gifts, but also careful preparation and training, which apparently were in short supply in England.

The state of the clergy was deplorably low in Greenham's day, especially by puritan standards. In the majority of English parishes, the clergy could not and did not preach. In many churches the same clerics who had sung mass during the Marian interlude were reading the prescribed services from the Prayer Book after the Elizabethan settlement. But they were not preaching. Less than half of the ministers in the diocese of London were licensed to preach early in Elizabeth's reign.[34] There is evidence that improvement came very slowly. In a 1586 "Supplication of the citie of London to the parliament," church leaders were still bemoaning the lack of preaching. The sun of the gospel has been "sore ecclipsed and darkned," through the "dimme Clowdes of Unlearned ministers," the document laments.[35] In 1593 Greenham's younger contemporary and good friend, Lancelot Andrewes, fresh out of Pembroke, described the clergy in language he might later have reconsidered when he became a bishop. He complained that most clerics were half-asleep, luke-warm, and tongue-tied. He called them "dumb-doges" who in their attempt to preach spew forth "incoherence" and "misshapen and evil-smelling

---

[33] Ibid., 53. "More accompted of"=held in higher esteem or value.
[34] Paul Seaver, *The Puritan Lectureships*, 130; see all of chapter 1.
[35] Albert Peel, ed., *The Seconde Parte of a Register*, 2 vols. (Cambridge: University Press, 1915) II, 185.

crudities." The church, he said, "is infested with as many fooleries of discourse as are commonly in the places where they shear sheep."[36]

That these views were shared by Greenham is indicated in his classic homily, "Of the mutuall duties betweene the Ministers and the people,"[37] a sterling exposition of his views on preachers and the preaching of the Word as means of faith and godliness. It is the lengthiest sermon in his *Workes*—twenty folio pages—and would have taken over two hours to deliver! Greenham occasionally preached at Great St. Mary's, the University Church in Cambridge,[38] and this sermon, addressed as it was to the "reverend Fathers and brethren beloved in our Lord Jesus," was probably delivered there. It is based on Hebrews 13:17: *"Obey them that have the oversight of you, and submit your selves, for they watch for your soules, as they that must give accounts, that they may doe it with joy, and not with griefe: for that is unprofitable for you."* Greenham interprets this text as having reference to the church's ministry, not to civil magistracy.

In the introduction, Greenham bases the church's vital need for ministers on their role as God's designated means to bring his people into his kingdom. The preaching of the Word is "the instrument which God hath appointed to pull his people into the sheepfold of Jesus Christ, where they are without daunger of destruction." He therefore despairs over the condition of churches without preachers, for "such horrible disorder is there, where Gods word is not truly preached." Any church of God that does not have a preaching pastor will be "devoured of their adversarie the divell" and "led away captive into hell."[39] Greenham subtly moves from the Word of God to the preacher himself as the means of faith. "Preachers are the onely meanes appointed by God to worke faith in his children," he declares. Consequently, the proclamation of the Word is the "necessariest thing in the world." Through the preacher, God accommodates himself to his people, for if he were to speak to them directly, they could not "abide the hearing of his voyce, but bee even swallowed up of feare." God mercifully chooses to bring his Word through mortal

---

[36] John Strype, *Whitgift*, III, 293 ff. See also the preface to Heinrich Bullinger's *Decades*, (Parker Society, 1849-52) I, 3-9.

[37] *Workes*, 339-58.

[38] Samuel Clarke, *Thirty-two Lives*, 13.

[39] "Of the mutuall duties between the Ministers and the people," *Workes*, 340.

men, "with whom we may talke familiarly."[40]

The duties of the godly preacher are fourfold according to Greenham: to read and study the Word and devote himself to prayer; to "come out of his study to teach and instruct his flocke" in wholesome doctrine; to live a godly life as an example for his people; and to give his life for the flock.[41] If parishioners are to learn the will of God from their preacher, he must become "as it were a storehouse of the Lord" through diligent study. What is taken in, however, must be poured out. The preacher must not remain in his study absorbing knowledge "till he become as full as a tunne that will not sound when one knocketh upon it,"[42] but he must come out and preach, teaching his parishioners the whole counsel of God. Just as law and gospel comprise the two elements of the Word of God, so also are they the two parts of the preacher's message. He must "beate downe the stiffenecked and obstinate sinners, by threatning the rigor of the law," and heal "the bruised and wounded consciences" with the "sweete promises of the Gospell."[43]

The minister must bring the Word not only in public, formal worship, but in private visits as well. Greenham himself was a model of this practice, for Samuel Clarke mentions that his "manner was to walk out into the Fields, and to confer with his Neighbours as they were at Plough."[44] In his sermon on ministry Greenham bases the practice of informal encounter upon the example of Jesus, who not only preached publicly in the synagogues, but spoke privately in people's homes. Private ministry is necessary "because that which is spoken generally to all, is regarded of very few or none," but when a word is spoken directly and privately, the recipient is unable to wriggle out of its demands by applying it mentally to others. The dutiful pastor must also engage regularly in prayer, for just as "the Minister is the mouth of God to speake unto the people, so must he be the peoples mouth, and pray unto the Lord both for himselfe and for them" so that God may bless the ministry of the Word to them.[45]

So as to be a Christian example to his flock, and to bring honor to

---

[40] Ibid., 341.
[41] Ibid., 342.
[42] Ibid., 343. "Tunne" is old English for "cask" or "wine-vessel."
[43] Ibid., 344.
[44] *Thirty-two Lives*, 15.
[45] "Of the mutuall duties betweene the Ministers and the people," *Workes*, 345. Cf., 564.

the Word of God which he proclaims, the minister must
conscientiously lead a godly life. Otherwise he gives occasion to the
enemies of God to slander the gospel of Christ. Moreover, if a pastor
is to be an adequate caretaker of others' souls, he must demonstrate
an ability to watch over his own. His proclamation of law and gospel
can only become authentic when confirmed by a godly life.[46]

Finally, the godly preacher must so dedicate himself to his
ministry and his people that he is even willing to give his life for them.
His flock should be "dearer unto him then his life." Just as St. Paul
declared his willingness to die for the name of the Lord Jesus, every
good minister, for the sake of his parishioners, should be "readie to
suffer all things, yea even to give his life for the confirmation of his
doctrine, the strengthening of...faith, and the glory of God." This
sacrificial attitude is modelled by one even greater than Paul. The
Lord Jesus is the supreme example of the shepherd who laid down his
life for his sheep.[47]

In one section of the sermon Greenham outlines the reciprocal
duties of the parishioners to their pastor. Here occurs a transparent
move toward "ministerial sacramentalism." Greenham presents a
portrait of a pastor who himself becomes a sacrament, a visible
"means of grace." Others have observed that in Puritanism, with its
emphasis on the "real presence" of Christ in the Bible, the Word
becomes a sacrament.[48] Greenham carries it a step further, suggesting
the real presence of Christ in the preacher. The preacher is the
visible, material, creaturely, flesh and blood substance in and through
whom Christ is conveyed to the people. This becomes most apparent
when Greenham enumerates the duties of the flock to the shepherd:
obedience, reverence, fear, and love. These obligations arise from the
subtle transfer of the properties of the Word of God, and even of God
himself, to the preacher. An editorial note in the margin sums it up:
"To disobey the Minister of God, is to disobey God himselfe and to
despise his word."[49] Greenham explicitly equates obedience to the
minister with obedience to Christ, for the messenger and the message
are indissolubly linked: "if thou confess it thy dutie to be obedient

---

[46] Ibid., 346.
[47] Ibid., 347-8.
[48] John S. Coolidge, *The Pauline Renaissance*, 142. Cf., Frere and Douglas,
*Puritan Manifestoes*, 76.
[49] "Of the mutuall duties betweene the Ministers and the people," *Workes*, 350.

unto Jesus Christ, I tel thee plainly thou oughtest no lesse to obey the Minister in that he bringeth the message of Christ, than if himselfe were present."[50] The minister is the "spirituall father" of his parishioners, who has "begotten them with the word of God"; therefore, the duties of obedience, reverence, fear, and love are incumbent upon the flock. When Greenham urges not only reverence, but even "fear" of the minister, the sacramental images become even more vivid. One who comes to the minister to ask a question, "must consider that he commeth to talke with the messenger of the Lord, whom he ought to heare as well as if the Lord himselfe were present." He adds, "where a faithful Minister is that doth sincerely and purely preach the word, it is all one as if the Lord himselfe dwelt personally among us." The Galatian church provides a model, for they received St. Paul "as an Angell of God, yea more than so, they received him as Jesus Christ himselfe."[51] This was the ideal Richard Greenham sought to incarnate in his Dry Drayton parish: the faithful shepherd prepared to lay down his life for his flock, followed by trusting parishioners who were to live in obedience, reverence, and fear for their master. God has given sacraments as means of conveying the gospel and increasing faith; for Greenham, the minister was the primary means of transmitting God's Word unto his children, and of increasing their faith in Jesus Christ.[52]

Given the prevailing level of learning and literacy, perhaps this emphasis was inevitable. In sixteenth century England, the puritan preacher seemingly had much to offer. He was a source of enlightenment and freedom, a means to a more significant life, a way to overcome fear, an avenue to spiritual adventure, the incarnate means to the goal of true happiness through a godly life.[53] Greenham's belabored discussion, however, suggests that this sanguine view of the minister did not arise naturally in the hearts of his parishioners. It had to be deliberately nurtured and Greenham rose to the task.

The "priesthood of all believers" notwithstanding, in Greenham's ecclesiology the preaching of the Word moved into a position formerly occupied by the sacraments. To some extent, the puritan

---

[50] Ibid.
[51] "Of the mutuall duties between the Ministers and the people," *Workes*, 352-3.
[52] Ibid., 351.
[53] William Haller, *The Rise of Puritanism*, 36-7.

passion for preaching aided and abetted the perpetuation of a
"priestly" class, with the preaching pastor regarded as the
indispensable mediator between God and his people. This protestant
sacerdotalism was balanced off, however, by the domesticating effects
of Greenham's Sabbath doctrine which called for extensive family
involvement in worship by means of preparation for and reflection on
what took place in public worship.[54]

## III

The reading and preaching of the Word is the primary means, for it
actually serves as the sperm that begets faith. All the others—prayer,
sacraments, discipline, affliction—are secondary but nonetheless
essential for the confirmation of faith and for growth in godliness. In
his catechism Greenham calls *prayer* "the next principall meanes"
which serves the strengthening and increase of faith. He defines prayer
as "the uplifing of the minde, and powring out of the heart before
God."[55] References to its necessity abound in his *Workes*, but he
gives little specific instruction about it apart from his "A short
treatise of prayer," based on Acts 2:21, where the apostle Peter
quotes Joel 2:32: *"Everyone who calls on the name of the Lord will
be saved"*[56] Greenham comments: "The holy ghost teacheth us that
all is nothing without prayer," for while the Word is the means by
which faith is engendered, prayer is the means "wherby this faith is
continued in us."[57] He urges private, family, and public prayer for
both the spiritual and political orders. "When thou shalt see no good
neither in Church nor in Common-wealth, then have recourse to
prayers, and thou shalt not onely be preserved from daungers, but
also thou shalt enjoy God his spirit with his graces."[58]

Greenham acknowledges the difficulty of prayer in adverse
circumstances, but this should not discourage or diminish its
practice, for "when we know not how to pray, Gods Spirit will teach
us how to crave, how to sigh, and how to pray, and the Lorde will

---

[54] See below, pp. 168ff.
[55] "A short forme of catechising," *Workes*, 90.
[56] Ibid., 236-40.
[57] Ibid., 237-8.
[58] Ibid., 239.

know the meaning of his owne Spirit crying in us."[59] He suggests that fervent prayer has a spontaneous quality. "For as the bullet out of the Gunne," he writes, "or an arrow out of a bow, so out of the abundance of our heart must our prayers proceede."[60] This could imply the superiority of free, spontaneous prayer over the prescribed prayers of the Church, but Greenham nowhere explicitly criticizes the *Book of Common Prayer.*

The Word and prayer are tied together closely, "for I dare say," he writes, "that all our power in prayer commeth from the word."[61] Furthermore, prayer is the essential element in preparation for both hearing the Word and applying it personally, once heard. After the public worship service, "change all that you remember into a prayer," asking God for divine aid to put the Word into practice.[62] Even the most powerful and fervent prayer, however, does not undermine the sovereign freedom of God. Prayer remains only a "means" that in itself is not to be trusted "as though wee could tye God to our praying."[63]

Regarding the practice of prayer, Greenham recommends the morning hours, for then, presumably, the mind is most awake and alert. He urges "cheerfulness" in prayer, and then bemoans his own lack of it.[64] In an unexpected bit of advice, he warns against praying too much at the expense of responsible attention to life's more ordinary demands. Praying, hearing sermons, and reading the Word are indispensable means of godliness, but it is also vitally important that time be taken to demonstrate the fruits of these spiritual exercises in deeds of love and mercy.[65]

In his catechism, Greenham uses the Lord's Prayer as the model, calling it the "prescript rule of Prayer left us in the Scriptures." His commentary on it is free and wide-ranging, even to the extent of a brief excursus on the Trinity. God's people are not tied to the precise words and phrases of the model prayer, but should use its various petitions as a guide to the appropriate content of prayer. The Lord's Prayer teaches, for example, that both praise for God's majesty as well

---

[59] "Meditations on the 119 Psalm," ibid., 484.
[60] "Of Prayer and Meditation," ibid., 777.
[61] "A third portion...of an hundred grave counsels," ibid., 54. Cf., 43.
[62] Ibid., 42.
[63] "The first portion of grave Counsels," ibid., 27.
[64] "Meditations on the 119 Psalm," ibid., 566.
[65] Ibid., 562.

as petitions for human welfare should be included. He begins a discussion of the first petition, but in the midst of it the catechism abruptly ends with a note from Henry Holland that the rest of the document could not be found.[66]

## IV

The Word is the primary means, and prayer "the next principall meanes," but the *sacraments* are not far behind. Greenham often mentions Word, prayer and sacraments together as means of faith and redemption: "the word carrieth the spirit of faith into thy heart; prayer giveth thee a feeling of thy faith; the Sacraments confirme both thy faith and feeling."[67] As prayer is powerless without the Word, the sacraments are meaningless without it, for the Word gives the promise which the sacraments confirm. The two sacraments, Baptism and Lord's Supper, are signs, seals, and pledges of the gospel promises of the Word. The sacraments must be observed publicly in the congregation's presence, for they are ordinances of the church and function not individualistically but communally in the life of the people of God.[68] Greenham insists on a proper understanding of the sacraments to ensure that they not be used superstitiously. Participation in the Lord's Supper, for example, should be preceded by a period of training followed by "some requisite trial" whose details he leaves unspecified.[69] The sacrament of Baptism is a "pledge of our washing in Christs blood," Greenham declares, and goes on to speak of other spiritual gifts it signifies: justification, union with Christ and other believers, dying to sin, and resurrection victory. Because Baptism is biblically prefigured by the rite of circumcision, it is to be administered to infant children. The sacrament does not mechanically and automatically save its recipients, but must nonetheless be observed because it is prescribed by the authority of Scripture.[70] He refutes "the popish opinion of the necessitie of Baptism," with an argument that hinges on the prescribed "eighth day" for the rite of circumcision: "for if this necessitie had been in

---

[66] "A short forme of catechising," ibid., 90-1.
[67] "The first portion of grave Counsels," ibid., 32.
[68] "A Treatise of the Sabbath," ibid. 157
[69] REM 524, fol. 2r.
[70] "A Treatise of the Sabbath," *Workes*, 157.

Circumcision, which they affirme to be in Baptisme, all that dyed before the eight day were condemned."[71] Greenham does not deny, however, the efficacy of a Roman Catholic-administered sacrament. Explicitly rejecting Donatism, he asserts that the power of the sacrament is not dependent upon the faith of the officiant, for even "the corrupt intent of the minister doth not hinder the blessing of God in the Sacraments, being his owne ordinance."[72] Not the officiant but the Holy Spirit determines the efficacy of the sacraments. The Spirit is the indispensable link between the sign and the thing signified. A person may be baptized a hundred times, Greenham exclaims, but if he has not received the Holy Spirit, he will die in his sins.[73] On the other hand, when used believingly, the sacraments are "conduits," through which "the graces of the holy Ghost" are "most plentifully powred on us."[74]

Receiving the sacrament of the Lord's Supper requires careful preparation. Those who are unable or unwilling to conduct a serious self-examination prior to participation must be excluded from the table. This includes children too young to properly examine themselves and others "wanting in wit," good judgement, and reason, as well as those who are ignorant "in the grounds of Religion," or whose lives are wicked and impenitent.[75] The purpose of the self-examination is to conduct a moral inventory, with God's Word as the standard, in order to determine worthiness for receiving the sacrament. This inventory should normally lead to participation in, not abstinence from, the table, for the Bible says, "and so eate: not so let him abstaine...." Greenham argues that the sacrament is abused not only by receiving it unworthily, but also by deliberate abstinence after appropriate self-examination.[76]

Greenham's emphasis on conscientious personal preparation for the Lord's Supper arises from his high view of the sacrament. The Lord's table in the church, he declares, is nothing less than a representation of God's table in heaven where the "glorious Trinity" is

---

[71] "Of Baptisme," ibid., 642.
[72] "The first portion of grave Counsels," ibid., 30.
[73] "Of Repentance and true sorrow for sinne," ibid., 281. Cf., William P. Stephens, *The Holy Spirit in the Theology of Martin Bucer*, 230-1.
[74] "Of Sacraments," ibid., 788.
[75] "A Treatise of examination before and after the Lords Supper," *Workes*, 190.
[76] Ibid., 191. "The neglect of Gods sacraments doth provoke him against us," "Of Sacraments," ibid., 787.

present. Here below, the body and blood of Christ are present in some special and unique way in the elements of bread and wine. On this crucial and controversial matter, Greenham avoids the "substantial presence" view on the one hand, and the "real absence" view on the other. His explanation reflects rather the "true presence" view of Calvin and Cranmer and the Thirty-Nine Articles— sacramentally, Christ is present. Participation in the Eucharist is an awesome privilege because of "the great reverence of the person with whom we are present." Communicants reverently participate in "the living body, yea the glorified body of the Lord." Greenham speaks of "the receiving of the body and blood of Christ" in the Eucharist, and even adds, "who so eateth of Christ, shall eate of life."[77] This is not a "carnall presence, as the Papists imagine, yet there is a true spirituall and effectuall presence of the things signified: and therefore we may certainly looke for the performance of the same, if by faith we can receive it."[78] Greenham cleverly reinterprets "transubstantiation" to mean that believing participants in the Supper, not the elements of bread and wine, are substantially changed. Whereas in ordinary eating the ingested food becomes part of the human body, "in receiving of the word & Sacrament, which feede the soule, they are not changed into the qualities of us, but we are changed into them."[79]

Although at one point Greenham sounds a bit Zwinglian when he says that the "principall end" of the Eucharist is the "remembrance of the death of Christ," the overall tendency of his sacramental theology is Calvinian, for ultimately he regards the Supper as more than a memorial meal. "The bodie of Christ represented by the Bread," he writes, "must have that effect in the soule, which bread hath in the bodie." What is gained is "spirituall strength for newnesse of life." The sacrament is a means of union with Christ, and "to a true receiver Christ is really given" in the elements. Similar to Calvin's emphasis on the Spirit lifting the believer into heaven for a sacramental union with Christ, Greenham writes that in the eating and drinking, believing participants become "as Eagles flying up to heaven" through the power of the Holy Spirit.[80]

---

[77] "A Treatise of examination," ibid., 187-8.
[78] "Of Sacraments," ibid., 788.
[79] Ibid.
[80] Ibid., 191-3.

## V

Although *discipline* is never omitted from the list in Greenham's frequent allusions to the means, he rarely pauses to expand on it. It is apparent, however, that his emphasis on discipline is closely tied to his doctrine of the church. Greenham speaks of this means exclusively in the context of the community of faith, never in terms of personal, individual, self-discipline. Personal responsibility is heavily emhasized in the over-all pursuit of godliness, but Greenham does not refer to this as "discipline." The term is used more formally and technically for the church's God-given, awesome responsibility to use the keys of the kingdom.

Because the Word of God ascribes such great dignity to the church, discipline must be faithfully exercised to maintain the church's purity. Greenham refers to the church as God's "peculiar people," and as "the Lords Jewel." Christ gave himself for the church and the angels of God are its servants. "The Church is the fulfilling of Christ, so that Christ is as it were maimed without it, and what can be said more of it?" Greenham does say more, much more, when he boldly states: "The Church is partaker even of God his owne nature."[81] But the church is also a very human institution, with faults and failings that must be curbed by the means of discipline.

If Greenham harbored any sympathy for presbyterianism, it remains well hidden in his comments about church discipline. The line of authority extends from Christ, through the apostles to whom he entrusted the keys of the kingdom, to the current "Ministers" of the church. There is no hint of a populist view of discipline through a shared lay-ministry. "The discipline which Christ hath instituted is committed to the Church," he writes, and is now carried out by the church's ministers: "the Lord hath committed into the hands of the Ministers the execution of life and of death." Their judgment is such that "they shall surely be condemned whom the Church bindeth." That the keys of the kingdom of heaven have been entrusted to human agents is for Greenham a miracle. "Behold, and heare a miracle, heaven placed under the earth: where as in all other things heaven is above earth...." He marvels that in creation God assigned to human beings the task of ruling the earth, and now, in redemption,

---

[81] "Of Discipline and Excommunication," ibid., 842.

has given them the rule of heaven as well. In a somewhat undisciplined comment, Greenham adds that this rule extends over the Angels, and even over God himself, "so that now God cannot loose them whom the Church hath bownd: so that although he doth many things without us, yet when we hath done this, he doth not otherwise."[82]

This awesome responsibility, Greenham observes, had fallen upon hard times in the dark days of Roman Catholicism, but the church is of such "high dignitie" that when human beings neglect the keys, the angels take over. Even the angels are the church's servants. The church is superior to the angels, for God has made the church "the bodie of his Sonne." Christ is the door to the kingdom, and "the keye of the dore hath he committed to his faithful Ministers."[83] Theirs is a daunting responsibility, for censure by the Church is "worse than five deaths," yet it is a duty not to be shirked.[84]

## VI

Although throughout his writings Greenham extols the creative, positive uses of *affliction* for Christian growth, it is nonetheless surprising to find it actually listed along with the others as one of the means of faith and godliness, for it seems to belong to a different order. The Word, sacraments, discipline—and even prayer to some extent—are more objective, institutional means, effected through the church. Affliction, on the other hand, is much more subjective, experiential, and personal in character. It is also different from the other means in that it is experienced more passively. Important as it is for Greenham, he comes short of suggesting that we should actively pursue affliction. In this case it is primarily a matter of properly and Christianly dealing with the miseries that inevitably accompany life in this sinful world.

The topic is introduced on the very first page of Greenham's *Workes*. "It is a most certaine thing in God's children," he writes, "that the more their afflictions grow, the more their faith groweth: the more Sathan striveth to draw them from God, the more they draw

---

[82] Ibid., 843-4.
[83] Ibid.
[84] Ibid., 842.

neer to God...."[85] His inclusion and explanation of affliction as one of the means of faith demonstrate the importance of the cross in Greenham's theology. Blessings and gifts from God will be and should be accompanied by "some crosse." The life of Christ, which featured cross-bearing, is the supreme model for a Christian. Christ's example teaches that "there is no readier way to obtaine life, than to offer ourselves unto death."[86] Wherever the Christian goes, "the Crosse would follow him, because that Christ would follow him...."[87] The believer, therefore, should not stumble because of affliction in his life, but rather should "profit by the grace" that comes with it.[88]

Greenham links affliction to God, for divine sovereignty is comprehensive. He does not, however, ascribe it to the cold, raw power of God, but presents it as a demonstration of his wisdom and mercy designed for the "preserving of his children." God sends "fire, theeves, and oppressions" to afflict his children, least they "should be too ranke, and grow into a surfet." Sinful pride sometimes requires that God "break them with some crosse, untill their harts be bruised."[89] At one point Greenham implies that affliction is a measure of last resort, employed when all else fails. When the other means seem ineffectual or insufficient, God provides "this last remedie" to bring about "his fatherly correction."[90] More frequently, however, affliction is presented as a completely normal state of affairs that every Christian must experience.

The ends and purposes of affliction in the Christian life are at least these six: to generate anger against sin; to win the sinner to repentance; to test whether he is open to correction; to prune the faith so that it flourishes even more; to separate the believer from wickedness; and to bring about greater conformity to Christ.[91] Afflictions make the Christian more amenable to God's instruction. When "reason and affections are tamed by miserie, calamitie, sicknes, and inward griefe, then we are very teachable."[92] Afflictions experienced by the non-Christian "reprobate," are punishments for

---

[85] "The first portion of grave Counsels," ibid., 1.
[86] "Of Humilitie," ibid., 271.
[87] "The first portion of grave Counsels," ibid., 4.
[88] Ibid., 2.
[89] Ibid., 34.
[90] "Meditations on the 119 Psalm," ibid., 604.
[91] "Of Affliction," ibid., 640.
[92] "A direction for the reading of the Scriptures," ibid., 175.

their sins—"here they suffer some, in hell they shall suffer all torments"[93] —but for the Christian, sufferings are "medicines against sinne."[94] They promote good works, for "wee are fuller of the exercise of weldoing in trouble than otherwise."[95]

Affliction sometimes comes in the form of personal, spiritual insecurity, which paradoxically can be spiritually productive. Consequently, Greenham, in spite of his reputation as the physician for troubled consciences, occasionally seems to advocate a measure of insecurity.[96] Sometimes, for example, the child of God upon hearing the promises of salvation will experience the "cold fear" of personal unworthiness. Such a person, says Greenham, "may hope well of himself."[97] In other words, feeling insecure because of personal unworthiness is a good sign. Christians must "suspect themselves, and think humbly of themselves" in order to trust fully in God.[98] Such insecurity is spiritually enriching, for it spurs the afflicted to greater spiritual effort. In order to gain personal peace and security, adversity and trouble must be experienced. Adversity is itself the route to freedom from adversity; affliction the pathway to eternal bliss. Summing up this Catch 22 logic, Greenham writes, "There is no greater miserie, than to bee without miserie; nor greater sorrow, than to be without sorrow."[99]

Greenham's most systematic and extended treatment of the doctrine of affliction appears in a separately published work entitled, *A Garden of Spiritual flowers*, co-authored by William Perkins, Richard Rogers, George Webb, and Greenham. Greenham's contribution was apparently a treatise entitled, "Afflictions the Lot and Portions of the Righteous: a Benefit to those to whom they be Sanctified."[100] Both personal experience and Scripture teach that the "dearest of Gods Children" often suffer affliction "with variety, extremity and continuance." The Bible is filled with examples of this—

---

[93] "Another or second portion of...grave Counsels," ibid., 45.
[94] "A short forme of catechising," ibid., 84. Cf., 334.
[95] "Meditations on the 119 Psalm," ibid., 555.
[96] It is important to note here, however, that Greenham distinguishes between the blessed assurance that comes as a gift from God to those with a confident but humble faith, and arrogant self-assurance which constitutes the vain "security" against which he warns.
[97] "Of Gods promises," ibid., 753.
[98] "Meditations on the 119 Psalm," ibid., 495.
[99] "Another or second portion of...grave Counsels," ibid., 46.
[100] *A Garden of Spiritual Flowers* (London, 1687) 16-54.

Jacob, Job, Solomon, Hezekiah—and the Psalmist declares that the troubles of the righteous are many. In the Scriptures, afflictions come in assorted varieties: wicked children were the burden of Noah, Abraham, Isaac, Eli, Samuel, and David; open contempt was suffered by Job, the father of all afflictees; imprisonment was the fate of many bibilical figures such as Joseph, Jeremiah, Peter, Paul, and Silas; shipwreck was experienced by the apostle Paul; the loss of a dear friend by David; and "inward fear and Horrour of Conscience" by Job, David, and Hezekiah. In all, Greenham proffers no less than seven pages of biblical examples of affliction![101]

The children of God do not experience affliction as punishment, however, for Christ fully bore the punishment for sin. Those who follow Christ suffer affliction as a means of sanctification. "Affliction is the Lords Pruning Knife," says Greenham, "wherewith he cutteth away from us all withering and unprofitable Branches" such as pride, carnal security, and seduction by the world. Affliction is given to "further our Conversion" and is a special means God uses to "make the Godly much better."[102] It stirs God's children to prayer, and weans them from love of this world. "We are in this World as in a Sea of Misery," he laments, "never out of one danger or other, yet such is our Folly, we love to be here still: what would we do if we had nothing to molest us?"[103] Afflictions "do fit and prepare us for the Kingdom of Heaven,"[104] for, as he says in another treatise, they lead to "more earnest contempt of this life" and "more hungrie longing for the life to come."[105] Greenham closes his treatise on affliction with a list of exercises for coping with adversity: self-examination, prayer, fasting, repentance, reading of the Word, and meditation on the future life.

## VII

Before the close of this chapter on Greenham's means of faith, one additional spiritual exercise he persistently advocates should be mentioned. It is *meditation*, which for Greenham is the basic

---

[101] Ibid., 19-25.
[102] Ibid., 35-8.
[103] Ibid., 41.
[104] Ibid., 42.
[105] "How to profit and examine our selves, when friends forsake us," *Workes*, 686.

devotional practice that should accompany all of the means. The historical roots of the meditative tradition lie in medieval spirituality, but it was a tradition carried forward in early English Protestantism through the likes of Thomas Becon, Edward Dering, and John Bradford.[106] It is to be distinguished from eastern meditation, which is more mystical and abstract. Western meditation calls for mental and spiritual reflection concretely focussed on the Word of God, the created world, the believer's relationship to God, salvation, God's providential care, material and spiritual blessings, and Christian conduct. Greenham defines meditation as "that exercise of the minde, whereby we calling to our remembrance that which we knowe, doe further debate of it, and applie it to our selves, that we might have some use of it in our practice."[107] He regards it as a requirement for the effectiveness of the various means. Meditation makes them all "more fruitfull," for it constitutes the "very life and strength of reading, hearing, prayer, and the sacraments, without which they are made weake and unprofitable unto us."[108] Meditation on the Word of God promotes practical obedience to God's will. It also aids the memory, for what is read becomes internalized by meditating on it. Since scholars of "most excellent wit" cannot attain to great learning without meditating on what they read, ordinary mortals who are "dull and blind" certainly need to meditate on spiritual things. Meditation is also important for personal application of the preached Word "because we are most privie to our owne estate." Greenham provides a list of rules for proper meditation including concentration on the Word, focussing on one thing at a time, deliberate avoidance of "all lets," prayer for the Spirit, and thankfulness to God.[109] Since it is meditation that gives life to the means, he recommends that we use the means "often" but meditation "continually."[110]

-----

[106] Chan calls meditation "utterly basic" to the puritan conception of the Christian life, and regards Greenham as important in the early development of a theory of meditation, "which recognizes its distinct role in the life of devotion." Simon Chan, *The Puritan Meditative Tradition*, 15, 38. Cf., Richard McCabe, *Joseph Hall: Study in Satire and Meditation* (Oxford: University Press, 1982) 146.

[107] "The first portion of grave Counsels," *Workes*, 22.

[108] "Meditations on the 119 Psalm," ibid., 459.

[109] "The first portion of grave Counsels," ibid., 22-4.

[110] "Meditations on the 119 Psalm," ibid., 459. See 659-62 for his "Meditation of Death."

In the Greenham corpus, the doctrine of means is very much in the foreground. Study of this doctrine reveals some of Greenham's basic theological convictions. His God was one who respects the created order and uses it to bring about his desired ends. Grace is not in conflict with nature; the spiritual world works in harmony with the created order; eternal verities are worked out in human history. In this process the divine institution of the church plays a significant role. The doctrine of means also implies confidence in the capabilities of redeemed humankind. Human activity counts; human choices are important; responses to God are meaningful. God is absolutely sovereign, but in his sovereignty he honors creation and history. Later puritans would fit the means of faith into the larger framework of the doctrine of the covenant, but before they did so, the basis for a cooperative theory of God's sovereignty and human responsibility had already been well established.

# 7

# THE MEANS OF THE MEANS

## I

The jewel in the crown of Richard Greenham's program for godliness was the Sabbath. It fit perfectly his vision for a godly people in a godly church in a godly nation, for to achieve this goal, the means had to be assiduously employed, especially the primary ones of Word, prayer and sacraments. Each Sunday, God's people were to gather together in public worship to read and hear his Word, to offer up prayers of thanksgiving, praise and petition, and to celebrate the sacrament. The godly were expected to devote some time to the Word and to prayer every day of the week, but the weekly payload came on the Sabbath, "the school day, the faire day, the market day, the feeding day of the soule." On that day, God's people "shall see how they may recover themselves from sinnes alreadie past, arme themselves against sin to come, grow in knowledge, increase in faith, and how much they shall be strengthened in the inner man."[1] The Sabbath was *The Means* of the means.

What Greenham regularly promoted in sermons, he embodied in practice. Fuller calls him "a strict observer of the Lord's day," and gives testimony to his nation-wide influence on Sabbath-keeping, calling Greenham a "great advancer thereof through the whole realm, by that treatise which he wrote of the Sabbath."[2] Greenham made a name for himself by "that treatise." "No book in that age made greater impression on people's practice," Fuller adds, in a grander assessment than Greenham would have made based on the more limited sample of his Dry Drayton parish. Had he written nothing else, "that treatise" would have been enough to ensure his place in

---

[1] "A Treatise of the Sabbath," *Workes*, 129.
[2] Thomas Fuller, *The Church History of Britain*, III, 148.

English puritan history, for Greenham is regarded, more than any other, as the pioneer of English Sabbatarianism.[3]

Twentieth century studies of "Puritan Sabbatarianism" make necessary a bit of nuancing at this point, for the appropriateness of that label has been called into question. Already in the 1930s, William Whitaker presented compelling evidence that there was a strong Sabbath tradition in England, dating back to the earliest years of the Reformation, probably antedating the puritans.[4] More recently, another scholar, after reviewing the evidence, has arrived at a more boldly stated conclusion, namely, that the so-called "Puritan Sabbath" at the end of the sixteenth century did not really exist, but was a misnomer cleverly concocted by anti-presbyterians in an attempt to prejudice official opinion against the puritans. Their "sabbatarian novelties" were just another example of their trouble-making tendencies in the church. First presbyterianism, then sabbatarianism, what next?[5]

The milder Whitaker thesis is closer to the truth. Early English Protestants like John Hooper, Hugh Latimer, Alexander Nowell, Thomas Becon and others did take the Sabbath very seriously as a special day of rest and worship. There is evidence that the Church of England from the beginning adopted a strong view of Sunday observance and that the nation enjoyed for several decades a peaceful consensus on the matter. But there is equally strong evidence that this consensus broke down in the 1580s, that heated debates about the meaning of the Sabbath took place, and that in the course of these debates, Richard Greenham and others refined and developed the meaning of the fourth commandment into a full-blown Sabbatarianism that went considerably beyond earlier teaching about Sunday.[6]

In these late-century developments, Richard Greenham was a pivotal figure. His "Treatise of the Sabbath," probably written around 1580, is presumed to be the first of legions of tracts that appeared

---

[3] John B. Marsden, *The History of the Early Puritans*, 240-1; DNB on Greenham.

[4] *Sunday in Tudor and Stuart Time* (London: Houghton, 1933).

[5] Kenneth Parker, *The English Sabbath: A Study of Doctrine and Discipline from the Reformation to the Civil War* (Cambridge: University Press, 1988) 1-7. Cf., John H. Primus, *Holy Time: Moderate Puritanism and the Sabbath* (Macon, GA.: Mercer University Press, 1989) 1-13.

[6] Primus, *Holy Time*, Part I, 17-99.

during the following half century, all of them touting Sabbath views that prompted lively controversy.[7] It is apparent from Greenham's treatise that he was in a fighting mood when he wrote it. Much of it is polemical in tone, with many pages devoted to answering the objections of unnamed opponents. His treatise, along with the Dedham debates on the Sabbath in the early 1580s,[8] evince the end of the peaceful consensus, and the beginning of some innovative developments in both the theology and practice of the Sabbath.

According to Henry Holland, Greenham's Sabbath treatise is the purest example of his writing, the least sullied by editors' hands.[9] In over-all quality it is outstanding, probably the best item that appears in his *Workes*. It is not only impressive in form, structure, and rhetoric, but also in thoroughness and sophistication of argument.[10] Although it probably began as a sermon or series of sermons—*Dearly beloved in the Lord*, Greenham intones in the opening words—it was later developed with care and erudition into a forty-three page treatise so efficiently packed with the sabbatarian essentials of doctrine and practice that it set the standard for the scores of studies to follow. Nicholas Bownd, who borrowed heavily from his step-father and made the dubious decision to expand on him, was much more prolix, ending up with two volumes on the fourth commandment, the first one 286 pages, the second a breathtaking 459.[11] Despite their length, there is little in Bownd's works that is not already present in embryo in Greenham's treatise.

---

[7] It was not published until 1599 when it appeared in the first edition of his *Workes*. Lancelot Andrewes's Pembroke lectures on the decalogue, including an extensive treatment of the fourth commandment, were delivered in the late 1570s but not published until 1630.Greenham probably heard these lectures—he and Andrewes were good friends—and borrowed from them. There are distinct similarities in the arguments. Cf., Lancelot Andrewes, *Pattern of Catechistical Doctrine* (Oxford: Parker, 1846), and Primus, *Holy Time*, 55-9.

[8] REM 874, fols. 237ff. Cf., Primus, *Holy Time*, ch. 2.

[9] In his Preface to the Reader, after citing difficulties in gathering materials, Holland says, "In that one treatise of the Sabbath I found his owne hand...." The treatise is on pages 128-71. The *Workes* include also a shorter, three-page treatise "Of the Sabbath," 809-12.

[10] Its exceptional quality may be due, in part, to the "help" he received from Andrewes.See n. 7 above.

[11] *The Doctrine of the Sabbath* (London, 1595), and *Sabbathum Veteris* (London, 1606).

## II

The biblical materials in "A Treatise of the Sabbath" are particularly noteworthy. Of all the works of Greenham, this treatise provides the best clues regarding his use of Scripture. Nearly half of the document is devoted to the refutation of arguments advanced by those whom he cryptically refers to as "some men," who have invented "such reasons" that "prejudice the trueth" of the Sabbath. These "reasons against the Sabbath" are all falsely based on Scripture. With painstaking detail Greenham examines and interprets (and reinterprets) every biblical passage used by the opposition against his views on the Sabbath, especially against his convictions regarding a moral and perpetual Sabbath. The many quotations from Scripture, although not always letter perfect, indicate his use of the Geneva Bible.

From the Old Testament he deals at length with Exodus 31:13-17, and Isaiah 56:1,2; 58:13,14; 66: 23. From the New—Matthew 11:1-8, Mark 2:27, Romans 14:1-6, Galatians 4:10, Colossians 2:16, and Hebrews 4:3-11. In the interpretation of these passages, Greenham makes reference to dozens of additional verses to reinforce his argument. Throughout, the unity of Scripture is implied, with virtually equal deference given to the Old and New Testaments. The rule of Old Testament fulfillment in Christ, however, is explicitly employed in his distinction between the ceremonial and moral aspects of law. He appeals to a "general rule" by which to determine which "figures and ceremonies end in Christ, and what morall precepts belong to us."

> When a thing is urged to the Jewes: and hath a peculiar reason made properly to the Jewe, and appertaineth nothing to the Christian; then as it begunne with the Jewes, as they were Jewes, it ceased with the Jewes: but when the reason of the thing urged is not peculiar to the Jewes, but also belongeth to the Christians; then the  thing  commanded  is not proper to the Jew, but common to the Jew and Gentile. Wherefore let us square out the reason by the line of this generall rule.[12]

---

[12] Ibid., 138.

Greenham's interpretive method is literal/historical without a hint of an allegorical approach. At several points, in explicit references to rules of interpretation, he reveals allegiance to a self-conscious hermeneutical method. In an argument against the notion that a separate weekly Sabbath is an Old Testament ceremony foreshadowing a New Testament understanding of the whole of life as one continual Sabbath, Greenham includes an admonition to deal with Scripture contextually. The absurdity of the opposition will be readily apparent, he says, "if we consider diligently what goeth before, & what commeth after: which rule is worthilie to be followed in sifting out the true sense of the places in the Scriptures."[13]

The principle of biblical accomodation to human understanding is employed when Greenham reflects on the nature of God's rest after the six days of creation. "Neither would I have any to thinke," he writes, "that the Lord had neede of any refreshing, who being infinite, cannot be subject to distractions or wearines: but we must know, that where the Lord is said, that he refreshed himselfe, by taking view of his creatures, he commendeth his love to usward, in shewing rather what ought to be in us, than what was in him."[14]  In the same context, Greenham alludes to the "plaine sense" of the passage.

On another occasion, Greenham brings extra-biblical sources to bear on the text. Commenting on Romans 14:2, *"One beleeveth that hee may eate of all things: and another which is weake, eateth herbes,"* Greenham notes that some think the reference to the "weak" who eat herbs is an allusion to Jews in Rome. "But this seemeth not to be a sound opinion, in that we reade not in any Ecclesiasticall historie, that the Jewes were at Rome....Againe, we cannot gather out of the records of the writers, that the Jewes did eate herbes alone."[15]

In his treatment of Galatians 4:10, Greenham again displays some hermeneutical sophistication when he warns "that we must not stand upon the titles of letters, but observe the scope of the writer and weigh the drift of the epistle." He proceeds to set the letter in its historical context, describing the Galatian problem with Judaizers

---

[13] Ibid., 142.
[14] Ibid., 138.
[15] Ibid., 149.

who upset the gentile Christians with their demands that the "same civill policie of religion should be there, which was among the Jews," and who "went about to intermingle the superstitions of Judaisme."[16] Finally, in a discussion of the meaning of the Sabbath references in Hebrews 4, Greenham appeals to yet another interpretive principle.

> There is a generall rule in Divinite to be observed, *that of one place of Scripture there is but one naturall and proper sense: although by consequence, searching out the contraries, the causes, the effects, and such like, other things may be also gathered out of it.* If the words be more proper and naturall, the sense is more proper and naturall: if the words be borrowed and metaphoricall, then is the sense borrowed and metaphoricall.[17]

He then makes reference to biblical "allusions" which are to be read not as proofs and confirmation of the matter, but "for the amplifying and illustrations of the same."[18]

The nineteen pages of biblical study in his Sabbath treatise are a testimony to Greenham's considerable hermeneutical skills, to an astonishing knowledge of both the scope and detail of Scripture, and to hours and hours, if not days and weeks, of laborious biblical study and cross referencing done at a time long before the availability of work-saving, modern reference tools.

## III

"A Treatise of the Sabbath" begins on a familiar note with references to the two enemies on the right and the left: papism and familism. The papists, he charges, "make the Sabbath day but an ordinance, and ceremonie of the Church" not unlike other ceremonies and holy days; the familists, "thinking it to containe nothing morall, crie out against it, as willing to have it wholie abrograted, seeing all ceremonies have had their end in Christ."[19] Fie on both, says Greenham, for the Sabbath is nothing less than a holy

---

[16] Ibid., 151.
[17] Ibid., 153-4.
[18] Ibid., 154.
[19] Ibid.

institution established by God himself, and of absolute importance to the Christian faith. Such is the argument of the entire treatise, which Greenham proceeds to divide into two basic parts, each of these in turn, in good Ramist fashion, infinitely subdivided into scores of additional twosomes. The two main parts, however, may be labelled "doctrine" and "observance." Since doctrine informs the judgment, it must precede the exhortation to practice; "for want of this order," he says,"many excellent Sermons have little effect."[20]

The distinguishing characteristics of Greenham's view of the Sabbath are four in number. They are not necessarily brand new and innovative, but Greenham elaborates on them in much more detail than ever before in English Reformation literature. They are, first, the explicit elevation of the fourth commandment above all the others in the decalogue; second, an unambiguous affirmation of the creational and therefore moral character of the fourth commandment; third, a bold declaration of a divinely authoritative transfer of the Sabbath from the seventh to the first day of the week; and fourth, a passionate insistence on scrupulous observance of the Sabbath commandment. These are the defining features of Puritan Sabbatarianism.[21] In subsequent puritan Sabbath treatises, all four features appear with monotonous regularity.

## IV

Without intending to diminish the importance of the other nine, Greenham elevates the fourth commandment to a special position of strategic significance in the decalogue. A small hint of what is to come appears already in the opening sentence of the treatise, in which he claims that "there is no commandement of Gods part more urged, and of our parts less observed," than this Sabbath command. He continues, more boldly, to assert that the keeping of the Sabbath is the key commandment, for "in the booke of God, when the Lord will urge the observation of the whole law, he often doth it under this one word of *keeping the Sabbath.*"[22] The fourth commandment is strategically positioned between the two tables of the law precisely

[20] Ibid., 130.
[21] For more on definition, see Primus, *Holy Time*, 8ff.
[22] Ibid., 129.

because its purposes extend in both directions. These purposes are the pure worship of God and the true love of neighbor. It is significant that, from the outset, the puritan Sabbath had strong ethical, as well as theological, implications. Faithful sabbath-keeping contributes enormously to Christian fulfillment of these two fundamental obligations. It is, says Greenham, "the schoole of all the other commaundements."[23]

There is additional evidence for the special character and uniqueness of the fourth commandment. It is stated in both affirmative ("remember") and negative ("thou shalt not") terms whereas all the others are expressed in either one or the other. The length of the commandment is also remarkable, its only competitor in this category being the second, on graven images. These two receive the most explanation in the decalogue because obedient observance of them requires more conscious, deliberate effort. The shorter, more "naked" commandments, says Greenham, surprisingly sanguine about human nature, are more naturally and instinctively obeyed.[24] The use of the word "remember" also makes the fourth commandment unique among the ten. Greenham dwells on the signficance of this word at some length.[25] It leads him to one of the more distinctive assertions of late sixteenth century sabbatarians, namely, the insistence that the fourth commandment was given "in expresse words" to Adam and Eve in Paradise.[26] This surprising claim was also made by William Perkins, and most emphatically by Nicholas Bownd, who appeals to a passage in the writings of the Heidelberg theologian, Jerome Zanchius, for support. Perhaps Greenham read Zanchius also, but there is no explicit reference to him in the text or margins.

## V

The claim that God gave the Sabbath commandment in express words to the parents of the human race is closely related to the second mark of sabbatarianism: the creational, and therefore moral, character of the fourth commandment. Since it was supra- rather than

---

[23] Ibid., 132.
[24] Ibid., 130.
[25] Ibid., 131 ff.
[26] Ibid., 131, 154.

infra-lapsarian, given in the garden rather than later in the wilderness, the Sabbath partakes of the very nature of perfectly created reality. It is embedded in the universe as God made it and in human life as God intended it. The commandment, therefore, has perpetual and universal scope. It "was given not onely to the posteritie of Abraham, but the whole posteritie of Adam"; therefore, it is a commandment not only for the Jews, but for the entire human race.[27] He grants that there is a ceremonial aspect to it that has been fulfilled by the coming of Christ, but it is more substantially, at its core, moral in character. Greenham defines what he means by "moral" and "ceremonial" in this discussion, albeit somewhat vaguely: "That I call morall, which doth informe mens manners either concerning their religion to God, or their duties unto man: that I meane figurative, which is added for a time in some respect to some persons for an help to that which is morall...."[28] He then alludes to Deuteronomy 5, anticipating the argument that the redemption (rather than creation) setting of the fourth commandment (remember that you were slaves in Egypt, etc.) might be used as an argument against its creational-moral character. Greenham argues that the Deuteronomic words, "Remember that thou wast a servant in the land of Egypt," were simply a figurative, temporary aid toward the end of obedience to a basically moral law. The Jews had a special cause for worshipping God because of their deliverance from Egypt. This was "a reason why they did keepe the Sabboth," but not the only, nor even the basic, reason for doing so. Moreover, the Deuteronomy passage does not entail that the Sabbath was for the Jews only, since the Exodus 20 account clearly roots the obligation in creation.[29]

In his discussion of the moral character of the fourth commandment, the menace of the Family of Love again looms large in Greenham's thought. Very early in the treatise he criticizes this sect for abandoning the Sabbath because of their ceremonial interpretation of the fourth commandment. In reaction to the incipient gnosticism of the familists, Greenham is even more naturally inclined to move toward a stronger creational view of the Sabbath.

The main argument for the moral nature of the fourth

---

[27] Ibid., 133.
[28] Ibid., 132.
[29] Ibid., 133.

commandment is one of timing, i.e., *when* the commandment was first given. As already noted, Greenham emphasizes that it was given by God in paradise, before the fall. It is, therefore, a creation ordinance that comes with at least as much fundamental moral authority as the other commandments, none of which appear to be as explicitly present in the creation story. In humanity's pre-lapsarian condition, the Sabbath was intended as a means to keep paradise free from sin.

> Our first father then had a Sabbath to be put in minde of the Creator, and that without distraction he might the better be put in minde of the glorious kingdome to come, that more freely he might give himselfe to meditation, and that he might the better glorifie God in six daies.[30]

The argument is obvious. If Adam needed the Sabbath "in innocencie," surely it is even more necessary now to use the Sabbath "to recover us, and to continue us in our recoverie."[31]

Long before the law was given at Sinai, "this, and all the other commaundements were written in the harts for our forefathers."[32] Such laws are not abrogated or annulled by the coming of Christ. He came to remove the "curse of the Lawe" and to fulfill the ceremonial law, but the moral law remains fully in force.[33] Greenham makes an interesting distinction among the commandments in terms of "natural law." Nature and "the light of reason" lead most people to believe in God, to honor parents, to protect life and property, and to abhor adultery. Other commandments, however, including the fourth, do not come naturally, but "fight against the reason of man." To believe in God is one thing; how to worship him quite another. "But if yee aske how this God is to be worshipped, and what times wee must sanctifie to that use: we shall see how many Countreys, so many religions: how many men, so many devises."[34]

Greenham's Sabbath doctrine differs somewhat from that of John Calvin, who not only called for a weekly day of worship, but especially

---

[30] Ibid., 137.
[31] Ibid.
[32] Ibid., 131.
[33] Ibid., 133.
[34] Ibid., 131.

emphasized the Sabbath as a sign of the eternal rest from sin. That the Sabbath is primarily a sign of spiritual rest, "as some have phantasticallie thought," borders on heresy in Greenham's view.[35] His extensive treatment of relevant biblical passages includes some comments about Hebrews 4, where the author speaks of an eternal Sabbath in which the children of God enter into God's rest. Greenham questions, however, whether this eternal Sabbath in any way diminishes the need for the weekly Sabbath. The imitation of God enjoined in Hebrews by entering into his rest can surely not be a resting from sin, for God does not rest from sin on his Sabbath day. When Adam was called to share in God's Sabbath, it was not for him a resting from sin either, for sin had not yet entered the world. Therefore, Greenham argues, the Sabbath is not primarily a resting from sin. Hebrews 4 is simply a picture of the Kingdom of Heaven given in terms of an eternal Sabbath. Greenham seems primarily concerned that the eternal rest not exclude the weekly Sabbath. He too believes that there will one day be an eternal rest from "our ordinarie callings," and, indeed, an eternal rest from sin. In the meantime, the godly must observe a weekly rest from their callings. Since these callings are subject to much corruption, resting from them will also involve withdrawing from sin, "which kind of rest in fulnes we must not looke for in this life."[36]

There is one additional creational/moral element built into the structure of the fourth commandment according to Greenham. It is the rule of equity. This "rule" is already suggested in Eve's conversation with the serpent in the garden, when reference is made to all of the trees in the garden given graciously by God for human use, save one: the special tree of which Adam and Eve are not to eat. Likewise, God has given seven days in the week, all of which are to be used for daily callings except one which is to be devoted solely to God's worship. This rule of justice should inspire obedience, says Greenham. If God provides six days for human vocation, it seems eminently fair that humans dedicate one to divine worship. Greenham is careful about making too sharp a distinction between the day of worship and the days of vocation. The Lord "granteth us six dayes for our bodies, and the seventh day for our soules: not that we must

---

[35] Ibid., 134.
[36] Ibid., 153.

thinke, that other dayes are to be separated from this use, but that this day must be wholly severed from other for that use."[37] Although the Sabbath is to be dedicated entirely to the worship of God, the six days should include "seasons" of worship also. Private worship and devotion require daily exercise. Even public worship is appropriate any day of the week, as Greenham's own version of "early mass"—four sunrise sermons per week—attests. This week-day worship must be so scheduled that it not interfere with "our lawfull and necessarie callings."[38] Greenham does not, however, speak of worship *within* those "ordinarie callings," or of the sanctification of vocations through worship.[39] Worship and daily vocations are in this sense separated from one another.

Greenham calls the fourth commandment's reference to six days of labor, "the permission" of the six days. Here he differs from his colleague, William Perkins, who regarded this reference as a commandment to labor for six days. Greenham turns this discussion into another argument for the perpetual, moral character of the fourth commandment. "Now if the permission of the sixe daies appertaine to us, is not the sanctifying of the Sabboth day also commanded to us?" In other words, if the reference to six days of labor is applicable for all times, then so also is the reference to the Sabbath. If the commandment were ceremonial, so would be the permission. If the permission is moral and perpetual, so is the commandment.[40]

Another argument for the moral nature of the fourth commandment is drawn from the "law-giver" and owner of the day. Since it is the "Sabboth of the Lord thy God," it is morally incumbent on humankind to dedicate it wholly to the Lord. The Bible explicitly speaks of ten commandments; "not the Church, but the word of God setteth down this computation." If the fourth commandment were merely ceremonial, "then it would follow that there were but nine commandments."[41] This oblique reference to the church's authority in distinction from the Bible's authority is

---

[37] Ibid., 134.
[38] Ibid., 135.
[39] The only exception in the entire treatise is in his later discussion of Sabbath observance. At one point he says that "as our callings serve to Gods worship, so Gods worship sanctifieth our callings," ibid., 163.
[40] Ibid., 135.
[41] Ibid.

significant, for it hints at possible trouble brewing between puritan pastors and the establishment over the Sabbath. The controversy would eventually focus on the question of authority, precisely the same issue that had lurked beneath the surface in the earlier vestments controversy, and subsequently became the key element in the presbyterian debates. Is the institution of the Sabbath in the contemporary church primarily a matter of the church's prerogative, or is it settled and binding by the Word of the Lord as revealed in Scripture? This would become an especially pivotal question in the debates about the specific day designated for worship.

## VI

The alteration of the day, from seventh to first, is the third distinguishing mark of Greenham's Sabbath theology. This, in fact, is the most important element in the definition of puritan Sabbatarianism.. The Church of England took the fourth commandment seriously from the earliest days of the Reformation. In both official and unofficial pronouncements regarding observance of a weekly day of worship, it is evident that the Church regarded the Sabbath commandment as having at least some ongoing moral significance. But what about the particular day for worship? The fourth commandment explicitly mentions the "seventh day," i.e., Saturday in the Jewish week. It connects the six and one pattern of human work and rest to God's work and rest in Genesis 1. Since his case for the moral character of the fourth commandment is grounded in the creational institution of the Sabbath, it appears that Greenham may have trapped himself in a biblical argument that would allow only for a perpetual Saturday Sabbath.

He addresses the issue boldly, but at first with traces of flexibility in his position, declaring that "it was never commanded nor appointed what one certaine day should be kept among seven, but that there should be observed a seventh day: which being kept, it is sufficient and the law remaineth unviolated."[42] From this statement it appears that any day will do, but such is hardly the case. Greenham is only establishing distance from any interpretation of the Old Testament commandment that would imply the establishment of the *seventh*

---

[42] "A Treatise of the Sabbath," *Workes*, 155.

*day* (Saturday) as the divinely authorized day of worship to be observed perpetually and universally. He is also distinguishing *a* seventh day from *the* seventh day. After this initial move, he articulates the principle of divinely authoritative apostolic example as the basis for the establishment of the first day and none other as the God-appointed day of worship. "And yet wee permit not, that any man at his pleasure should now change this day. For that which the Apostles did, they did not as private men, but as men guided by the spirit of God, they did it for the avoyding of superstition, wherewith the Jewes had infected it."[43]

The Apostles shifted worship from the seventh to the first day of the week primarily because the first was the day of Christ's resurrection. Greenham points out that there are additional reasons for the appropriateness of the change, namely, that the first day of the week was the first day of the creation of the world and later was the day divinely selected for Pentecost, when the Holy Spirit was poured out upon the church. Greenham concludes, therefore, that the alteration of the Sabbath from Saturday to Sunday is grounded upon nothing less than the supreme authority of the Triune God: "this day doth fitly put us in minde of our creation to be thankfull to God the Father, of our redemption to bee thankfull to God the Sonne, and of our sanctification to bee thankfull to God the holy Ghost." With this bold appeal to the Holy Trinity, Greenham clinches his argument for the transition of the Sabbath from the seventh to the first day of the week.[44] Elsewhere in his *Workes*, Greenham leaves no doubt that he had adopted an absolutist position on the crucial question of diurnal alteration. "That it should be changed once, it was meet, but never to be changed again: for as then the day of rest for the creation was most fit: so now the day of our redemption is most fit, seeing now the world is as if it were made new, and therefore cannot be changed."[45]

Greenham thereby took the step, which, more than any other, shattered the Church of England's consensus on the Sabbath. By whose authority the day of worship was established was also one of the most hotly disputed questions in the Dedham debates in the early 1580s.[46] It was the doctrine of alteration that especially provoked the

---

[43] Ibid., 155-6.
[44] Ibid., 156.
[45] "Of the Sabbath," ibid., 811.
[46] REM 874, fols. 237r-244r. Cf., Primus, *Holy Time*, 41-53.

vigorous anti-sabbatarian reaction in the 1590s and subsequently comprised the single most critical difference between the sabbatarians and anti-sabbatarians.[47] Sunday absolutism became sabbatarianism's key defining feature, for it affirmed the explicit transfer of the Old Testament Sabbath to Sunday, the first day of the week. Sunday became heir of the Old Testament Sabbath.

Underlying the disagreement was the troublesome issue of authority. The sabbatarians insisted that the Sunday-Sabbath had been established by biblical, apostolic authority; the anti-sabbatarians argued that the day is a matter of indifference, and that the Church, simply in the interest of good order, had designated Sunday as the Christian day of worship. This entailed that it was in the power of the Church to designate any other day as equally appropriate should practical considerations lead it to do so. It was a debate redolent of the earlier vestments disputes and of the battles over presbyterianism, for in these too, the authority and liberty of the Church was called into question. Each of the three—vestments, presbyterianism and sabbatarianism—in its own way presented a challenge to the Church's authority. Each raised similar questions relating to the view and use of Scripture, the definition of adiaphora, and the meaning of Christian freedom. And because they all represented challenges to the established order, each contributed to the national mood that led eventually to civil war.

Especially in the context of the concurrent battle over church government, the alteration question became extremely sensitive and potentially explosive.[48] Sunday absolutism was regarded by the establishment as another presbyterian attempt to nibble away at the Church's authority. Although materially presbyterianism and sabbatarianism were entirely different issues, on the formal question of the Church's authority, there was considerable overlap. William Perkins recognized the supreme importance of the issue when he identified as the "first and most principal question" pertaining to the Sabbath: "Whether it be in the liberty of the Church of God upon earth, to alter the Sabbath day from the seaventh day, to any

---

[47] Primus, *Holy Time*, 91ff.
[48] The "Admonition Controversy" starring Thomas Cartwright and John Whitgift took place in the 1570s; the "classis movement" in the 1580s. The scurrilous Martin Marprelate tracts appeared in 1588.

other?"[49]

Greenham was one of the first to articulate this most distinctive characteristic of puritan sabbatarianism. Whether he recognized the church government implications or not, he opened the way for others to make even stronger and more radical claims about the divinely established day of worship, for example, in the lengthy arguments of his step-son, Nicholas Bownd.

## VII

The fourth and final special feature of Greenham's treatise on the Sabbath is its extensive elaboration on how the day should be observed. He was not the first to address the issue of observance, but probably the first to do so at such length and in such detail. Greenham paved the way for the cataloging of Sabbath dos and don'ts that in his successors seems virtually without end. He began the process of sabbatarian codification that became so familiar in the subsequent decades.

The key to Greenham's lengthy recommendations for Sabbath practice can be stated in one word: *sanctification*. The unwavering focus of Greenham's discussion of observance is on the Sabbath as *The Means* of the sanctifying means. The Sabbath is to be observed first by "using the exercises of religion, whereby we may be sanctified," second, by using prayer, conference, reflection, meditation, etc., "whereby we may be furthered in our sanctification," and third, by engaging in "the exercises of love, wherby we may shew that wee are sanctified."[50] Conscientious observance is not to be regarded as an Old Testament, ceremonial obligation, but as an aspect of the moral, perpetual character of the commandment, "as needful for us as for the Jewes." The continuing purpose of the Sabbath is defined and tested by Christ's summary of the law: "Hereby is insinuated unto us, that in this day wee should grow in love towards God, and tender affection to our brethren." With such growth comes assurance that the Sabbath is kept aright.[51]

The two main demands of the Sabbath are rest and worship.

---

[49] *Workes*, vol. II, 105. His answer was an unequivocal "No." A lengthy discussion follows, 105-7.
[50] "A Treatise of the Sabbath," ibid., 132.
[51] Ibid., 156.

Greenham's discussion of Sabbath rest is particularly interesting, for he advocates not an inactive rest, but one that is devoted to service leading to further sanctification. It is the opposite of indolence, for "by bathing our bodies in our beds on that day more than on any other," we use the day selfishly for our rest rather than spiritually for the Lord's rest.[52] The work of "ordinarie callings" must cease on the Sabbath, but only in order to provide time for another kind of work: worship, spiritual improvement, increased godliness, and loving service to others. In Greenham's vision for a proper Sabbath, the day is filled with socio-religious enterprise. It should be a day of almost feverish activity, some of it mental and reflective to be sure, but without a moment of idleness. Again, God himself is the model, for although he ceased from the work of creation on the seventh day, "the workes of God his providence" have to be done every day. Since human beings are the instrumental means of carrying out God's providence, the Sabbath is not only a day of worship, but also a special day in which God, through his obedient people, provides for the sick and needy. Literal, physical rest is not the primary intent of the Sabbath; it should be used to provide for the spiritual and physical needs of humankind. This, says Greenham, is the meaning of Mark 2:7, that "the Sabbath was made for man and not man for the Sabbath." The text supports his functional view of Sabbath rest, for it suggests that "the Sabbath, that is, the rest, was made for mans good and comfort, and not man for the rest alone, but for the sanctifying of the Sabbath." This emphasis protects Greenham from rigid legalism in the exercise of Sabbath rest. He defines a Sabbath day's journey, for example, as "that distance, as a man conveniently may travaile for some holie purpose, without any hinderance of the ordinarie exercise of that day, and without wearisomnes either to bodie or minde, whereby he should be the unfitter for the Lords worship, or his duties."[53]

Greenham displays some flexibility about physical labor on the Sabbath, but advises caution about appeal to the loophole of "necessary work." The "milking of kine, making of beds, and dressing of meates" must be done, but, if possible, "done either early in the morning, or lately in the evening," so as not to interfere with

---

[52] Ibid., 158.
[53] Ibid., 143.

worship.[54] In a lengthy paragraph about mariners who are at sea with shipboard obligations on the Sabbath, he recommends that, if possible, one day in seven, even if it is not the first day of the week, should be set aside for worship. For in such instances, "the Lord accepteth the equitie of the law when upon necessitie we cannot observe the prescript time of the law."[55] The work of the "posts"[56] is addressed similarly. If on the Sabbath they "goe on the necessarie affaires of the land," and "speedie dispatching" would be "more profitable" to the realm, "libertie is permitted" proportionate to the "gravitie and slendernes of their affairs," but again, if the work is not truly necessary, "the rule of God his lawes take hold on them." The responsibility to make this judgment belongs to the Prince, "because Princes matters are not knowne to all men."

Greenham points out to his rural parishioners that harvesting on the Sabbath, even when it appears needful, should be resisted. Harvest time is precisely when God's bountiful blessings are most obvious, so farmers should, especially then, take a day each week to give him thanks. In that busy season, moreover, servants and their work animals need a regular day of physical rest.[57] Regarding saffron, produced in such abundance in East Anglia in the sixteenth century, it may sometimes "by the law of necessitie" be harvested on the Sabbath lest it perish if it remain ungathered.[58]

Although Greenham's emphasis in Sabbath observance is on its immediate sanctifying function and purpose, the eschatological implications are not wholly absent from his discussion. The Sabbath is an emblem of eternal rest according to Hebrews 4. Even for Adam before the fall, the Sabbath was a reminder of the Kingdom of God. The Sabbath continues to be a "resemblance of a thing not past, but to come." It calls for rest "from the worke of our callings, and consequently from the works of sin much more." But with the ever-present threat of the perfectionist Family of Love in mind, he adds that the Sabbath does not mean that "here we have our heaven." Although "resting from sinne is also enjoyned to the Christians as a pure use of the Sabboth," this does not negate the need for a weekly

---

[54] Ibid., 164.
[55] Ibid.
[56] Originally, those who delivered the king's mail. See OED.
[57] Ibid., 165-6.
[58] Ibid., 167.

Sabbath of rest from daily work for the purpose of worship and service.[59]

Although in Greenham's view of Sabbath observance, corporate worship is of critical importance, he spends relatively few pages discussing its various details. Early in the treatise, he states that the Sabbath is "sanctified," when "the meanes which hee hath appointed for his worship" are used.[60] Later, he briefly discusses these means, namely, "the word read and preached: then prayers fervently made with thanksgiving, singing of Psalmes, reverend administration of the Sacraments." At least twice a Sunday, the godly should gather to hear the Word of God. Various Old and New Testament passages are referenced in support of the centrality of the Word in the public service, as well as of the need for prayer and song.[61] As for the Sacraments, Greenham notes that in the apostolic church the Lord's Supper was administered every Sunday, but adds somewhat cryptically, "now adaies the ministers may not so doe, for the great ignorance & carnall securitie of people." With regard to baptism, Greenham raises the issue of public vs. private baptisms. Although the Scriptures do not explicitly state that this sacrament was administered on the Sabbath, "yet there are many good reasons" for doing so. "First, we know Circumcision was used on that day, & therefore Baptisme which is come into the place of Circumcision, is to be used on the Sabbath day." Furthermore, "Baptisme is a publike action of faith," by which members are received into the Church; therefore, the prayers of the congregation should be included, and the people in general should use the opportunity of public baptisms to recall for themselves the benefits of this sacrament.[62]

Following these few liturgical guidelines, Greenham devotes five pages to a lengthy discussion of "private exercises on the Sabbath" to be used before, between, and after the corporate services for the purpose of enhancing the meaningfulness and effectiveness of public worship.[63] He thereby contributed substantially to the puritan domestication of worship. Although preparation for worship is a home exercise, done privately in the context of the family, Greenham

---

[59] Ibid., 153.
[60] Ibid., 132.
[61] Ibid., 156.
[62] Ibid., 157.
[63] Ibid., 157-62.

deals with it at much greater length and detail than he does public worship, emphasizing it so heavily that it almost takes on a life of its own and becomes a ritualized part of Sabbath observance. A number of rules for preparation are formulated, beginning with the "stirring up of our selves" by a process of careful self-examination. Greenham notes that "at least once in the weeke" Dry Drayton farmers "search their bookes, cast their accounts, conferre with their gaine their expenses, and make even reckonings, whereby they may see whether they have gained, or whether they have lost." Such weekly accounting, he argues, is even more necessary in the spiritual realm in order to measure "how wee have gone forwarde in godly proceedings, or how wee have gone backward, that if we have holy increases, we may give thankes and glorie to God; if we come short, we must humble ourselves, and endevour the weeke following, to travaile with our selves the more earnestly to recover our former losse."[64] Following this spiritual inventory, additional preparation by means of reading, meditating, and praying is required. For Greenham, these private exercises actually take priority over the public, for they lay the groundwork for successful public worship.

> For what is the cause why in the prayers of the Church wee so little profit? what causeth the word to be of so small power with us? whereof commeth it that the Sacraments are of such slender account with us? Is it not because we draw neere to the Lord with uncatechised hearts, and uncircumcised eares, without prepared affections and unschooled senses: so that we come unto, and depart from the house of God with no more profit, than we get at stage plaies, where delighting our eyes and eares for a while with the view of the pageants, afterward we vainely depart?[65]

Although not emphasized with as much passion as the preparatory steps for worship, various applicatory techniques are encouraged for use between and after the public services so that the proclaimed Word may have its full effect. The soul must be thoroughly steeped by the Word through "reading, comparing of things heard, examining

---

[64] Ibid., 157.
[65] Ibid., 157-8.

and applying them to our selves, praying, thankesgiving, and meditating." Sabbath meditation is not soul-gazing introspection, but thoughtful, disciplined reflection on the spiritual and physical blessings of God. It is not focussed inwardly but outwardly, and includes the whole creation. Just as the sacraments are visible means to strengthen faith, so creation itself is a visible reminder of the creator God. Before the fall, Adam, "by the light of nature," beheld the created world and glorified the God who made it; now, "by the light of Gods grace and holy spirit," the godly may again perceive the Creator through meditation on his creation. Greenham avoids a gnostic Sabbath-spirituality by means of this emphasis on the physical, created world.[66]

There is another sense in which Greenham's private Sabbath exercises are directed outwardly: they include deeds of love and mercy toward others. The Sabbath is to be used not only for "hearing the word by preaching, but also of doing the word by practising." These exercises must to be devoted to both spiritual and physical need, and include teaching, admonishing, comforting, stirring up "them which be dul" in spirit, confirming and encouraging their faith. The Christian should respond to physical need every day of the week, but especially on the Sabbath, by visiting the sick and imprisoned, and "bestowing of our goods on them that are needie."[67] Greenham thereby contributed an admirable ethical dimension to the puritan Sabbath often ignored by its critics, yet consistently included in the multitude of Sabbath treatises published during the following fifty years.

## VIII

In Greenham's Sabbath treatise, three theological motifs emerge which may be regarded as central features of puritan thought—creation, resurrection, and sanctification—a trio of activities in which respectively, Father, Son, and Holy Spirit are at work. Greenham's Sabbath theology is grounded in and shaped by his doctrine of the triune God who ordained the Sabbath. In this important respect also, Greenham paved the way for all subsequent sabbatarians. The motifs

---

[66] Ibid., 159.
[67] Ibid., 160-1.

of creation, resurrection, and sanctification were consistently used in most of the Sabbath treatises to provide answers to the three most hotly disputed aspects of sabbatarianism: the institution, alteration, and celebration of the Sabbath.[68]

In his discussion about the moral and ceremonial aspects of the Sabbath, the doctrine of creation assumes a critical role. Central to Greenham's argument for the essentially moral and perpetual character of the fourth commandment is the creational establishment of the Sabbath. Deuteronomy 5 notwithstanding, the Sabbatarians held that the fourth commandment is not primarily a redemptive ordinance. It is pre-lapsarian, founded at Creation, etched indelibly on the human heart as certainly as all other moral laws, observed by the patriarchs before the time of Moses, and simply given written form at Sinai because of the sinfulness and weakness of mankind. Not only is the Sabbath commandment engraved in the heart; Greenham claims it was "in expresse words injoyned unto Adam and Eve in Paradise."[69] Step-son Nicholas Bownd elaborated on this claim, and even William Perkins argued that the Sabbath ordinance was one of only two commandments expressly articulated by the Creator to Adam and Eve in the garden.[70]

Beginning with Greenham, every Sabbath treatise focussed on the Exodus 20 rendering of the decalogue, rather than on the Deuteronomy 5 version. The redemptive emphasis in Deuteronomy, where the Sabbath is tied to the deliverance from Egypt, is only briefly mentioned by Greenham, and interpreted as an additional feature that became necessary after the fall, as a "helpe to that which is morall."[71] For Greenham and his fellow sabbatarians, the central meaning of the Sabbath is not to be found in the exodus from Egypt, but in the creation of the world. By keeping the Sabbath, God's people fit into the divine order for life established at the very beginning. The six/one, work/rest example set by God, is the creational pattern for human existence. To observe the Sabbath, therefore, is to share in the very life of God himself. God's example is, in fact, the most important motive for obedience to the fourth

---

[68] Primus, *Holy Time*, 147-63.
[69] Ibid., 131.
[70] *A Golden Chaine*, 20. The other was the commandment concerning the trees in the garden.
[71] "A Treatise of the Sabbath," *Workes*, 132.

commandment. Sabbath-keeping is not simply obedience to God's law; it is living like God does. It is, therefore, the heart-beat of the godliness for which Greenham was ever striving in his own life and in the lives of his Dry Drayton parishioners.

The doctrine of creation, so important to Greenham's view of the Sabbath, leads him to affirm the significance of the six days of labor as well. In his appeal to the equity of the fourth commandment, which illumines God's generosity in his provision of six days for human vocations while demanding just one for divine worship, Greenham asserts that the work days are also under God's direction and control. They are not simply to be used as humanity chooses, but are also modeled after the Creator whose six days of creative labor grace all human endeavor. The Creator calls humanity to labor also. Although the work of the six days is usually referred to as "ordinary," Greenham in no way diminishes or degrades this part of the weekly rhythm. In his reaction against the Family of Love, who asserted that every day is a Sabbath for the Christian, and also against the Roman Catholics, who appointed holy days throughout the week, Greenham distinguishes the six days of labor from the one of rest and worship, not only to preserve a day of worship, but also to protect a time for work. The labor of ordinary callings is not to encroach upon the Sabbath, but neither is worship to encroach upon the six days. Special moments of worship throughout the week must be so scheduled that they be "without any hinderance of our lawfull and necessarie callings."

Christopher Hill's Marxist interpretation of the economic implications of the puritan Sabbath may go too far,[72] but Greenham's Sabbath doctrine did include a this-worldly appreciation for ordinary, daily human labor, arising from the creation orientation of his Sabbath theology. Although he emphasized heavily the spiritual purpose of Sabbath-keeping, he did not remove the day from this earthly realm, but kept it firmly rooted in the world. For Greenham, the cosmic dance of the universe was set to 6/1 time. The Sabbath, therefore, was to be used as a means and aid to a deeper and fuller appreciation of this created world, explicitly including, in Sabbath meditation, "the beholding of God his creatures, as the heavens and

---

[72] *Society and Puritanism in Pre-Revolutionary England* (London: Secker and Warburg, 1964).

the scope, beautie, and continuall course thereof, and the earth, which should have been all as pleasant as the garden of Eden, if Adam had continued in his innocencie...."[73] Greenham suggests an intimate connection between worship and work, grace and nature, when he says, "as our callings serveth to God's worship, so God's worship sanctifieth our callings."[74]

The doctrine of the resurrection did not figure in Greenham's Sabbath as extensively and pervasively as the doctrines of creation and sanctification, but it nevertheless played an important role in his discussion of what was to become the most controversial issue in the debates about the Sabbath at the turn of the century: the alteration of the Sabbath from the seventh day to the first. Heavy emphasis on a Sabbath controlled directly by the Old Testament's fourth commandment, and on imitation of the Creator's pattern of work and rest, created a problem for the Sunday-Sabbath of the sabbatarians. The fourth commandment explicitly designates a certain day for worship, and it is not the first day of the week. Neither does Genesis indicate that God rested on that day. Greenham led the way, nevertheless, in the sabbatarian teaching that Sunday became the New Testament Sabbath. He defended the Sunday-Sabbath with appeals to apostolic example and to the mighty acts of God that took place on the first day of the week, namely, the work of creation, the Lord's resurrection, and the pentecostal outpouring of the Holy Spirit. But in his discussion about the change of the day of worship, he refers most frequently to Christ's resurrection as the pivotal, world-shaking event that made the first day of the week, in some very special way, the "Lord's Day."[75]

It was above all the resurrection emphasis that shaped the mood of Greenham's Sabbath. Christ's resurrection was the ultimate sign of his divine power, and represented ultimate victory after a life of struggle, opposition and affliction, wrought by the powers of sin and evil in the world. The observance of each Sabbath on the first day of the week reawakens in the Christian a sense of sharing in that resurrection victory after another six-day war with the sins of this world. Since every Sabbath is a miniature Easter, i.e., a weekly

---

[73] "A Treatise of the Sabbath," *Workes*, 159.
[74] Ibid., 163.
[75] Ibid., 150.

celebration of Christ's triumph over the powerful enemies of sin, death, and hell, the tone of Greenham's Sabbath treatise is basically positive and optimistic. For him, the Sabbath was the doorway to a full appreciation of the Christian's new life in Christ. He recommended a Sunday evening inventory of Sabbath-keeping in which one of the key questions was: "Hath the Sabbath been our delight?"[76] And his answer to a question about Sunday weddings reveals his convictions about the celebrative character of the day. "If it be demaunded," he said, "whether this day be fit for mariage or no: I answere, it is, because on that day of rejoycing, there is a more lawfull libertie of speech, and a more liberall use of cheerfull behaviour."[77] Greenham ultimately viewed the Sabbath as a day representing freedom rather than bondage, a day of joy rather than gloom.

No words appear more frequently in Greenham's treatise on the Sabbath than various forms of "sanctification." As indicated above in Chapter 5, the ideal of the sanctified life became the preoccupation of his Dry Drayton ministry. The Sabbath was the means to that ideal. Observance of the *fourth* commandment became the prerequisite to obeying the rest of them. He found a good reason for regarding the fourth commandment as the key to the door of sanctification: it is the only commandment that explicitly mentions "holiness."

Sanctification moves in three directions according to Greenham. First, God sanctified the Sabbath. Second, in *imitatio Dei*, humanity must also sanctify the Sabbath. Third, through divine and human sanctification of the Sabbath, the Holy Spirit sanctifies the believer. In each of these movements, the concept of *separation* is most important in understanding the meaning of sanctification. That God sanctifies the Sabbath means that he separates it from the other days, designating this one for rest and worship. Greenham says that God "sanctified, that is, put a part of the seventh day to his own worship, and blessed it with a peculiar blessing given to his worship appointed...."[78] He also states that God gave a "special blessing above the other days, unto this day."[79] In Greenham's scheme of things, the Sabbath was not inherently superior to the other days, and yet,

---

[76] Ibid., 161.
[77] Ibid., 168.
[78] Ibid., 136.
[79] Ibid., 137.

because of the special use for which it was set aside (i.e., sanctified), it has a "special blessing."

As God sanctified the Sabbath with his blessing, so the godly must sanctify it with their obedience. Both in their view of the day and in their use of it, sanctification is the controlling word. The Sabbath is to be regarded as providing holy time for worship, and in its use human behaviour is sanctified, for it is dedicated to holiness. Hence, the Sabbath becomes the microcosm of the Christian life.

The Sabbath rest provided opportunity for intense sanctifying activity, typically divided into four phases: preparation for worship; public worship; reflection, study, and conference; and performance of merciful deeds. In these, the Pauline pattern of sin, deliverance, and gratitude is discernible. Preparation for worship involved a personal inventory of sin, to examine "how we have gone forward in godly proceedings, or how we have gone backward...."[80] The later doctrine of "preparation for grace," may have grown out of these seeds planted by Greenham, for he explicitly emphasized that Word and Sacraments have little meaning unless we come to them with "prepared affections."[81] In public worship the gospel of deliverance is preached and the sacraments confirming that gospel received. The primary means of salvation are found in these exercises, for it is through the preaching and hearing of the Word that God saves all who believe. Finally, from the hearing of the gospel issues the good life of gratitude. As Greenham put it, "the Lord his Sabbath is not a day of knowledge alone, but of love"; and through exercises of love toward the needy, he says, "we may show that wee are sanctified."[82]

Sabbath sanctification is received in the context of corporate Christian experience. The church plays a pivotal role, but home and family also contribute significantly. Preparation for worship, self-examination, private and family prayer, conference, reading, and meditation, all take place within the home and are vital requirements for meaningful public worship. Much of the Sabbath's sanctifying power comes through the home. Greenham urges the use of "all such private exercise as may make the publike meanes profitable to my

---

[80] "A Treatise of the Sabbath," ibid., 157.
[81] Ibid., 158. On the doctrine of preparation for grace, see Norman Pettit, *The Heart Prepared* (New Haven: Yale University Press, 1966).
[82] Ibid., 160, 132.

selfe and to others."[83]

Creation, Resurrection, and Sanctification—these are the great biblical-theological themes that surface in Greenham's doctrine of the Sabbath. Sabbatarianism is intrinsically trinitarian, for the three themes find correspondence in the three persons of the trinity: the creator Father, the resurrected Son, and the sanctifying Spirit. The Sabbath, for Greenham, was a sacrament of the trinity. It was the ultimate means of godliness, for through it the Christian was provided with a glorious opportunity to connect with the triune God. Greenham quotes Ezekiel, who in turn speaks for God: "*I gave them my Sabbaths to bee a signe betweene mee and them, that they might know that I am the Lord that sanctifie them.*"[84] Greenham goes on to interpret these words covenantally.

> So that, in that the Lorde saith, *My Sabbath is a signe betweene mee and you*, it is as much in effect, as if he should say: "my Sabbath is a common instruction betweene you and me: of mee as the Creator, Redeemer, and Sanctifier: of you as created, redeemed, and sanctified: so that the Sabbath is a document and pledge of Gods will, whereby we should know, what hee is unto us, and wherein wee should learn what we should do to him.[85]

The Sabbath played a critical, defining role in Greenham's ministry, for it was directly related to his passionate concern for godliness. The godly life is nurtured by the *means* of faith, and the Sabbath provided time for the exercise of the means. To hear the preaching of the Word, to engage in prayer, to receive the sacraments—these take precious time, and especially in a rural setting, where work seems endless and time is not divided into eight-hour days and forty-hour weeks with weekends off, Greenham regarded it as spiritually indispensable that his parishioners should set aside one day in seven for the holy purpose of exercising the means of godliness. He would have insisted, of course, that time was not his to regulate and dispense. Time belongs to God who created it, rules over it, and gives

---

[83] "A short forme of catechising," ibid., 75.
[84] Ezekiel 20:12
[85] "A Treatise of the Sabbath," *Workes*, 132-3.

it to his creatures. God exercises his sovereignty over time by designating a rhythm of work and worship. Ideally, some time should be devoted to spiritual exercise each day, but God set aside a weekly day in its entirety to insure regular opportunity for worship. All time is God's. Six-sevenths of it is to be used for "ordinarie callings"; one-seventh for total immersion in worship and service. For Richard Greenham, keeping the Sabbath was the key to the moral, sanctified life. It was *The Means* of the means.

# 8

# CONCLUSIONS

## GREENHAM'S ANGLICAN, PURITAN PROTESTANTISM

It has been the intent of this study to use Richard Greenham as the lens through which to view the Protestantism of the Elizabethan Church. He serves very well in this regard, for he was a widely respected leader in that Church, not in the highly visible and dramatic way of a Thomas Cartwright or John Whitgift, but a powerful leader nonetheless in his role as a gifted and dedicated parish pastor. As such, he became a model for others in his own time not only, but also well into the seventeenth century, for through his writings his influence endured beyond that of the average Church of England pastor. This chapter will attempt to set forth a number of conclusions about Greenham and his ministry, some of which have already been drawn, but here summarized more briefly and systematically.

## I

Greenham's theology can best be described as eclectic Protestantism.[1] He was educated at Pembroke Hall, where theology was a refreshing mixture of continental protestant traditions. Greenham was ecumenical with respect to the continental reformers. He learned from Luther, Bucer, Calvin, Bullinger, and Melanchthon. He did not participate in their theological prejudices (except against the papists and anabaptists) or internal debates. His theology had a

---

[1] On the eclecticism of English Reformation thought, see Carl R. Trueman, *Luther's Legacy* (Oxford: Clarendon Press, 1994) 56, et. al.

wholesome, ingenuous air about it. It may be significant that Greenham was not one of the Marian exiles who were influenced especially in German and Swiss Reformed centers on the continent, and that the impact of these exiles seems to have been minimal at Pembroke Hall in the 1560s.

Greenham's theology is, at its core, a theology of grace, genuine reformational theology. One of its most basic motifs—the law/gospel dialectic—comes from the Lutheran side, transmitted through Tyndale and a little later by Melanchthon who was the main channel of Lutheranism into Cambridge by the 1540s. Greenham's sacramental theology is Calvinian, and his passionate spiritual and ethical concerns are reminiscent of both Bucer and Calvin, although Tyndale and Melanchthon could have been sources of these as well. On the practical level of hermeneutics and preaching, the law/gospel distinction rules supreme. His Sabbath doctrine comports with neither Calvin or Luther, but with Zanchius, the later Heidelberg theologian.

For Greenham, theology is not an end in itself, nor designed as a resource for debate propositions, but is a means of comfort and guidance, immediately applicable to Christian life in a difficult and confusing age. It is genuinely pastoral theology, applied at the parish level, devotional and experiential in nature.[2] Doctrine is evident but unobtrusive in his *Workes,* serving the purpose of deeper spirituality and devotion to God. Greenham intertwines doctrinal instruction with devotional teaching. The comfort he gives afflicted consciences is grounded in Christian theology, for correct doctrine is affective; it is primarily a source of comfort.

Biblical history is used for the same pastoral purpose. Greenham never tires of reminding his parishioners of God's mercies graciously bestowed upon his saints in the past, and of assuring them that God will live up to his past performances. Biblical teachings are means of comfort, inspiration, devotion, and piety, as well as stimuli to good works. Greenham's theology, therefore, as well as the Christian life based thereon, are upbeat, joyful, and positive in tone, quite contrary to "the received notion of Puritan piety as sombre, sad and altogether

---

[2] Charles Hambrick-Stowe, *The Practice of Piety* (Chapel Hill: University of North Carolina Press, 1982) 3. "The proper study of Puritanism begins with the spiritual experiences of Puritans," says Hambrick-Stowe.

in the minor key."[3]

## II

The fundamental theological device Greenham uses, both in his interpretation of Scripture and also in the practice of preaching and pastoral work, was the law/gospel dialectic. One of the most familiar phrases in the whole of the Greenham corpus is: "the threatenings of the law, and the promises of the gospel." Hermeneutically, he is as persistent as Luther himself in applying this dialectic to the Scriptures. The law and the gospel are the "principall parts of God's Word." The law "is that part of the Word that commaundeth all good, and forbiddeth all evill," and the gospel "is that part of the word which containeth the free promises of God made unto us in Jesus Christ, without any respect of our deservings."[4] For Greenham, the law functions almost exclusively as the teacher of sin, and the gospel as the primary instrument of "true and lively faith in Jesus Christ."[5] Over and over again the theme appears: the law reveals sin, the gospel cures sin; the law wounds, the gospel heals; the law kills, the gospel quickens; the law disturbs, the gospel comforts.

Greenham established his reputation in the two basic areas of ministry: preaching of the Word, and pastoral care for the afflicted. In both, the law/gospel dialectic functioned as the operative principle. He regarded his basic responsibility to be that of preacher of the Word, and saw his parishioners primarily as hearers of the Word. They had to be confronted, gripped, judged, and redeemed by the Word, which on the one hand condemns and judges, and on the other, promises and liberates. The law must first be preached in order to prompt a deep sense of sin, for then, and only then, will the gospel promises of Christ be appreciated and appropriated. He warns that preachers must not "so presse the Law, that [they] suppresse the Gospell."[6] The needs and circumstances of the auditors will determine where the emphasis should lie. If they are "alreadie humbled" they must have the promises; if they are still in ignorance

---

[3] Gordon Rupp, "A Devotion of Rapture in English Puritanism," in *Reformation, Conformity and Dissent*, R. B. Knox, ed., (London: Epworth Press, 1977) 127.
[4] " A Short Forme of Catechising," *Workes*, 72.
[5] Ibid.
[6] "Of Prophecie and Preaching," ibid., 772.

of sin, they must hear the law.[7]

The law/gospel dialectic also was applied in his pastoral work. Peace was brought to troubled consciences by means of the distinction, for attempts to pursue righteousness by means of the law and works can only add to the troubled, burdened conscience. The gospel proclaims the righteousness of Christ, received as a gift, and then actively integrated into Christian life.

Greenham's law/gospel doctrine is strikingly like Martin Luther's— right down to the hammer metaphor. In this respect, Greenham seems more Lutheran than Calvinistic. The law/gospel motif is present in both of these Reformation traditions, but receives more prominence in the thought of Luther. For Luther, just as for Greenham, it functions more obviously and more consistently as a basic hermeneutical principle. Leading analysts of Luther's theology typically include the law-gospel dialectic as one of the hallmarks of his thought,[8] hardly the case in surveys of Calvinism.

Not only is the dialectic more prominent and visible in Luther than in Calvin, but also their views of the relationship between law and gospel differ markedly. The antithesis between them is stronger in Luther. For Luther, the law is always the revealer of sin and of God's judgment. Law demands perfect obedience; hence it condemns the sinner. Gospel is always the promise of God's love and grace. It declares that the law's demands have been met in Christ; hence it redeems the believer. Law is the ministry of death; gospel the ministry of life. In Luther's words: "the true and proper function of the law is to accuse and kill; but the function of the gospel is to make alive."[9] This does not mean that Luther abandoned the law, or regarded it as irrelevant in a Christian context. Rather, in the proclamation of the Word of God, Christians need to hear the law to bring them to an understanding of their sinfulness and to an awareness of God's wrath against sin. But before they languish in despair, they must hear the gospel also. It is then that they realize that the law is not the final word, for when they cast themselves on God's mercy, the gospel

---

[7] "A third portion...of an hundred grave counsels," ibid., 59.
[8] See, for example, Paul Althaus, *The Theology of Martin Luther* (Philadelphia: Fortress Press, 1966) 251ff.; Gerhard Ebeling, *Luther: an Introduction to his Thought* (Philadephia: Fortress Press, 1970) 110ff.; and Philip Watson, *Let God Be God: An Interpretation of the Theology of Martin Luther* (Philadelphia: Muhlenberg Press, 1949) 152ff.
[9] Quoted in Althaus, ibid., 256, n. 40.

promises forgiveness. Law without gospel does not heal; but gospel
without law is incomprehensible for the gospel of forgiveness
presupposes law-revealed sin. Precisely these same emphases are found
in Greenham.

Calvin on the other hand, softens the antithesis between law and
gospel. He subdues the judgment character of the law somewhat by
making the gospel a confirmation of an already existing promise that
came with the Old Testament law. On occasion Calvin also speaks of
the accusing, condemning function of the law, but ultimately the
tension between law and gospel is resolved so that they function
harmoniously in the Christian life. Theologically, this harmony is
achieved by means of the doctrine of the unity of God. This doctrine
leads Calvin to a strong emphasis on the unity of the two testaments,
and to his delineation of a third use of the law in which the breach
between law and gospel is bridged by means of an emphasis on the law
as a gracious guide for the Christian life.[10]

For many later puritans, Calvin's reduction of tension between law
and gospel and development of a "third use" of the law was very
attractive, for it provided a theological basis for their appeal to the
works of the law as a measure of Christian piety and as a means to the
assurance of salvation. Earlier English reformers like Greenham,
however, found ways of exhorting believers to pious living without
abandoning a sharp distinction between law and gospel. The dialectic
seems to function in Greenham's thought somewhat more as a formal
hermeneutical principle and as a practical typology for his preaching,
than as a material theological doctrine consistently applied
throughout the entire system of his thought.

# III

Greenham's single most original and significant contribution to
English church and society, as well as to the history of the church at
large, is his doctrine of the Sabbath.[11]

---

[10] *Institutes,* II, vii, 12. See also John H. Leith, "Creation and Redemption: Law
and Gospel in the Theology of John Calvin," in Paul C. Empie, ed., *Marburg
Revisited* (Minneapolis: Augsburg, 1966) 141-52; and I. John Hesselink, *Calvin's
Concept of the Law* (Allison Park, PA: Pickwick Publications, 1992).

[11] Knappen calls it "a bit of English originality," and "the first and perhaps only
important English contribution to the development of Reformed theology in the
first century of its history," *Tudor Puritanism,* 442.

His "Treatise of the Sabbath," written in the early 1580s, lays claim to being the first English analysis of the fourth commandment with distinctive sabbatarian features; namely, that this commandment is a perpetual, moral law rooted in creation; that Sunday is the Christian Sabbath ordained by divine authority; and that the entire day must be devoted to worship and related spiritual exercises. This is another dimension of his thought in which he differs markedly from John Calvin, although later continental Protestants like Junius and Zanchius in the Calvinian tradition were also sending out sabbatarian signals by the 1580s.[12] It is impossible to determine how much the English sabbatarians were influenced by these continental Calvinists or vice versa.

Greenham's sabbatarianism may seem theologically puzzling, especially when viewed in conjunction with his law/gospel motif. Given his sharp distinction between law and gospel and his emphasis on the use of the law primarily as a teacher of sin, why did he become so enamored with the fourth commandment as to make it fundamental for the Christian life? Is there not an inconsistency here? To put it another way, if Greenham's law/gospel theology was more akin to Luther than to Calvin, how could it produce a "Puritan Sabbath"? Is not a Lutheran sabbatarianism inconceivable?

The name of Andreas von Karlstadt suggests, at a minimum, that sabbatarianism in a Lutheran environment is not inconceivable. Karlstadt was Luther's eccentric colleague in Wittenberg, whose treatise, "Of the Sabbath," has been called the "precursor" of the puritan sabbatarian tradition.[13] To call him a "Lutheran," however, is to stretch the term to the breaking point. Although he was in basic agreement with Luther's theology of grace, there are several respects, especially in the area of law and freedom, in which he launched out on his own. Luther's treatise, "Against the Heavenly Prophets," is a blunt repudiation of many of Karlstadt's ideas, including those on the Sabbath. Karlstadt, he said, misunderstands and misapplies Mosaic law, making it too restrictive and binding on Christians. Old Testament regulations are applicable to the Christian community

---

[12] John H. Primus, *Holy Time,* ch. 6, "Sabbatarian Appeals to the Continent," 119-45. See also, Primus, "Calvin and the Puritan Sabbath," in *Exploring the Heritage of John Calvin,* ed. by David Holwerda (Grand Rapids: Baker, 1976) 40-75.

[13] Gordon Rupp, *Patterns of Reformation* (London: Epworth Press, 1969) 123.

only when they express the "natural law" written in human hearts. The Sabbath commandment is essentially "ceremonial," and Karlstadt's interpretation of it does not allow adequate room for Christian discretion and liberty.[14] Perhaps Luther would have responded to Greenham as he did to Karlstadt, for Greenham, especially in his discussion of Sabbath observance, also verges on legalism. And yet, Greenham's Sabbath theology was quite different from Karlstadt's. "In the end," writes Gordon Rupp, "Karlstadt's Sabbath is under the sign of the Law rather than of the Gospel."[15] Greenham's Sabbath, on the other hand, was essentially *in the service of the gospel.* For Karlstadt, the day tended to be one of sadness; for Greenham, it was "the Lord's Day," the day of resurrection joy and victory, a day of gladness.

Total consistency is an unrealistic expectation from any theologian, but even so, Greenham himself saw no inconsistency between his law/gospel doctrine and his emphasis upon the Sabbath. At one point in the Sabbath treatise, he specifically refers to the law/gospel distinction: "And where the word is administred in any power and sinceritie, there doubtlesse the preaching of the law striketh us, and the preaching of the Gospell bringeth us to Christ."[16] Here he affirms again the primary function of the law as hammer of God's wrath, and of the gospel as awakener of faith. This does not mean, however, that the law can be abandoned once sin has been acknowledged and faith aroused. Although its primary function is to disclose sin, and although by itself, without the gospel, it is powerless to enable obedience, the moral law is nonetheless the revealed will of God, etched in the human heart, woven into the fabric of the created universe. Luther said, in response to Karlstadt, that Mosaic law is not binding on Christians unless it expresses moral, natural law. Greenham would have agreed, and the fundamental argument of his Sabbath treatise is precisely in support of the basically moral character of the fourth commandment.

Although theologically the point is relatively unemphasized, it is obvious that for Greenham the law, *with the gospel,* is enormously important for revealing the way of godliness. The good works that

---

[14] *Luther's Works,* vol. 40, Conrad Bergendoff ed. (Pennsylvania: Muhlenberg Press, 1958) 93-8.
[15] *Patterns of Reformation,* 130.
[16] *Workes,* 139.

proceed from repentance and faith are "such as God hath commanded in his Law." Law and gospel "agree in this, that they bee both of God, and declare one kinde of righteousnesse," even though they differ sharply in their ability to enable that righteousness.[17] The law is powerless to bring about renewal of life, but once the gospel has taken over, the law is a dependable guide to the will of God. This is Greenham's emphasis with regard to the Sabbath; it teaches, it instructs, it is a school for godliness. For Greenham, the fourth commandment is law, but the Sabbath itself is gospel, that is, the Sabbath has a gospel purpose—it provides time for worship, prayer, the proclamation of the Word, and administration of the sacraments. Greenham insists that the Sabbath command was given to Adam in the garden; he needed it even in a state of perfection, not, in his case, as the revealer of sin. The moral law in general, and the Sabbath law in particular, was not initially designed for sinners. The Sabbath was established in creation when God rested from his works on the seventh day. These convictions, which lie at the heart of Greenham's doctrine of the Sabbath, go far toward explaining how his understanding of the significance of the fourth commandment does not necessarily conflict with his law/gospel theology.

The puritan Sabbath had lasting impact in England both theologically and sociologically. Peace-loving though he was, with his doctrine of the Sabbath Greenham ushered a highly controversial topic into the Church of England, the first genuinely theological issue over which "puritans" and "anglicans" divided, antedating the Arminian issue by a decade. The Sabbath issue was hotly debated for at least fifty years, right up to the Civil War. Sociologically, the view of time divided into the routine of six days of labour followed by the Sabbath rest was firmly established in English society by the end of the seventeenth century. It replaced the medieval notion of a church year filled with all manner of special holy days, which, as the sabbatarians were quick to observe, tended to undermine a high view of the Sabbath. As Christopher Hill points out, sabbatarianism contributed to the development of industrialization in England by introducing a pattern of weekly time conducive to regular, disciplined labor.[18]

---

[17] "A Short Forme of Catechising," ibid., 88.
[18] *Society and Puritanism in Pre-Revolutionary England*, 146.

Greenham's sabbatarianism offers some important clues regarding the developing key notes of puritan theology.[19] The doctrine of creation, so important in the development of the puritan argument regarding the universal, moral character of the fourth commandment; the doctrine of the resurrection, used as the basis for the Sunday-absolutism of sabbatarianism; and the doctrine of sanctification, which is highlighted especially in the emphasis on Sabbath observance—these can be used to identify the triple foundational pillars of puritan theology. They constitute a much more interesting and fruitful way of understanding Puritanism than, say, through the doctrines of predestination or the covenant.

## IV

Puritan theology is commonly regarded as Calvinistic particularly in its emphasis on the doctrine of predestination. It is a stubbornly persisting error to make that doctrine the touchstone of Calvinism,[20] even though it is beyond dispute that all of the leading continental reformers held to the doctrine, and that Luther had a more rigidly double-predestinarian view than Calvin himself. Since predestination is the biblical (and logical) extension of the doctrine of grace, it is included in Greenham's theology, but it did not occupy a central, controlling position in his thought. He was a moderate predestinarian.

The "experimental predestinarianism" that became common among late sixteenth century puritans and which placed election and personal assurance at the center of practical divinity, is also virtually absent from Greenham's theology. For Greenham, election is a source of comfort and the "spurre to good workes,"[21] rather than the cause of immobilizing anxiety. The practical syllogism of Beza is nowhere evident in his writings. Assurance of salvation is to be found in a combination of exercises, including examination of one's Christian walk—Greenham lists fifteen "sweet and sure signs of election"[22]—but personal security ultimately hinges not on introspection, but on the

---

[19] Primus, *Holy Time*, 147-63.
[20] A recent example may be found in Nicholas Tyacke, *Anti-Calvinists: The Rise of English Arminianism* (Oxford: Clarendon Press, 1987) 1.
[21] "Of Workes," *Workes*, 838.
[22] Ibid., 122.

hearing of the gospel, trust in God's promises, and the testimony of the Holy Spirit.

The category of "the elect" seems to be somewhat fluid and open-ended for Greenham. In a sermon in which he chastises parents who neglect to instruct their children, he says they seem to "have no care to increase the Church of Christ, and the number of the elect...."[23] Greenham's emphasis is decidedly on human responsibility to proclaim and hear the Word, as the means of implementing divine redemption. God does not operate on the basis of a fixed, rigid plan determined by eternal decree. In fact, Greenham even makes an occasional Arminian-sounding comment, as when he says that Christ did not commit himself to all men because "hee knewe what was in their hearts."[24] Had he remained in Dry Drayton and lived to the end of the century, he might have become embroiled in the Barrowist controversy at Cambridge.[25]

Greenham did not hold to double predestination. He consistently attributes the "cause of destruction" not to God, but to sinful humanity.[26] God elects, but the reprobate suffer the consequences of their sins. "The afflictions of the reprobate are the punishments of their sinnes: here they suffer some, in hell they shall suffer all torments...."[27] The elect experience afflictions also, but these become for them means of spiritual growth and development. Greenham suggests, indeed, that a life without affliction has its drawbacks, for personal security is more likely to be found through affliction than through the absence of it. He refuses to speculate on why some believe and others do not: "I am rather to thanke God that I believe, then to search out a reason, why another doth not beleeve."[28]

## V

Greenham combined his theology of grace with deep, ethical concern. In his view, puritan piety was worthless unless it led to

---

[23] "Of the education of children," *Workes,* 277.
[24] Ibid.
[25] See Porter, *Reformation and Reaction in Tudor Cambridge,* 277ff.
[26] "Of the education of children," ibid., 280.
[27] "Another or second portion...of grave Counsels," ibid., 45.
[28] "The first portion of grave Counsels," ibid., 14. Harry Porter calls this non-speculative approach "the Pembroke contribution to English theology." *Reformation and Reaction in Tudor Cambridge,* 342.

ethical sensitivity and a life of good works. He followed in the
footsteps of those who extended the principle of reform beyond
doctrine and polity to the Christian life. This emphasis on piety,
devotion, and the good life was not absent from the original
continental reformers—Martin Bucer certainly promoted and
encouraged it in Cambridge—but it was especially prominent in
England, evident from the very beginning of the Reformation in the
likes of Tyndale, Latimer, Barnes, and Frith.

The Lutheran emphasis on grace did not lead these reformers
down the libertine path of antinomianism, but rather to a recognition
that salvation by the love of God calls believers to love one another.
All of these early reformers had a strong sense of social justice shown
especially in their compassion toward the poor. Interestingly,
Greenham displayed the same, stating that certain unspecified
experiences at the time of his ordination led him to a great sense of
responsibility toward the poor. This was concretely worked out in Dry
Drayton in the economic measures he initiated to help the poor, and
also at Cambridge where he gained a reputation for his project to aid
needy students. Luther's doctrine of the imputation of Christ's
righteousness became, on English soil, the doctrine of the
impartation of righteousness, with a consequent emphasis on
sanctification. Thus, by the time the influence of the Reformed wing
of Protestantism reached England, Zwingli's, Bucer's, and Calvin's
emphasis on sanctification simply confirmed what had already been
established. Greenham stands firmly within the tradition that kept
sanctification closely tied to justification.

This combination was ideal for the typical, sixteenth-century,
English protestant parishioner, who had been spiritually programmed
by medieval semi-pelagianism. For such, Greenham's law/gospel
approach to the Bible and its proclamation was used effectively, for it
was designed to bring people who were still Roman Catholic in
religious mentality to the protestant message of salvation by grace.
The law reveals sin; the gospel proclaims forgiving grace. Obedience
follows as a grateful response but will not earn heaven. Without
compromising his whole-hearted commitment to the universe of
grace, Greenham ceaselessly expounded on the importance of the
good life. As indicated above, he managed to do this in spite of his
sharp law/gospel distinction, without appeal to a third use of the law,

and without reliance on a reciprocal covenant doctrine. Rather, he used another teaching characteristic of the earlier English reformers: the doctrine of means. This for Greenham was the primary implementing device for his emphasis on good works.

This emphasis did not compromise or soften his insistence upon salvation by grace alone, for sanctification is also by grace through faith, and good works inevitably issue from grace. "As we are carefull to use the meanes of our salvation," he writes, "so must we wholly referre the blessing of the meanes to the grace of God: neither, as some doe, thinke that we can obtaine or continue the grace of God in us without using the meanes,...neither, as the manner of some is, so to trust in the meanes, as neglecting to pray for the grace of God in them: which is but a preposterous zeale of such as are not rightly instructed in the way of their salvation."[29]

In Greenham's view, grace brings about an inner spiritual transformation that results in good works. Hence, a righteous life is not simply the outcome of human obedience to divine commands; rather, righteousness arises from the very being of the triune God who gave the holy commandments. To be graciously saved by this God means the redemption and renewal of God's image in humankind. Furthermore, union with Christ supplies the power for good works, and regeneration through the Holy Spirit establishes a connection between grace and good works through the Spirit's "effectual call" to the good life.

## VI

The church played a very important part in Greenham's Puritanism. His main concern was for the practice of piety defined by the Word of God, which can only be appropriated through the work of the Holy Spirit in the context and fellowship of the church. It is a mistake to understand Puritanism as "a movement toward immediacy, towards direct communion with God through his Holy Spirit in independence of all outward and creaturely aids."[30] Greenham's Puritanism was heavily dependent on the "outward and

---

[29] "The first portion of grave Counsels," *Workes*, 15.
[30] Geoffrey Nuttall, *The Holy Spirit in Puritan Faith and Experience* (Oxford: Basil Blackwell, 1946) 91, 134-5.

creaturely" church, where the Word is to be faithfully preached and the sacraments purely administered. In Greenham's view of things, all earthly blessings are given for the church's sake. God has given to the church the "keys of the kingdom," i.e., the power to loose and to bind under Christ the church's head. "Behold a miracle," he writes, "heaven made subject to the earth!" He cites no less than 25 biblical metaphors for the church in order to demonstrate its exalted nature.[31]

Although Greenham emphasized piety and devotion, he put little stock in feeling and emotion. Perhaps in reaction to the Family of Love, he combined his emphasis on piety with a rather cognitive approach to spirituality. Faith is to be built upon knowledge of the Word, thoughtful participation in the sacraments, and intelligent prayer—all promoted and cultivated in the church. This churchly Puritanism had a rational, intellectual side to it that made thorough preparation in the university necessary for aspiring pastors. Greenham called the universities, "polished Saphires to garnish the house of the Lord," and spearheaded an effort to help poor university students.[32] Sectarians like the familists touted spirituality too, but they did not study at the universities.

On the practical side, it has already been noted that church attendance, the hearing of the preached Word, participation in corporate prayer, and regular use of the sacraments, were basic essentials in Greenham's understanding of the Christian faith and how it is generated and nurtured. These are indispensable means to faith and it is especially in his doctrine of the means that Greenham's emphasis upon the church becomes apparent. His doctrine of the church is summed up nicely in the following quotation.

> Wherefore if wee doe professe our selves to bee of God, and to worship him, then must we joyne our selves to the Church of God, which with us doth worship God. And this must we doe of necessitie, for it is a branch of our beleefe, that there is a Communion of Saints in the Church: and if we beleeve that there is a God, we must also beleeve that there is a remnant of

---

[31] "Of the Church," *Workes,* 648-9.
[32] "Of Knowledge and Ignorance," *Workes,* 734; "Rules concerning the power and priviledges of Gods word," ibid., 864.

people, unto whom God revealeth himselfe, and commun-
icateth his mercies, in whom we must have al our delight, with
whom we must communicate, according to the measure of
grace given unto every one of us.[33]

Greenham stands in contradiction to any understanding of
Puritanism as the individualising of the Christian faith through an
immediate mystical experience of God. His emphasis is rather on the
communal aspect of Christian experience, on Christians gathered in
congregations, on an organic national church, and on one holy
catholic church. One's identity as a Christian individual is found in
the context of the corporate body of believers.[34]

Not only was Greenham's emphasis on the church important for
religious practice, but it also provided the theological basis for his
cooperative Puritanism. His antipathy toward political controversy
was closely related to his ecclesiology. Greenham's view of the
Christian life emphasized the social, corporate character of the faith.
His ecclesiology included a recognition of the body of Christ beyond
the local congregation. Christ's body is the church on a national and
international level; it is ultimately the holy, catholic church spanning
all time and space. Separatism, however, violates the catholicity of
the church, for separatism is, by definition, individualistic. It leads
ultimately to the lone individual, living in splendid isolation because
of his failure either by temperament or by settled conviction to live in
harmony with others. Greenham's doctrine of the church led to the
ecumenical, cooperative spirit that was so characteristic of
mainstream Puritanism in the Elizabethan era.

## VII

Greenham, like all good puritans, contributed to the
domestication of the church by emphasizing the important role of
home and family in spiritual nurture.[35] His very first published work,

---

[33] "Of divers Christian instructions," ibid., 318.
[34] John S. Coolidge, *The Pauline Renaissance in England*, 147.
[35] For discussions of the puritan emphasis on worship and education in the
home, see Charles Hambrick-Stowe, *The Practice of Piety* chs. 5 & 6; John Morgan,
*Godly Learning* (Cambridge: University Press, 1986) ch. 8; and Christopher Hill,
*Society and Puritanism in Pre-Revolutionary England*, ch. 13.

in 1584, was *A godly Exhortation, and fruitfull admonition to vertuous parents and modest Matrons.*[36] Greenham believed that both the laws of the state and the message of the church require the full cooperation of parents in the home, who are called to exemplify in their own lives biblical principles and Christian values. This recognition of the important teaching role of the home, however, did not undermine his strong doctrine of the church. Family and church are never in tension in his writings, but exist in a supplementary or reciprocal relationship. Families supplement the proclamation of the gospel carried on in church. He states that the "Church of God" must be brought "into our households,"[37] but never does he suggest that the family can supplant the church. He simply recognizes that families (and individuals for that matter) are agents to carry God's truth proclaimed by the church into every corner of the land.

> And surely if men were careful to reforme themselves first, and then their own families, they should see Gods manifold blessings in our land upon Church and Common-wealth. For of particular persons come families; of families, townes; of townes, provinces; of provinces whole realmes: so that conveighing Gods holy trueth in this sort from one to another, in time, and that shortly, it would so spread into all parts of this kingdome.[38]

Greenham here displays remarkable insight into the sociology of education, but he cannot be used to support the suggestion that in Puritanism the household became the essential unit of religion rather than the parish.[39] The church is absolutely essential for the proclamation of the Word and the administration of the sacraments; the home is the primary locus in society where the work of the church is put into practice. In that sense, "we must bring it [the church] into

---

[36] This was incorporated later in his *Workes* (1612) as the sixth sermon in Part III, "Of the education of Children," 276-81.

[37] "Of Parents, Education of Children, Governours of youth, and care of Posterity," *Workes*, 799. Cf., REM 524, fol. 62v.

[38] "Of the education of children," *Workes*, 278-9.

[39] Christopher Hill says that in Puritanism the household rather than the church was the "lowest unit" in the hierarchy of spiritual discipline, *Society and Puritanism in Pre-revolutionary England,* 443.

our households and nourish it in our families."[40]

Although Greenham did not elevate the doctrine of the covenant to a primary position in his theology, he appealed to it in his discussion of family responsibilities. He compares every father to "our father Abraham," who first received the blessing to be the "blessed father of a blessed seede." That same blessing is available to all fathers and is fulfilled when Christian fathers bring their children "within the covenant," by making their natural sons and daughters children of God by grace. The gracious promise is historically realized through obedient and God-fearing parents.[41]

In Greenham's ideal Sabbath, the household plays an important part. Parents are responsible for bringing their families to public worship, but also for preparing their families for worship and, after the corporate gathering, leading family conferences in which the sermon is discussed and digested. For all practical purposes, the master of the household was the primary agent for faithful and obedient Sabbath-keeping.

Education is the primary task of the home. The spate of catechisms that appeared in the sixteenth century was stimulated in large part by the felt need to provide families with instruments of Christian instruction in the home. Some of them specifically mention that they were designed for use by households. Greenham's *Workes* includes a brief treatise directed to parents on the importance of catechizing their children.[42] On this score, Greenham would agree with William Gouge who challenged families to become "excellent Seminaries" for the church and commonwealth.[43] The puritan goal of total reformation was to be achieved by producing a godly laity through the cooperative efforts of church and home.

---

[40] "Of Parents, Education of Children, Governours of youth, and care of Posterity," *Workes*, 799. This is the closest Greenham comes to calling Christian families "little churches" as a number of his puritan colleagues do." See, for example, William Perkins, *Workes*, III, 670; Henry Ainsworth, *The Communion of Saints* (n.p., 1628) 308; and Paul Baynes, *Briefe Directions unto a godly life* (London, 1618) 338.
[41] "Of the education of children," *Workes*, 279.
[42] "Of Catechizing and instruction of youth," ibid., 662-6.
[43] "Epistle Dedicatory," *Of Domesticall Duties*, (London, 1622), fol. A3.

## VIII

Neo-Calvinists who believe that Christians must attempt to transform this world's culture, and who have adopted a modified "realized eschatology," will likely be disappointed in the example set by early puritans like Richard Greenham, for in his worldview, the "pilgrim" metaphor is more prominent than creational and cultural affirmation. Greenham's worldview begins and ends with God—the creator, redeemer, and sanctifier. God created the world and, of course, it was good, even very good. Mysteriously, sin entered the world through the fall in paradise, and Greenham is unrelenting in his emphasis on the presence of sin and disastrous results of the fall.[44] The fall, in fact, has devolutionary momentum. He says, "our times are worse, than the times wherein the Prophet lived, and wee are easier and readier to take harm by evill example than he was...."[45] Yet, God's redemption worked out by Christ and applied through the power of the Holy Spirit is ultimately triumphant. Greenham, however, views redemption in primarily personal rather than cultural or cosmic terms. The biblical vision of an eternal kingdom made up of a new heaven *and new earth* is present, but only in shadowy form in Greenham's thought.

Christians are "strangers" and pilgrims on this earth.[46] They have here "no long abiding place." The eternal paradise "is our native countrie, and we in this world be as exiles and as strangers: we dwell here as in Mesech, and as in the tents of Kedar."[47] In this world, Christians "have fewe friends and many enemies," and Christian instruction is needed for shielding and reinforcement. The chief enemies are human corruption itself, the vanities of this world, the evil example of the wicked, "and the great enemie of mankinde the divell."[48]

Only occasionally does a world-affirming perspective appear in

---

[44] On the good but fallen creation see, for example, "Of Christian warfare," *Workes*, 307 ff.

[45] "Meditations on the 119 Psalm," *Workes*, 493.

[46] On puritans as pilgrims, see Charles Hambrick-Stowe, *The Practice of Piety*, ch. 3.

[47] "Of our generall and speciall calling," *Workes*, 645.

[48] "Meditations on the 119 Psalm," ibid., 405-6. The "divell" is mentioned on nearly every page of this, the longest of Greenham's treatises. But the "word" and the "spirit" are mentioned even more frequently.

Greenham's writings. In a passage reminiscent of John Calvin, Greenham reflects on prosperity and adversity, and concludes:

> ... too much austeritie is not commended, for why then should there bee such divers tastes in meates? And wine was given not only to quench the thirst, but also to make the hearts of men glad...and therefore the children of Israel were commaunded to eate and to bee merrie before the Lord.[49]

In a similar vein, Greenham occasionally calls for a fuller and deeper appreciation of the created world in his treatise on the Sabbath. Greenham's sabbatarianism leaned heavily on the doctrine of creation; his entire argument would have collapsed without it. The Sabbath commandment is not post-lapsarian, intrinsic only to redemption, but it is pre-fall, given to Adam and Eve in the creation of the world. God's own example of work and rest is the force field for the Sabbath and for Sabbath keeping. Sabbatarianism, therefore, involved deep respect for the six days of labor as well as for the day of rest, an emphasis that pulled Greenham into the affairs of this world. The Sabbath was not lifted out of daily life, but was part of the cosmic pattern and rhythm of life. In the context of the Sabbath, Greenham ascribed a sacramental function to the natural, created world.

> Now as with the exercise of the word we have the Sacraments to strengthen our faith; so with the meditating of the workes of God we are to strengthen our selves with the beholding of God his creatures, as the heavens and the scope, beautie, and continuall course thereof, and the earth, which should have been all as pleasant as the garden of Eden, if Adam had continued in his innocencie, whose worke as it was by the light of nature to view the creatures of God, so also is it our worke by the light of Gods grace and holy spirit to doe the same.[50]

Perhaps Greenham was ultimately too Reformed, or simply too

---

[49] "Of Prosperity and Adversity," ibid., 769. Cf., Calvin's *Institutes*, III, 10.
[50] "A Treatise of the Sabaoth," *Workes*, 159.

biblical, to ignore the created world. Although the pilgrim theme is dominant, one can find in his worldview small hints of a creational, cultural perspective.

## IX

Finally, to return to the introductory comments about Richard Greenham as a puritan prototype: he was indisputably a superb example of sixteenth-century English Puritanism. That brief, innocent-looking assertion, however, needs substantial explanation, for he was not a puritan in the original (and popular) sense of that term. He himself expressed misgivings about Puritanism. He mentions it only three times in his *Workes,* usually somewhat negatively. On one occasion he ridicules the "foolish preciseness of puritanisme."[51] On another, he reflects on the name-calling strategy employed in the heat of ecclesiastical battle: "This is the practice of men in these daies, to deface the persons by calling them Puritanes, and the cause that it will overthrow states."[52] And in one of his sermons on the Psalms, in the midst of a stern warning against even the appearance of idolatry in the church, he writes: "This seemeth precisenes and puritanisme to the world, ... but if we urge upon puritie, wee are counted precisians. Well, if it be so, then David was a precisian."[53]

Greenham's ambivalence toward Puritanism stems from the way the word was used in his day. The term was born in the early 1560s during the heated debates of the vestments controversy—precisely when Greenham was studying at Pembroke Hall—and it suffered a birth injury from which it has never fully recovered. It was first used as a term of reproach and ridicule against those who refused to don the surplice. Hence, it entered history laden with negative, emotional baggage, a problem that intensified as the years passed. In the 1580s, at the height of Greenham's pastoral career and in the midst of the presbyterian debates, the term was used as a weapon against the more radical, separatist element in the Church of England. "This name Puritan," wrote Archbishop Whitgift, "is very aptly given to these

[51] "Meditations on the 119 Psalm," *Workes,* 602
[52] Ibid., 431.
[53] "Of divers Christian Instructions on Psalm 16," ibid., 321.

men; not because they be so pure...but because they think themselves to be *mundiores ceteris,* `more pure than other,'...and separate themselves from all other churches and congregations, as spotted and defiled: because also they suppose the church which they have devised to be without all impurity."[54]

In such an atmosphere, Greenham, keenly sensitive to political correctness, was naturally reluctant to be tagged a "puritan." Indeed, in the original sense of the term, he was not a puritan, did not regard himself as a puritan, and was not regarded by others as a puritan. He was simply a diligent Church of England pastor, utterly loyal—although not uncritically so—to church and crown. Non-conformity was not his style, and he was emphatically not a separatist, probably not even a presbyterian. Although he was somewhat sympathetic with those who had liturgical and governmental complaints about the church, he loved the church as his mother. He felt alienated from the sinful world, not from the church. The world, the flesh, and the devil—embodied in papism and the Family of Love—these were the battlefronts for Greenham as they were for most pious and dedicated Church of England pastors. If, therefore, he is to be called a puritan, the word has to be expanded beyond its popular negative usage as a term for narrow, mean-spirited people who were hostile toward the religious and political establishments.

Actually, from the very beginning, Puritanism was two-dimensional. It had an external or political side; and an internal, more spiritual side. Although the term "puritan" was first used in the mid-1560s for the political type—those who refused vestments—it soon became evident that something deeper was involved, that the political aggression was generated by certain internal convictions. On the political spectrum, a puritan was measured by how he dealt with controversy in church and state, that is, how far he carried into practice his misgivings about such things as vestments, kneeling at the Eucharist, and hierarchical church government. But internally, Puritanism had to do with zeal, devotion, and spirituality. In the minds of some, the two sides were inseparable, for it was precisely great zeal for godliness in the church and commonwealth that led to more radical political action in liturgy and polity.

There were many puritans, however, who managed to separate the

---

[54] *Works* (Parker Society, 1851) I, 171.

two dimensions. They were spiritual rather than political puritans. If Puritanism had initially been defined in spiritual terms, Greenham would likely have been content with the label. His was a non-aggressive, non-revolutionary, apolitical brand of Puritanism. With hundreds of colleagues, he longed for thorough reformation of the Church of England, but in personal, spiritual terms. Greenham rarely used the word "reformed," and when he did, he typically applied it to *persons*, rather than to *institutions*. He spoke of the opportunity God has given, "wherein we might reforme ourselves." He expressed concern about people "being so little reformed," and lamented that "our heart is reformed but in part."[55] The reformation Greenham sought was one that would especially touch the depths of people's hearts and lives, not one that would result in division and hostile relationships in the church. Greenham was one of the earliest of the many Elizabethan pastors who refocussed the meaning of Puritanism. As one of those who displayed a special zeal for God and godliness, he is an excellent example of the more internal type. His writings are characterized by an intense spirituality and a burning commitment to God. He sought to bring people into spiritual communion with a personal God, who has come near to his people through Jesus Christ and the Holy Spirit. This was at the heart of the puritan version of the Reformation. It is not enough to worship a divine being who is distant in the heavens; rather, a close relationship with the triune God must be cultivated through almost unceasing devotional exercises.

Such Puritanism had little enthusiasm, and very little time, for ecclesiastical politics. Since it involved spiritual dynamics more than political action, it was a Puritanism without clear institutional demarcations, a feature that created difficulties of definition and identification. It was "at root experiential in nature,"[56] and could be detected only by a difference of degree on the zeal thermometer. In this regard, whether definable or not, there can be no doubt about Greenham's Puritanism, for he was a veritable volcano of spiritual passion. But ecclesiastically and politically, he was a "cooperative puritan." Such cooperative Puritanism was the normative pattern in the sixteenth century Church of England, so pervasive that A. G.

---

[55] "Meditations on the 119 Psalm," *Workes*, 528, 532.
[56] Richard Greaves, "The Nature of the Puritan Tradition," in *Reformation, Conformity and Dissent*, R. B. Knox, ed. (London: Epworth Press, 1977) 257-8.

Dickens could even speak of "the Puritan character of the Elizabethan Church."[57] Richard Greenham was, along with scores of other Church of England clerics of his time, a puritan anglican.[58]

---

[57] *The English Reformation,* 313-14. Dickens also states that "the vast majority of Elizabethan Englishmen who cared deeply about religion were either Roman Catholic or Anglican Puritans." See also Patrick Collinson, *Godly People,* 534-5.
[58] See above, p. 5-6.

# EPILOGUE

Richard Greenham's life and ministry ended not in the serene village of Dry Drayton, but in the teeming city of London. Both Clarke and Fuller suggest that the difficulty of ministering to the stubborn, unmalleable inhabitants of the rural Cambridgeshire village had something to do with his decision to depart in 1591. This step did not come easily, however, and occurred only after considerable cajoling from his friends. His tabletalk records that he was "often laboured unto to remove from his place and to plant a church elsewhere," but at first he staunchly resisted this advice, setting forth three stringent conditions for such a move: that his stipend not be "one penny more" than he was receiving in Dry Drayton, that he would be allowed to choose his own successor there, and that wherever he might move, it not be too far away so that he could continue to maintain pastoral contact with his former parishioners.[1] The move to London indicates that he dropped the third of these stipulations. Whether the others were met is uncertain, but it is likely that there was an overriding consideration, one mentioned later in the tabletalk. If it ever appeared to Greenham that the Lord was "denying his grace and blessing" in his ministry, he would "publickly in the congregation to the glory of God and shaming of himself confes his unhability and unwoorthines of the place and so depart."[2]

His friends appealed not to Greenham's unworthiness, but Dry Drayton's. They were convinced that his considerable talents were being wasted in that "poor and peevish" country parish. Dry Drayton, they thought, was like a bushel that hid the light of his witness, while London would be a candlestick for all to see.[3] Greenham was not easily persuaded in spite of his own frustrations about the response to

---

[1] REM 524, fol. 2r.
[2] Ibid., 67v.
[3] Thomas Fuller, *The Church History of Britain*, III, 147.

to his ministry.[4] One can imagine the self-effacing little man modestly resisting the advice, however much its implicit praise may have pleased him inwardly. His puritan rules of behaviour would only have stiffened his resolve not to take compliments and flattery seriously, nor to seek fame in London. This after all was the Greenham who said, "I care not who have the praise...so that by any means god may bee glorified and others profited,"[5] and who lived by the proverbial axiom that a "hauty minde goeth before destruction."[6] But in the end he relented—against his own better judgment according to Fuller—and decided to leave Dry Drayton (population 250), in order to "cast his nets" in the "ocean of people" in London[7] (population 200,000).

Greenham left Dry Drayton without illusions about his twenty-one year ministry there; but rather, with an assessment surprisingly modest even for him. His successor in Dry Drayton was Richard Warfield, who reportedly conversed with Thomas Fuller's father in Impington, another suburb of Cambridge. In this conversation Warfield indicated that Greenham had passed the torch to him with these somber words: "Mr. Warfield, God blesse you, and send you more fruit of your labours than I have had: ffor I perceive noe good wrought by my ministerie on any but one familie." He added a prediction—made perhaps with secret hope—of God's vengeance on an unidentified enemy he was leaving behind, a man "who I am perswaded will never goe out of this world without some heavie stroake of God's visible wrath and judgement on him," for he was not only "verie wicked," but a "profound scoffer at all pietie and religion."[8] In spite of these feelings at the time of his departure, Fuller reports that Greenham later "repented his removal from his parish."[9] He was not as sanguine as his friends had been about life and ministry in the big city.

The move to London is shrouded in mystery. If Fuller is right, Greenham went with no settled parish commitment. He may have been that city's first itinerant evangelist, for he initially preached "up and down in no constant place" and had "no cure, but the curing of

[4] See above,
[5] REM 524, fol. 22r.
[6]"Of Humilitie," Workes, 268.
[7] The Church History of Britain, III, 147.
[8] Notes and Queries, Sixth series, Vol. 7, Jan.-June 1883, 366.
[9] The Church History of Britain, III, 148.

consciences." He soon tired of this "erratical and planetary life," however, and became officially attached to Christ Church on Newgate street, in the west end of the old city, just a five minute walk from St. Paul's Cathedral.

Christ Church was located on the site of an earlier church built in 1228 as the worship center of a Franciscan monastery. The following century, Queen Margaret, wife of Edward I, replaced the original structure with a new and much larger one completed in 1337. This was a grand edifice 300 feet long, 89 feet wide, and 64 feet high, paved with marble, and with at least three side chapels and some eleven altars.[10] It was here Greenham preached in the 1590s, in a building that could not have contrasted more dramatically with the humble little church in Dry Drayton.

It had been known as the "Church of the Greyfriars," in deference to the Franciscan monks who worshipped there. It was closed down at the time of the dissolution of the monasteries in 1538, and used for nearly a decade as a storehouse for spoils of wars with the French. The "modern history" of the Church began in January, 1546, when the building was used for worship once again. The parish was revived as a part of the King's letters patent reconstituting London's greatest hospital, St. Bartholemew's, a short distance away in West Smithfield. The newly formed parish, called Christ Church, was made up of the Greyfriars' Church combined with the parishes of St. Nicholas and St. Ewen, and was placed under the supervision of the hospital's board of governers. The new parish was a large and busy one, so provision was made for a vicar, another priest called, "Visitor of Newgate Prison," five additional priests, who were to assist the vicar especially in divine service of the sacrament, and two parish clerks.[11]

---

[10] This building was totally destroyed in the Great Fire of 1666. It was replaced by Christopher Wren with one of his largest churches but still much smaller than the original. The Wren church measured 114 by 81 feet, 46 feet high. It was, in turn, destroyed by German bombing in December, 1940. Only the tower remained intact. It has been preserved, and a lovely rose garden was laid out in 1989 copying the floor plan of the Wren church. The site is maintained by the Corporation of London.

[11] John Stow, *A Survey of London* (1598), edited by Henry Morley (London: George Routledge and Sons, 1890), 301-5; and Norman Moore, *The History of St. Bartholemew's Hospital*, 2 vols. (London: C. Arthur Pearson Ltd., 1918), 151-6. The vicar was to receive 25 pounds, 13 shillings, and 4 pence per year; the visitor of Newgate prison, 10 pounds; each of the five priests 8 pounds; and each of the parish clerks, 5 pounds per year. The large staff reflects not only an expanded parish, but also the growth of the city, from 50,000 in 1500 to 200,000 in 1600.

Christ Church in its earliest years was caught up in the religious vacillation and uncertainty created by the royal succession from Henry VIII to Edward VI to Mary to Elizabeth. When the latter took the throne, however, the Marian exiles and others eager for more complete reformation of the church, gained the upper hand in the diocese of London and certainly at Christ Church. From that point on, the Church had a history of leadership sympathetic to the puritan vision, some of it from outstanding ministers.[12] The well-known former exile, Thomas Becon, was instituted as vicar of Christ Church in 1559. Becon had moderate puritan leanings, but trouble developed when the more radical Richard Allen was appointed to assist him. Allen was a young Cambridge-trained minister with non-conformist tendencies, lacking in tact and diplomacy. He became an issue and within a short time was suspended by the bishop of London, Edmund Grindal. Allen had some supporters at Christ Church, however, who appealed the decision with the result that he was reinstated for another year. He soon became embroiled in the vestments controversy, and was one of the thirty-seven London ministers suspended by Archbishop Parker for failure to conform. Thomas Becon was another, but he quickly conformed after his suspension.

Becon died in 1567 and was succeeded as vicar by Henry Bedel, another early non-conformist, who likewise relented after he was suspended. During Bedel's tenure, there is evidence of continuing unrest in the church, particularly over the conduct and performance of curates and part-time lecturers, who served the parish. Christ Church parishioners had become sufficiently reformed to enable them to distinguish between ineffective and edifying preaching, and to evaluate over-all ministerial quality. After Bedel was dismissed for moving his place of residence outside of the parish, the tradition of securing puritan vicars continued with the appointment of Thomas Gattacre. He did not get along with his assistants, especially with a curate whom he sought to have removed for reasons of incompetence. Gattacre himself resigned as vicar, and was succeeded by John Bell, chaplain to the bishop of Winchester, a position he retained along with his post at Christ Church.

---

[12] The account that follows is based on H. Gareth Owen, "Tradition and Reform: Ecclesiastical Controversy in an Elizabethan London Parish," *Guildhall Miscellany*, Vol. II, No. 2, July, 1961, 63-70.

It was during Bell's incumbancy that controversy at the Church reached its peak. Because of his duties at Winchester, Bell was often absent from Christ Church, leaving the worship services to assistants who had not been trained to preach. The majority of the parishioners rebelled against these "singing priests," and in 1580, under the skillful lay leadership of Thomas Fanshaw, the church succeeded in having all five of these priests removed. Provision was made to replace them with ministers who could preach, one of whom was Thomas Gattacre. Christ Church thus became a prime example of the "puritan"—or, more broadly, "reformed-protestant"—emphasis on biblical preaching as the fundamental requirement for ministers, with the church's musical tradition increasingly the object of scorn and suspicion.[13] The parishioners of Christ Church remained faithful to their reputation as knowledgeable assessors of good preaching through the remainder of the 1580s, occasionally petitioning the governors to remove a preacher who was not up to standard.

It was at this time, when puritan sympathizers had firm control of Christ Church and the concern for godly preaching had reached its apex, that the services of Richard Greenham were secured. The able and influential Fanshaw was actively involved in the negotiations. He held the prestigious and lucrative position of Remembrancer of the Exchequer (i.e., chief royal bill collector), with a resumé including education at Jesus College, Cambridge and membership in the Middle Temple, one of the distinguished Inns of the Court. He became Remembrancer of the Exchequer in 1568, and achieved wealth in office holding properties in various counties. He had strong puritan leanings and was very active in church affairs, serving on several commissions for causes ecclesiastical. The evidence suggests a special kinship between Fanshaw and Greenham, possibly tracing back to university days.[14] In the first edition of Greenham's *Workes* (1599), the third section includes a dedicatory epistle to Sir Dru Druie and "Master Thomas Fanshaw Esquier, the Queenes Remembrancer in her Highnesse Court of Exchequer."[15]

---

[13] For puritan views on church music, see Percy A. Scholes, *The Puritans and Music* (London: Oxford University Press, 1934), esp. ch. XVI, 253-69.

[14] Although the matriculation records do not indicate exactly when Fanshaw was at Jesus College, it was probably in the 1560s when Greenham was at Pembroke Hall.

[15] Greenham's *Workes* (1599) 219.

In what Owen calls "the ecclesiastical scoop of the day," Fanshaw arranged for the appointment of Greenham as lecturer (preacher) at Christ Church.[16] The substantial political influence of Fanshaw is indicated by his success in arranging for Greenham to receive his license to preach in the London diocese without having to subscribe to Archbishop Whitgift's twelve articles for the regulation of the clergy and for uniform observance of the laws of the church.[17] In London, Fanshaw was not only Greenham's parishioner and friend, but also close neighbor, for they both resided on Warwick Lane, virtually in the shadow of St. Paul's. It is likely that Fanshaw arranged for Greenham to live there, just a few hundred feet from Christ Church. Very little is known of Greenham's ministry in these final years, other than that some of the controversy that characterized Christ Church's history continued, although not at boiling point. The hospital records suggest that after Greenham's arrival, there was debate over how precisely to fund his ministry. On two occasions a motion was considered that would have jeopardized the place of the four part-time assistant preachers, for it was moved that Greenham be paid from the combined hospital funds normally used to pay the assistants. This would likely have entailed the termination of their employment, with Greenham, in effect, replacing all four. The records indicate no final resolution of the matter.[18]

Presumably, he preached regularly in the huge edifice, and carried on pastoral work in the teeming parish. The needs were great—the population of London had increased two and a half times in the reign of Elizabeth and there was desperate overcrowding, especially in the west end. He also continued to be an irenic influence in the church at large. One recorded incident confirms that his reputation for moderation preceded him to London. In April of 1593, he was part of a clerical deputation commissioned to confer with the militant separatist, John Penry.[19] Penry (1559-93) was the chief author of the

---

[16] H. Gareth Owen, "Tradition and Reform," 69.
[17] GLRO, Consistory Court of London, Liber Vicarii Generalis, 1590-99, fol. 60v. John Strype, *The Life and Acts of John Whitgift*, I, 227ff.
[18] SBHA, Ha/1/3, fols. 86r&v, 109v.
[19] John Waddington, *John Penry, The Pilgrim Martyr* (London: W. and F. Cash, 1854) 122-4. On Penry see also William Pierce, *John Penry, His Life, Times, and Writings* (London: Hodder and Stoughton, 1923); and Donald J. McGinn, *John Penry and the Marprelate Controversy* (New Brunswick: Rutgers University Press, 1966).

Martin Marprelate tracts, the scurrilous writings that appeared in the 1580s excoriating the episcopal hierarchy and discipline of the church. Greenham had indicated his disapproval of the tracts in a sermon at Great St. Mary's in Cambridge, observing that they "make sin ridiculous, whereas it ought to be made odious."[20]

After many years of flight from the authorities, Penry was finally arrested in 1592 and imprisoned in the Poultry Compter in London. D. Crooke,[21] a Mr. Temple, and Greenham visited him there on April 2. They apparently were commissioned by London diocesan authorities to reason with Penry, persuade him to retract, and convince him that moderation was a wiser course. Considering the abundance of clerics to choose from in London, which had more than a hundred parishes in the 1590s, it is significant that Greenham, a relative newcomer, was chosen by Bishop Aylmer to be a part of this deputation. It indicates the considerable esteem in which Greenham was held in the church, as well as confidence in his persuasive peace-making abilities. Nevertheless, the trio were not successful. In a letter to his wife, Penry stated that after "much needless speeches" the delegation departed.[22] On April 10, Henry Fanshaw (son of Thomas) and Mr. Justice Young examined Penry. He was charged with inciting insurrection and rebellion in the land, was found guilty as charged and sentenced to death. On May 29, 1593, Penry was hanged.

The contrast between Penry and Greenham is striking and brings Greenham's cooperative Puritanism into sharp relief. Sympathetic though Greenham was to Penry's theology and concern for reform, they were miles apart in strategy and in their convictions about legitimate lines of authority. To the very end, Greenham was faithful to church and crown, and showed little interest in reforming church government.

In April of 1594, "godly Greenham" died.[23] He was only in his early fifties, active nearly to the end, preaching weekly at Christ Church throughout the "tyme of great sicknes,"[24] a reference to a London epidemic that snuffed out more than ten thousand lives in

---

[20] Samuel Clarke, *Thirty-two lives*, 13.
[21] Crooke is also mention in Henry Holland's preface as one of those who helped collect Greenham's works for publication.
[22] BL, Add. MS. 48064, fols. 20v, 21r.
[23] GLRO, Liber Vicarii Generalis, 1590-99, fol. 174v.
[24] GLMS 9163, fol. 305r.

twelve months. The city, says Fuller, was "filled with funerals," one of them Greenham's, for he too was "mortally visited with the plague."[25]

Nothing is known of Greenham's final days, but Samuel Clarke says that whenever he was ill, he wanted no one to watch over him "so he might more freely converse with God."[26] These conversations no doubt included the subject of death, for although he did not welcome it, he certainly did not fear it. His stance was one of acceptance of, rather than longing for, death. "As I would have you to thinck of lyfe, as being content to dy," he said to one who came to him with dark fears of death, "so thinck of death as you could bee content to live." He thought it better to "measurably fear" death, than to rejoice in it. For a Christian to fear death even in the moment of dying is no mortal sin, "for wee shal not be judged according to that particular instant of death, but according to our general cours of lyfe," and if God's mercy has been "sealed" before, in one's "vocation and sanctification," it can be fully trusted in death.[27]

Although his age was replete with reminders of human mortality, Greenham still found it necessary to admonish people about the brevity of life. In a meditation on the shortness of life and on death, Greenham notes that Scripture consistently speaks of the transitory nature of earthly existence. Life is "a bubble, a sleepe, a vapour," he writes; it is a "booth or tent" that does not last. And yet, it is human tendency to defer serious thoughts of death, to believe that "our Lord will be long in comming," and to think that "the plague shall not come yet." The Psalmist, on the other hand, urged God's people to number their days. Human beings number all sorts of things, observes Greenham—their sheep, their money, their lands. "But to number our daies is a rare kind of numbering, it is a strange Arithmetic...a numbering, wherewith we are unacquainted."

He proceeds to do some calculating. If an average life span is seventy years and about half of that is spent in sleep, thirty-five years remain. Subtract another fourteen for the years of youth, "wherein we are unfit to glorifie God or doe good to man"—a dim view of childhood to be sure. There are also other empty times of sickness, lust, and worldliness, leaving finally very little time consciously and

---

[25] *The Church History of Britain*, III, 146.
[26] *Thirty-two Divines*, 15.
[27] REM 524, 56r&v.

single-mindedly to glorify God, maybe only seven or eight years. The days past are gone and the days to come are not yet, so there is "consequently...none but the present time" to praise the Lord. Therefore, Greenham urges, labour to attain wisdom, which is "a continuall thinking, that death is nigh." It is a "maine point of wisedome to learne to die," for "they that before had no delight in the word, if once they take this account, that every day they thinke they drawe their last breath, the word will be full of comfort to them."[28] Richard Greenham, who spent his life teaching people how to live, taught them also how to die.[29]

His panegyrist, Henry Holland, says that "the day before his departure out of this life, his thoughts were much troubled, for that men were so unthankfull for that strange and happy deliverance of our most gratious Queene, from the dangerous conspiracies and practices of that time."[30] This is undoubtedly a reference to the "Lopez affair," for Rodrigo Lopez,[31] personal physician to the Queen, in February just prior to Greenham's death, was found guilty of conspiring with the hated Spanish to poison Elizabeth. Lopez was hanged in June of 1594. Greenham died in April, loyal to constituted authority to his dying breath, the non-revolutionary character of his Puritanism thoroughly intact.

Greenham's burial site is unknown. There is no record of a will. He left the scene as he entered it, quietly and unannounced. Fuller's gentle, closing comment is appropriate here: "Thus godly Greenham is fallen asleep: we softly draw the curtains about him, and so proceed to other matter."[32]

---

[28] "Of the shortnesse of our life, and the Meditation of Death how profitable," *Workes*, 660-61.

[29] Sixteenth century English protestants developed it into an art form, the *ars moriendi*. See, for example, William Perkins's "A Salve for a Sicke Man," *Workes* (London: J. Legatt, 1616-18) I, 487-514.

[30] "The Preface to the Reader," Greenham's *Workes* .

[31] See DNB.

[32] *The Church History of Britain*, III, 148.

# BIBLIOGRAPHY

Ainsworth, Henry. *The Communion of Saints.* n.p., 1628.

Althaus, Paul. *The Theology of Martin Luther.* Philadelphia: Fortress Press, 1966.

Angier, John. "An Helpe to Better Hearts," in *Life of John Angier of Denton*, Ernest Axon, ed. Manchester: The Chetham Society, 1937.

Armstrong, Brian G. *Calvinism and the Amyraut Heresy.* Madison: University of Wisconsin Press, 1969.

Attwater, Aubrey. *Pembroke College Cambridge: A Short History.* Cambridge: Pembroke College, 1973.

Baker, J. Wayne. *Heinrich Bullinger and the Covenant: The Other Reformed Tradition.* Athens, Ohio: Ohio University Press, 1980.

Barfield, Samuel. *Thatcham, Berkshire, and its Manors.* 2 vols. Oxford and London: James Parker and Co., 1901.

Bauckham, Richard. *Tudor Apocalypse.* Abingdon: Sutton Courtenay Press, 1978.

Baxter, Richard. *A Christian Directory.* London: Robert White, 1673.

____ *The Reformed Pastor.* London, 1656.

Baynes, Paule. *Briefe Directions unto a godly Life.* London, 1618.

Beaty, Nancy Lee. *The Craft of Dying: A Study in the Literary Tradition of the Ars Morendi in England.* New Haven and London: Yale University Press, 1970.

Bennett, Henry S. *English Books and Readers 1558-1603* Cambridge: Cambridge University Press, 1965.

Bernard, Richard, *The Faithfull Shepherd.* London: 1621.

Bolton, Robert. *Two Sermons Preached at Northhampton.* London, 1635.

Bonini, Cissie Rafferty. "Lutheran Influences in the Early English Reformation: Richard Morison Re-examined," *Archiv für Reformationsgeschichte*, Vol. 64 (1973): 206-224.

*A booke of the forme of common prayers, administration of the Sacraments etc. agreable to Gods worde, and the use of the reformed churches.* Middleburgh: Richard Schilders, 1586.

*The Book of Common Prayer 1559*. John E. Booty, ed. Charlottesville: University Press of Virginia, 1976.

Bond, Nicholas. *The Doctrine of the Sabbath*. London: 1595.

____. *Sabbathum Veteris*. London: 1606.

Bradford, John. *The Writings of John Bradford*. Parker Society, 1848.

Breward, Ian. *The Life and Theology of William Perkins* (unpublished Ph.D. diss., Manchester University, 1962-63).

____, *The Work of William Perkins*. Appleford: Sutton Courtenay Press, 1970.

Brewer, Henry W. *Old London Illustrated*. 9th ed. London: The Builder, Ltd., 1962.

*A Brief Discourse of the Troubles Begun at Frankfort in the year 1554 about the Book of Common Prayer and Ceremonies*, reprinted from the Black Letter Edition of 1575. London: John Petheram, 1846.

Browne, Robert. *A True and Short Declaration*, 1583, in Peel, Albert, and Carlson, Leland, eds., *The Writings of Robert Harrison and Robert Browne*. London: Allen and Unwin, 1953.

Bullinger, Heinrich. *Decades*. 5 vols. Parker Society, 1849-52.

Calvin, John. *An Admonicion against Astrology Judiciall*. G. Gylby, 1561.

____. *Institutes of the Christian Religion*, John T. McNeill, ed. Philadelphia: Westminster Press, 1960.

Chan, Simon K. H. *The Puritan Meditative Tradition 1599-1691* (unpublished Ph.D. diss., Cambridge University, 1986).

Christianson, Paul. "Reformers and the Church of England under Elizabeth I and the Early Stuarts," *Journal of Ecclesiastical History*, Vol. 31 (October 1980): 463-482.

Clarke, Samuel. *The Lives of Sundry Eminent Persons*. London, 1683.

____. *The Lives of Thirty-Two English Divines*. London, 1677.

Clebsch, William A. *England's Earliest Protestants*. New Haven and London: Yale University Press, 1964.

Cole, C. Robert, and Moody, Michael E., eds. *The Dissenting Tradition*. Athens: Ohio University Press, 1975.

Collinson, Patrick. *Archbishop Grindal 1519-1583*. London: Jonathan Cape, 1979.

____. *The Birthpangs of Protestant England*. Basingstoke & London: Macmillan, 1988.

____. "A Comment: Concerning the Name Puritan", *Journal of Ecclesiastical History*, Vol. 31 (October 1980): 483-488.

____. "Cranbrook and the Fletchers: Popular and Unpopular Religion in the Kentish Weald," *Reformation Principle and Practice*, ed. P. W. Brooks. London: Scholar Press, 1980, 173-202.

____. *The Elizabethan Puritan Movement*. Berkeley and Los Angeles: University of California Press, 1967.

____. *English Puritanism*. London: The Historical Association, General Series 106, 1983.

____. *Godly People: Essays on English Protestantism and Puritanism*. London: The Hambledon Press, 1983.

____. *The Religion of Protestants*. Oxford: Clarendon Press, 1982.

Coolidge, John S.. *The Pauline Renaissance in England*. Oxford: Clarendon Press, 1970.

Cooper, Charles H. and Thompson. *Athenae Cantabrigienses*, 2 vols. Cambridge: Deighton, Bell, and Co. and Macmillan and Co., 1861.

Corrie, George E. *A List of Books Presented to Pembroke College*. Cambridge Antiquarian Society, 1960.

Curtis, Mark H. *Oxford and Cambridge in Transition 1558-1642*. Oxford: Clarendon Press, 1959.

Dent, Arthur. *The Plaine Mans Path-way to Heaven*. London: 1601.

Dent, Christopher M. *Protestant Reformers in Elizabethan Oxford*. Oxford: Oxford University Press, 1983.

Dering, Edward, and More, John. *A briefe and necessary Catechisme* London, 1573.

Dever, Mark. *Richard Sibbes and the "Truly Evangelicall Church of England": A Study in Reformed Divinity and Early Stuart Conformity* (unpublished Ph.D. diss., Cambridge University, 1992).

Dickens, Arthur G. *The English Reformation*. London: B.T. Batsford LTD, 1964.

Donnelly, John P. *Calvinism and Scholasticism in Vermigli's Doctrine of Man and Grace*. Leiden: E. J. Brill, 1976.

Duffy, Eamon. *The Stripping of the Altars*. New Haven & London: Yale University Press, 1992.

Ebeling, Gerhard. *Luther: an Introduction to his Thought*. Philadelphia: Fortress Press, 1970.

Ekwall, Eilert. *The Concise Oxford Dictionary of English Place-Names*, 4th ed. Oxford: Clarendon Press, 1960.

Emerson, Everett H. *English Puritanism.* Durham, N.C.: Duke University Press, 1968.

Foxe, John. *The Book of Martyrs.* London, 1732.

Frere, Walter H. and Proctor, Francis. *A New History of the Book of Common Prayer.* London: MacMillan & Co., 1902.

Frere, Walter H. ed. *Visitation Articles and Injunctions,* 3 vols. London: Longmans, Green & Co., 1910.

Fuller, Thomas. *The Church History of Britain,* 3 vols. London: William Tegg, 1868.

Garrett, Christina H. *The Marian Exiles.* Cambridge: University Press, 1938.

Geree, John. *The Character of an Old English Puritan.* London, 1646.

Gifford, George. *A Briefe discourse of certaine points of the religion, which is among the common sort of Christians, which may be termed the Countrey Divinitie.* London, 1612.

____. *A Catechisme conteining the summe of Christian Religion.* London, 1583.

Gilpen, Bernard, *A Godly sermon preached in the Court of Greenwich.* London, 1552.

Gouge, William. *Of Domesticall Duties.* London, 1622.

Grabo, Norman S. "The Art of Puritan Devotion," *Seventeenth Century News,* Vol. xxvi, No. 1 (Spring, 1968): 7-9.

Greaves, Richard L. "The Nature of the Puritan Tradition" in *Reformation, Conformity, and Dissent,* R. B. Knox, ed. London, 1977.

____, "The Origin and Early Development of English Covenant Thought." *The Historian XXXI,* 1 (Nov. 1968): 21-35.

Greenham, Richard, Rogers, Richard, and Perkins, Wm., et al. *A Garden of Spiritual Flowers.* London, 1687.

Greenham, Richard. *A godly Exhortation, and fruitfull admonition to vertuous parents and modest Matrons.* London, 1584.

____. *Propositions Containing Answers to Certaine demaunds in divers spirituall matters, specially concerning the Conscience oppressed with the griefe of sinne. With An Epistle against hardnes of heart.* Edinburgh, 1597.

____. *Two Treatises of the comforting of an afflicted conscience.* London, 1598.

____. "The Apologie or aunswere of Maister Grenham, Minister of Dreaton, unto the bishop of Ely, being commonded to subscribe and to use the Romish habite, with allowance of the com. booke," *A parte of a register*. n.d.n.p., 86-93.

____. *The Works of the Reverend and Faithful Servant of Jesus Christ M. Richard Greenham, Minister and Preacher of the Word of God*. London, 1599.

____. The *Workes of the Reverend amd faithful servant....M. Richard Greenham*. London: Felix Kingston, 1601.

____. The *Workes...of Richard Greenham*. London: Felix Kingston, 1605.

____. *Workes of R. Greenham*. London, 1612.

Haigh, Christopher. *Reformation and Resistance in Tudor Lancashire*. Cambridge: University Press, 1975.

Hall, Joseph. *Heaven Upon Earth*. London, 1606.

Haller, William. *The Rise of Puritanism*. New York: Columbia University Press, 1938.

Hambrick-Stowe, Charles E. *The Practice of Piety*. Chapel Hill: The University of North Carolina Press, 1982.

Hamilton, Alistair. *The Family of Love*. Cambridge: James Clarke and Co., 1981.

Hawes, Robert, and Loder, Robert. *The History of Framlingham*. Woodbridge, 1798.

Heal, Felicity. *The Bishops of Ely and Their Diocese During the Reformation Period: 1515-1600* (unpublished Ph.D. diss., Cambridge University, 1972).

____. "The Family of Love and the Diocese of Ely," in *Schism, Heresy and Religious Protest*, Studies in Church History, Vol. 9. Cambridge: University of Cambridge Press, 1972, 213-222.

Herbert, George. *A Priest To The Temple, or, The Country Parson, His Character, and Rule of Holy Life*. London, 1675.

Hesselink, I. John. *Calvin's Concept of the Law*. Allison Park, PA: Pickwick Publications, 1992.

Hill, Christopher. *Society and Puritanism in Pre-Revolutionary England*. London: Secker and Warburg, 1964.

Hoskins, William G. "The Rebuilding of Rural England 1570-1640," *Past and Present*, 4 (1953): 44-59.

Howell, Wilbur S. *Logic and Rhetoric in England, 1500-1700*. Princeton: University Press, 1956.

Hunt, William. *The Puritan Movement*. Cambridge, Mass.: Harvard University Press, 1983.

Ingram, Martin. "Religion, Communities and Moral Discipline in Late Sixteenth and Early Seventeenth-Century England: Case Studies," in *Religion and Society in Early Modern Europe 1500-1800*, Kaspar von Greyerz, ed. London: Allen and Unwin, 1984, 177-193.

Jacobs, Henry E. *The Lutheran Movement in England*. Philadelphia: G. W. Frederick, 1890.

Jenkins, Elizabeth. *Elizabeth the Great*. London: Panther Books, 1958.

Jenkins, R. B. *Henry Smith: England's Silver-Tongued Preacher*. Macon: Mercer University Press, 1983.

Jensen, Peter F. *The Life of Faith in the Teaching of Elizabethan Protestants* (unpublished Ph.D. diss., Oxford University, 1979).

Jewel, John. *Works*, 4 vols. Parker Society, 1845-1850.

Knappen, Marshall M. "The Early Puritanism of Lancelot Andrewes," *Church History*, II (1933): 95-104.

____. *Richard Greenham and the Practical Puritans under Elizabeth*. (unpublished Ph.D. diss., Cornell University, 1927).

____. *Tudor Puritanism*. Chicago: University of Chicago Press, 1939.

Knewstub, John. *A confutation of monstrous and horrible heresies, taught by H. N. and embraced of a number, who call themselves the Familie of Love*. London, 1579.

Knott, John R. Jr. *The Sword of the Spirit: Puritan Responses to the Bible*. Chicago: University of Chicago Press, 1980.

Lake, Peter. *Anglicans and Puritans? Presbyterianism and English Conformist Thought from Whitgift to Hooker*. London: Unwin Hyman, 1988.

____. "Calvinism and the English Church" *Past and Present*, 114 (February, 1987): 32-76.

____. *Moderate Puritans and the Elizabethan Church*. Cambridge: Cambridge University Press, 1982.

Lang, August. *Der Evangelienkommentar Martin Butzers*, in *Studien zur Geschichte der Theologie und der Kirch*, Bonwetsch and Seeberg, eds. Leipzig: Dieterich'sche Verlags-Buchhandlung, 1900.

Laslett, Peter. *The World We Have Lost*. London: Methuen and Co., 1979.

Leader, Damian R. *A History of the University of Cambridge*, Vol. 1. Cambridge: University Press, 1988.

Leedham-Green, Elisabeth S. *Books in Cambridge Inventories*, 2 vols. Cambridge: University Press, 1986.

Leith, John H. "Creation and Redemption: Law and Gospel in the Theology of John Calvin," in *Marburg Revisited*, Paul C. Empie, ed. Minneapolis: Augsburg Press, 1966, 141-52.

Lever, Thomas. *Sermons*, Edward Arber, ed. London, 1870.

Macfarlane, Alan. *Reconstructing Historical Communities*. Cambridge: University Press, 1977.

____. *Witchcraft in Tudor and Stuart England*. London: Routledge and Kegan Paul, 1970.

Manschreck, Clyde L. *Melanchthon on Christian Doctrine*. New York: Oxford University Press, 1965.

Marsden, George. "Perry Miller's Rehabilitation of the Puritans: A Critique," *Church History*, Vol. 39 (March, 1970): 91-105.

Marsden, John B. *The History of the Early Puritans*. London: Hamilton, Adams, & Co., 1850.

Marsh, Christopher W. *The Family of Love in English Society, 1550-1630*. Cambridge: Cambridge University Press, 1994.

Maunsell, Andrew. *The First Part of the Catalogue of English printed Bookes*. London, 1595.

McCabe, Richard. *Joseph Hall: Study in Satire and Meditation*. Oxford: University Press, 1982.

McGiffert, Michael. "Grace and Works: The Rise and Division of Covenant Divinity in Elizabethan Puritanism," *HTR* 75:4 (1982): 463-502.

McGinn, Donald J. *The Admonition Controversy*. New Brunswick: Rutgers University Press, 1949.

____. *John Penry and the Marprelate Controversy*. New Brunswick: Rutgers University Press, 1966.

McGoldrick, James E. *Luther's English Connection*. Milwaukee: Northwestern Pub. House, 1979.

McGrath, Patrick. *Papists and Puritans under Elizabeth I*. London: Blandford Press, 1967.

Meads, Dorothy M., ed. *Diary of Lady Margaret Hoby*. London: Routledge & Sons, 1930.

Miller, Perry. *Errand Into the Wilderness*. Cambridge, Mass.: Belknap Press, 1956.

Moore, Norman. *The History of St. Bartholomew's Hospital*, 2 vols. London: C. Arthur Pearson Limited, 1918.

Morgan, Irvonwy. *The Godly Preachers of the Elizabethan Church.* London: Epworth Press, 1965.

Morgan, John. *Godly Learning: Puritan Attitudes Towards Reason, Learning, and Education, 1560-1640.* Cambridge: University Press, 1986.

Moss, Jean Dietz. "The Family of Love and English Critics," *The Sixteenth Century Journal*, VI, 1 (April, 1975): 35-52.

Muller, Richard A. "Perkins' *A Golden Chaine*: Predestinarian System or Schematized *Ordo Salutis*?" *The Sixteenth Century Journal* IX, 1 (1978): 69-81.

Mullinger, James Bass. *A History of the University of Cambridge.* London: Longmans, Green, and Co., 1888.

Musculus, Wolfgang. *Commonplaces of Christian Religion.* London, 1563.

Muskett, Joseph J. "Cambridgeshire Church Goods," *Notes and Queries*, vols. 6 (1895-6) -10 (1903-4).

New, John F. H. *Anglican and Puritan: the Basis of Their Opposition, 1558-1640.* London: Adam and Charles Black, 1964.

Nicolas, Josias. *The Plea of the Innocent.* n.p., 1602.

Nowell, Alexander. *Catechismus.* London: R. Wolfe, 1572.

____. *A Catechism*, G.E. Corrie, ed. Parker Society, 1853.

Nuttall, Geoffrey F. *The Holy Spirit in Puritan Faith and Experience.* Oxford: Basil Blackwell, 1946.

____. *The Puritan Spirit.* London: Epworth Press, 1967.

O'Day, Rosemary. *The English Clergy.* Leicester: University Press, 1979.

Owen, H. Gareth. "Tradition and Reform: Ecclesiastical Controversy in an Elizabethan London Parish," *Guildhall Miscellany*, Vol. II, No. 2 (July, 1961): 63-70.

Page, Frances Mary. *The Estates of Crowland Abbey.* Cambridge: University Press, 1934.

Pagitt, Ephraim. *Heresiography or, A description of the Hereticks and Sectaries of these latter times.* London, 1645.

Palmer, William M., and Saunders, Herbert W., eds. *Documents Relating to Cambridgeshire Villages*, No. VI (December, 1926).

Parker, Kenneth. *The English Sabbath: A Study of Doctrine and Discipline from the Reformation to the Civil War.* Cambridge: Cambridge University Press, 1988.

Pearson, Andrew F. Scott. *Thomas Cartwright and Elizabethan Puritanism 1535-1603.* Cambridge: Cambridge University Press, 1925.

Peel, Albert and Leland Carlson. *Cartwrightiana.* London: Allen and Unwin, 1951.

Peel, Albert, ed. *The Seconde Parte of a Register,* 2 vols. Cambridge: Cambridge University Press, 1915.

Perkins, William. *A Golden Chaine.* Cambridge: J. Legatt, 1591.

____. *Workes,* 3 vols. London: J. Legatt, 1616, 1617, 1618.

Phillimore, William P. W., and Young, Evelyn, eds. *Cambridgeshire Parish Registers-Marriages,* Vol. III. London: Phillimore and Co., 1909.

Pierce, William. *John Penry, His Life, Times, and Writings.* London: Hodder and Stoughton, 1923.

Porter, Harry C. *Reformation and Reaction in Tudor Cambridge.* Cambridge: University Press, 1958.

____. ed. *Puritanism in Tudor England.* Columbia: University of South Carolina Press, 1971.

Poynet, John. *A Short Catechism.* London: Seeley, Jackson, and Halliday, 1865.

Primus, John H. *Holy Time: Moderate Puritanism and the Sabbath.* Macon: Mercer University Press, 1989.

____. *The Vestments Controversy.* Kampen: J. H. Kok, 1960.

Rait, Robert S. *Life in the Medieval University.* Cambridge: University Press, 1912.

Ravensdale, John R. "Landbeach in 1549: Ket's Rebellion in Minature," *East Anglican Studies,* L. M. Munby, ed. Cambridge: Heffer, 1968, 94ff.

Reaney, Percy H. *The Place-Names of Cambridgeshire and the Isle of Ely.* Cambridge: University Press, 1943.

Reed, Antony C. *Law and Gospel in the Theology of Philip Melanchthon* (unpublished Ph.D. diss., Cambridge University, 1973).

*The Registers of Christ Church, Newgate,* Willoughby A. Littledale, ed. London, 1895.

Ridley, Nicholas, *Works.* Parker Society, 1841.

Rogers, John. *The Displaying of an horrible Secte of grosse and wicked Heretiques, naming themselves the Family of Love.* London, 1579.

Royal Commission on Historical Monuments. *An Inventory of Historical Monuments in the County of Cambridge,* Vol. 1, West Cambridgeshire, 1968.

Rupp, Gordon. "A Devotion of Rapture in English Puritanism," in *Reformation, Conformity and Dissent,* R. B. Knox, ed. London: Epworth Press, 1977.

____. *Patterns of Reformation.* London: Epworth Press, 1969.

____. *The Righteousness of God.* London: Hodder and Stoughton, 1953.

Scholes, Percy A. *The Puritans and Music.* London: Oxford University Press, 1934.

Seaver, Paul S. *The Puritan Lectureships.* Stanford: University Press, 1970.

Short, K.R.M. "A Theory of Common Education in Elizabethan Puritanism," *Journal of Ecclesiastical History,* Vol. 23 (Jan. 1972): 31-48.

Smith, Alan W. "Popular Religion," *Past and Present,* 40 (1968): 181-186.

Sprunger, Keith L. *The Learned Doctor William Ames.* Urbana: University of Illinois Press, 1972.

Spufford, Margaret. *Contrasting Communities.* Cambridge: University Press, 1974.

Stephens, William P. *The Holy Spirit in the Theology of Martin Bucer.* Cambridge: University Press, 1970.

Stoeffler, Fred Ernest. *The Rise of Evangelical Pietism.* Leiden: E.J. Brill, 1965.

Stoute, D. A. *The Origins and Early Development of the Reformed Idea of the Covenant* (unpublished Ph.D. diss., Cambridge University, 1980).

Stow, John. *A Survey of London 1598,* Henry Morley, ed. London: George Routledge and Sons, 1890.

Strype, John. *Annals of the Reformation.* Oxford: Clarendon Press, 1824.

____. *The Life and Acts of J. Whitgift,* 4 vols. Oxford: Clarendon Press, 1822.

Tanner, Thomas. *Bibliotheca Britannico-Hibernica.* London, 1748.

Thirsk, Joan, ed. *The Agrarian History of England and Wales,* 8 vols. Cambridge: University Press, 1981.

Thomas, Keith. *Religion and the Decline of Magic*. London: Weidenfeld and Nicholson, 1971.

Trexler, Richard C. "Reverence and Profanity in the Study of Early Modern Religion," in *Religion and Society in Early Modern Europe 1500-1800*, Kaspar von Greyerz, ed. London: Allen and Unwin, 1984, 245-69.

Trueman, Carl R. *Luther's Legacy: Salvation and English Reformers, 1525-1556*. Oxford: Clarendon Press, 1994.

Tyacke, Nicholas. *Anti-Calvinists: The Rise of English Arminianism*. Oxford: Clarendon Press, 1987.

Tyacke, Nicholas, and White, Peter. "Debate: The Rise of Arminianism Reconsidered," *Past and Present*, 115 (May, 1987): 201-229.

Tyndale, William. *Doctrinal Treatises*. Parker Society, 1848.

Underdown, David. *Revel, Riot, and Rebellion*. Oxford: Clarendon Press, 1985.

Usher, Roland G. *The Presbyterian Movement in the Reign of Queen Elizabeth*. London: Royal Historical Society, 1905.

Vander Molen, Ronald J. "Anglican Against Puritan: ideological origins during the Marian exile," *Church History*, xlii, (1973): 45-57.

Venn, John, and Venn, J. A. *Alumni Cantabrigienses*, Part I, Vol. II. Cambridge: University Press, 1922.

____. *The Book of Matriculations and Degrees: A Catalogue of those who have been Matriculated or been admitted to any Degree in the University of Cambridge from 1544 to 1659*. Cambridge: University Press, 1913.

Venn, John, ed. *Grace Book*. Cambridge: University Press, 1910.

Waddington, John. *John Penry, The Pilgrim Martyr, 1559-1593*. London: W. & F. G. Cash, 1854.

Wakefield, Gordon Stevens. *Puritan Devotion*. London: Epworth Press, 1957.

Walker, Francis A. *A History of the Parish of Dry Drayton*. London: T.P. Newman, 1876.

Wallace, Dewey D. "George Gifford, Puritan Propaganda and Popular Religion in Elizabethan England," *The Sixteenth Century Journal*, IX, 1 (1978): 27-49.

Wallace, Dewey D. Jr. *Puritans and Predestination*. Chapel Hill: University of North Carolina Press, 1982.

Warde, William. *God's Arrowes*. London: 1607.

Watson, Philip. *Let God Be God: An Interpretation of the Theology of Martin Luther*. Philadelphia: Muhlenberg Press, 1949.

Whitaker, William. *Sunday in Tudor and Stuart Times*. London: Houghton, 1933.

.White, Peter. "The Rise of Arminianism Reconsidered," *Past and Present*, 101 (November, 1983): 34-54.

Whitgift, John. *Works*, 3 vols. Parker Society, 1851-53.

Wilkins, John. *Ecclesiastes, or, A Discourse Concerning the Gift of Preaching*. London: 1646.

Wren, Matthew. *De Custodias Pembrochianus*, transcribed by Thomas Baker, CUL - MS Baumgartner 10.

____. *Memoriae, Veritati, Virtuti, Sacrum LAVRUM Pembrochianam*. Cambridge, 1617.

Wrightson, Keith, and Levine, David. *Poverty and Piety in an English Village*. New York, London: Academic Press, 1979.

Wrightson, Keith. *English Society, 1580-1680*. London: Hutchinson, 1982.

# INDEX

*Richard Greenham: Portrait of an Elizabethan Pastor*
John H. Primus

Published by Mercer University Press
April 1998
Book design by Marc A. Jolley.
Camera-ready pages composed on a Macintosh Performa
    6300CD, via Microsoft Word 6.0.1.
Text font: Caslon 11/13.
Printed and bound in the United States.
Cased and covered with cloth, smyth-sewn, and printed on
    acid-free paper.